ACTS OF THE APOSTLES

ACTS OF THE APOSTLES

RONALD J. ALLEN

Fortress Press
Minneapolis

ACTS OF THE APOSTLES

Fortress Biblical Preaching Commentaries

Copyright © 2013 Fortress Press. All rights reserved. Except for brief quotations in critical articles or reviews, no part of this book may be reproduced in any manner without prior written permission from the publisher. Visit http://www.augsburgfortress.org/copyrights/ or write to Permissions, Augsburg Fortress, Box 1209, Minneapolis, MN 55440.

Scripture quotations are from the New Revised Standard Version Bible, copyright © 1989 by the Division of Christian Education of the National Council of the Churches of Christ in the USA. Used by permission. All rights reserved.

Cover design: Laurie Ingram

Library of Congress Cataloging-in-Publication Data is available

Print ISBN: 978-0-8006-9872-0

eBook ISBN: 978-1-4514-2644-1

The paper used in this publication meets the minimum requirements of American National Standard for Information Sciences—Permanence of Paper for Printed Library Materials, ANSI Z329.48-1984.

Manufactured in the U.S.A.

This book was produced using PressBooks.com, and PDF rendering was done by PrinceXML.

*To
West Street Christian Church
(Disciples of Christ),
a congregation of glad and generous hearts*

CONTENTS

Series Foreword ix
Preface xi
Index of Passages from the Book of Acts in the Revised Common Lectionary
Introduction lxv
1. The Coming of the Realm of God: The Main Theme of the Book of Acts
   Acts 1:1—2:13 15
2. You Will Be My Witness in Jerusalem and in all Judea
   Acts 2:14—8:3 33
3. You Will Be My Witnesses in Samaria
   Acts 8:4-25 71
4. You Will Be My Witnesses to the Ends of the Earth
   Acts 8:26—28:29 77

Appendix 1: The Chiastic Structure of Luke-Acts 209
Appendix 2: Table Correlating Lectionary Readings from Luke with Chiastic Parallels from Acts 219
Appendix 3: Sermon Series from the Book of Acts: Representative Texts, Characters, and Themes 223
Appendix 4: Suggestions for Further Reading 229

Series Foreword

A preacher who seeks to be creative, exegetically up to date, hermeneutically alert, theologically responsible, and in-touch with the moment is always on the hunt for fresh resources. Traditional books on preaching a book of the Bible often look at broad themes of the text with little explicit advice about preaching individual passages. Lectionary resources often offer exegetical and homiletical insights about a pericope with little attention given to broader themes and structures of the book from which the lection is taken. *Fortress Biblical Preaching Commentaries* provide the preacher with resources that draw together the strengths of these two approaches into a single text aid, useful for the moment of preparation halfway between full scale exegesis and a finished sermon.

The authors of this series are biblical scholars who offer expositions of the text rooted in detailed study and expressed in straightforward, readable ways. The commentators take a practical approach by identifying (1) what the text invited people in the ancient world to believe about God and the world and (2) what the text encouraged people to do in response. Along the way, the interpreters make use of such things as historical and cultural reconstruction, literary and rhetorical analysis, word studies, and other methods that help us recover how a text was intended to function in antiquity. At the same time, the commentaries offer help in moving from then to now, from what a text meant (in the past) to what a text means (in the present), by helping a minister identify issues, raise questions, and pose possibilities for preaching while stopping short of placing a complete sermon in the preacher's hands. The preacher, then, should be in a position to set in motion a conversation with the text (and other voices from the past and present) to help the congregation figure out what we today can believe and do.

The commentators in this series seek to help preachers and students make connections between the various lections from a given book throughout the lectionary cycle and liturgical year in their sermons and studies. Readers, preachers, and their parishioners will have a deeper appreciation of the book's unique interpretation of the Christ event and how that influences their approach to living the Christian faith in today's world. The most life-giving preaching is nearly always local in character with a minister rooted in a particular congregation, culture, and context encouraging listeners to think specifically about how the text might relate to the life of the congregation and to the surrounding community and world. *Fortress Biblical Preaching Commentaries* are set forth in the hope that each volume will be a provocative voice in such conversations.

PREFACE

The Book of Acts nears its climax with a sea voyage. I began writing this commentary on the open deck of a ship on my first voyage at sea, and through the feel of the ship, I felt a certain resonance with Paul and with the larger story of Acts. The main theme of the Gospel of Luke and the Book of Acts is the coming of the Realm of God—the confidence that God is seeking to restore the present old and broken world so that all things will fully manifest God's purposes for all to live in love, peace, justice, and abundance. From Luke's point of view, this restoration is already underway in nascent form through the ministry of Jesus, though Luke believed it would come fully only with Jesus's return.

Beginning to write at sea affected my work. It called attention to differences between the world of Acts and the world of today. The ships on which Paul rode would have fit in the control room of my vessel. Yet we visited ports in which people struggle for survival, evidence the need for the manifestation of the Realm of God is as urgent today as then.

This commentary seeks to spark conversations with Acts that respect the otherness of the text—the differences in its world from the world of today—while exploring points at which this conversation continues to offer hope.[1] At times, Acts points a way forward for today's community. At other times—when elements of a passage in Acts are theologically or ethically problematic—the conversation sets in motion theological reflection that can help us chart a course towards a world more like the Realm.

As a heterosexual male of European origin in the upper middle class, I enjoy the best the old age offers, often at the expense of women and people of other racial and ethnic communities. Yet, I hope this book can be a companion to preaching that sails on a journey of transformation toward a world ever more in the model of the Realm of God.

After a brief Introduction, this commentary moves passage by passage through Acts. Each discussion contains three elements. First, it interprets the passage in light of its historical, literary, and theological function in Acts. Second, because I see the Gospel of Luke and the Book of Acts as a giant chiasmus, I mention how the chiastic passage in the Gospel illumines our understanding of the passage in Acts. This chiastic structure is explained in Appendix 1. Third, each discussion offers suggestions for sermons. Since most of my exegetical observations are found in the standard commentaries, I cite other scholars only at points at which a distinct viewpoint has a direct effect on this work.[2]

I pause now over the titles "Old Testament" and "New Testament." The names "Old" and "New" are theologically problematic: "old" can suggest outdated, in need of replacement, whereas "new" can refer to new and improved. These designations contribute to anti-Judaism, anti-Semitism, and supersessionism (the notion that Judaism is no longer valid and that Christianity has superseded or replaced Judaism). Preachers today increasingly use alternate terms such as Hebrew Bible or First and Second Testaments. These ways of speaking are not quite satisfactory because "First" and "Second" can imply first place and second place, and "Hebrew Bible" is not strictly accurate since parts of the "Hebrew Bible" are in Aramaic. In this commentary, I lean toward "Torah, Prophets, and Writings" for the first thirty-nine books and "Gospels and Letters" for the second twenty-seven books.[3] This designation has the advantage of implying that the one Bible is composed of these different but theologically parallel parts.

I have previously ventured into the waters of Luke-Acts. *Preaching Luke-Acts* suggests that preachers develop sermons on themes that stretch across the Gospel of Luke and the Book of Acts.[4] The theme is essentially the text of the sermon. Readers interested in a more detailed consideration of introductory matters can consult my chapters on the Gospel and Acts in *The Chalice Introduction to the New Testament*.[5]

I thank the Trustees of Christian Theological Seminary for the sabbatical that made this writing possible. I thank David Lott for encouragement, support, and good-humored emails. I thank the advisors of this series for judicious guidance: Luke Powery, Dawn Ottoni-Wilhelm, and David Lose. The Book of Acts played a seminal role in the emergence of the movement of which I have been a lifelong part, the Christian Church (Disciples of Christ).

Just as Paul often traveled with companions, so Linda McKiernan-Allen, minister of West Street Christian Church (Disciples of Christ) in Tipton,

Indiana, was not only a companion on my sea voyage but is a continuing partner on the great journey of life.

The Book of Acts envisions a church so full of the Holy Spirit its interior life embodies the Realm of God and its external witness is irrepressible. It envisions a church whose message and life are magnetic to people from every race, tribe, people, and tongue. It envisions a church with the courage to face the most savage powers of its time to invite repentance as the first step on the journey to restoration and to the Realm. I send this book forward with a prayer that the church of our time may be such a community.

Notes

1. On the text as other, see Ronald J. Allen, *Preaching and the Other: Studies in Postmodern Insights* (Saint Louis: Chalice, 2009).

2. A brief list of works for further reading, including many standard commentaries on the Gospel of Luke and the Book of Acts, is found in Appendix 4.

3. See further Ronald J. Allen, "A New Name for the Old Book: Torah, Prophets, Writings, Gospels, Letters," *Encounter* 68 (2007), 53–62.

4. Ronald J. Allen, *Preaching Luke-Acts*, Preaching Classic Texts (Saint Louis: Chalice, 2000).

5. Ronald J. Allen, "The Story of Jesus According to 'Luke' and "The Story of the Church According to 'Luke,'" in *The Chalice Introduction to the New Testament*, ed. Dennis Smith (Saint Louis: Chalice, 2004), 175–219.

Index of Passages from the Book of Acts in the Revised Common Lectionary

Acts	Liturgical Date	Page Number
The Realm of God		
Acts 1:1-11	Ascension: ABC	15–20
Acts 1:6-14	Easter 7: A	17–23
Acts 1:15-17, 21-26	Easter 7: B	23–25
Acts 2:1-21 (alt)	Pentecost: ABC	26–31
You Will Be My Witness in Jerusalem and Judea		
Acts 2:14a, 22-32	Easter 2: A	26–29
Acts 2:14a, 36-41	Easter 3: A	26, 36–38
Acts 2:42-47	Easter 4: A	38–40
Acts 3:12-19	Easter 3: B	42–44

Acts 4:5-12	Easter 4: B	45–50
Acts 4:32-35	Easter 2: B	50–53
Acts 5:27-32	Easter 2: C	57–59
Acts 7:55-60	Easter 5: A	68–69

You Will Be My Witnesses in Samaria

| Acts 8:14-17 | Baptism of Jesus [1]: C | 74–76 |

You Will Be My Witnesses to the Ends of the Earth

Acts 8:26-40	Easter 5: B	78–83
Acts 9:1-6 (7-20)	Easter 3: C	83–89
Acts 9:36-43	Easter 4: C	91–93
Acts 10:34-43	Baptism of Jesus [1]: A	97–99
Acts 10:34-43 (alt)	Easter: ABC	97–99
Acts 10:44-48	Easter 6: B	99–101
Acts 11:1-18	Easter 5: C	101–104
Acts 16:9-15	Easter 6: C	128–132

Acts 16:16-34	Easter 7: C	132–135
Acts 17:22-31	Easter 6: A	141–143
Acts 19:1-7	Baptism of Jesus [1]: B	148-150

Introduction

With the shadow of next Sunday's sermon falling over the study, the preacher using this commentary may be tempted to bypass the Introduction and go directly to the passage that is the starting point for the sermon. However, a commentary does not simply string together discussions of particular passages. A commentary offers a holistic interpretation of the biblical book based on a particular reconstruction of the world to which the biblical book was written, and the purposes and distinctive features of that book. This information not only helps a preacher understand a particular passage but often makes its way into the sermon. Since the central focus of *Fortress Biblical Preaching Commentaries* is sermon development, I straightforwardly indicate my perspectives on such matters in this Introduction. Preachers who want to delve into details of scholarship can consult more technical commentaries.

THE SERMON: THE TWENTY-NINTH CHAPTER OF ACTS

I once heard a preacher announce the title of her sermon as "The Twenty-Ninth Chapter of Acts." The congregation became restive—we knew that Acts contains only 28 chapters. But the preacher made an important point: Luke intended for the congregation to whom Luke wrote to continue the story told in Luke-Acts by witnessing in its own time much as Luke depicted Jesus, the apostles, and the church in their earlier times. The saga begun in Luke-Acts will not be complete until Jesus returns. In the meantime, congregations add new chapters to the story.

The sermon today is not itself the Twenty-Ninth chapter of Acts. That congregation writes that chapter in its life and witness. In the sermon, the preacher urges the congregation to witness faithfully to the presence and coming of the Realm. By the time we reach the end of the Book of Acts, Luke wants readers to ask, "How will we write *our* chapter in the movement toward the Realm? Will we continue faithfully in the line of Jesus, the apostles, and Paul even as we await the end of this age?"

Who Was "Luke?"

Many people in North America today are interested in the personalities and personal lives of public figures. Those who follow the contemporary cult of personality are often disappointed when encountering biblical figures because we can know so little about these ancient personalities and personal stories. In this vein, we do not know the name, the personality, or many other facts about the author of Acts. The earliest records that attach the name "Luke" to the Gospel and Acts do not appear in our records until the second century. To be sure, biblical materials refer to a figure named Luke (Col. 4:14; 2 Tim. 4:11; Philem. 24). But the Bible itself gives no indication that this Luke is the author of the Gospel and Acts. Nevertheless, the church has long used the name Luke when referring to this writer, and I follow this custom.

Because Colossians 4:14 describes someone named Luke as "beloved physician," many Christians have imagined Luke as a medical doctor. However, no major scholars today think Luke was a physician. While the picture of Luke as a "beloved physician" created a warm feeling about Luke-Acts, it added nothing of substance to our understanding of the theological meaning of these materials.

Scholars continue to debate whether Luke was a Jew or a gentile. In my view, Luke has such a profound knowledge of the Septuagint (the translation of the Torah, Prophets, and Writings into Greek), it is difficult to imagine a gentile acquiring such a deep and intuitive resonance. I think Luke was Jewish. This possibility is reinforced when we remember that many Jewish people regarded the primary mission of Judaism as being a "light to the gentiles" (for example, Isa. 40:7; cf. Gen. 12:1-3). For Luke the life, death, and resurrection of Jesus were a light through which God sought to reach out to gentiles in the last days of the present age. Of course, Luke is critical of some Jewish people, which I regard as a family fight.

Who Was Theophilus?

Luke dedicates both the Gospel and Acts (Luke 1:1; Acts 1:1) to Theophilus. Scholars ponder whether Theophilus was an actual person or whether the name is a symbol. If a person, then Theophilus was likely Luke's benefactor or patron—a wealthy person who subsidized Luke writing these materials. Some scholars think this situation accounts for the relative sympathy toward wealthy people in Luke-Acts. At the same time, the name Theophilus could be a theological symbol whose meaning is revealed in the two parts of the name:

"Theo" is from the Greek word for God, and "philus" is from a Greek expression for "one who loves" or "beloved." Thus the name Theophilus could refer to all who love God or to all who are beloved of God.

In either event, Luke 1:4 indicates that Luke's congregation was already acquainted with stories of Jesus and the church. Luke envisions readers whose mindset will be reframed by Luke's retelling of the story. Luke's purpose is similar to that of the preacher today: to help a community already familiar with the broad lines of the story discern more adequately the leading of God.

Date, Place of Composition, and Location of Addressees

Most scholars think Luke wrote between 80 and 90 CE. We do not know either the precise place Luke wrote these materials or the location of the congregation to whom Luke wrote. Yet clues within the materials suggest that Luke wrote to a congregation in an urban environment influenced by Greek culture. For example, Luke modifies some details in the Gospel to appeal to urban residents. In the Markan version of the story of the friends who lower a paralyzed person to Jesus through the roof, the friends dig through roof of a typical Palestinian small-town house, whereas in the Lukan version they remove the tiles on the roof of a more prosperous urban house (Mark 2:4; Luke 5:19). The narrative in Acts moves from city to city and regards Rome as the destination of the story. Luke quotes Greek authors as theological authorities (for example, Acts 17:28; 26:24b).

One Story: The Gospel of Luke and the Book of Acts

The Gospel and Acts tell one continuous story. The narrative that begins in Luke 1:1 does not reach its climax until Acts 28:31. To read the two volumes in separation is to rend asunder what Luke intended to join together. When preaching from the Gospel, the preacher should trace the main themes of the passage from the Gospel into Acts. When developing a sermon from Acts, the preacher should explore how themes of the passage emerged in the Gospel. To treat a passage from Luke-Acts in isolation is to violate one of the fundamental axioms of biblical interpretation: the interpreter should always explore a passage in its literary context.

Special Feature: The Chiastic Structure of the Gospel of Luke and the Book of Acts

In my view, the Gospel of Luke and the Book of Acts form a giant chiasmus. Chiasm was a commonplace literary structure in antiquity in which an author arranged the elements of a text in inverted parallelism. A chiasm could be as short as one verse or as long as an entire document. The center element of the chiasm reveals the central concern.

In a chiasm, the parallel elements interpret one another. The Gospel tells the story of how Jesus came to ascend to God. The Book of Acts draws out the implications of the ascended Jesus for the witness of the church. The geographical movement of Luke-Acts helps us see the chiastic structure. The story begins in out-of-the-way Jewish settlements of Luke 1–2 with the news that through the ministry of Jesus, God is bringing the Realm of God to its final manifestation. The story moves toward Jerusalem where the central revelatory events occur, especially the center of the chiasm, the ascension of Jesus (Luke 24:44-53 and Acts 1:6-11). The story ends with the news of the Realm going from Jerusalem to Rome, the heart of the power structure of the old age and symbol of the gentile world.

As noted below, Luke's congregation was likely in a season of difficulty. By placing the ascended Jesus at the center of the story, Luke assures the congregation they can continue to witness to the coming of the Realm in the confidence that the promises God made through Jesus are trustworthy.

The chiastic structure is set out in Appendix 1. In connection with each passage from Acts, I briefly discuss how the parallel element from the Gospel enriches our understanding of Acts. The element in the Gospel typically provides background for understanding the element in Acts. The element in Acts typically draws out the implication of the element in the Gospel for the witness of the church. The preacher who wants to make full use of the chiasmus in preaching could print two texts for each sermon—one from the Gospel and one from Acts.

A Companion to Preaching from the Gospel of Luke

Because of the chiastic pattern just discussed, a preacher can use this commentary on the Book of Acts as an immediate companion when developing a sermon from the Gospel of Luke. A preacher working with a text in Luke can use Appendix 1, "The Chiastic Structure of Luke-Acts," to locate the passage in Luke and its parallel in Acts, and then turn to the commentary proper for exegetical and homiletical discussion. The preacher who is preparing a message from the Revised Common Lectionary can use Appendix 1 in the way just described or can turn to Appendix 2, "Table Correlating Lectionary Readings from Luke withy Chiastic Parallels from Acts." This latter appendix lists passages from the Gospel of Luke and their chiastic parallels from Acts in the order of the days of the Christian Year for lectionary years A, B, and C. In a sense, this work on Acts is really a commentary on two books of the Bible at once.

THE END-TIME WORLDVIEW OF ACTS: LIVING THROUGH A DELAY IN THE END

Luke shared the main lines of Jewish end-time theology (apocalypticism). This viewpoint is found in nascent form in Isaiah 56–66 and Zechariah 9–12 and is fully developed in Daniel 7–12. It was popular in Jewish circles beginning about 300 BCE. The end-time theologians believed that God created the world as an Eden in which all things manifest God's purposes. However, Eve and Adam accepted the invitation of Satan (the snake) to transgress by eating the forbidden fruit. As punishment, God cursed the human beings and the world. As an act of grace, God did not destroy the world but promised to restore it.

The end-time theologians thought of history from the fall to the restoration as an old age in which existence was broken. Satan and the demons had great power. The old creation was an age of idolatry, injustice, exploitation, enmity with nature, violence, and death. However, at a moment God had predetermined, God would end the old age and replace it with the Realm of God—a time in which God's rule would prevail in every circumstance and which was marked by worship of the living God, love, justice, mutual support, social equality, abundance, health, a relationship of blessing between humankind and nature, peace, and everlasting life. The means of transition from the old to the new would be an apocalypse in which God would invade the world, destroy the old age, and restore all things. The old creation included empires that idolatrously sought ultimate allegiance and demanded subservience. The Roman Empire was a prime example.

Luke modified this end-time theology in three respects. First, Luke interpreted the ministry of Jesus, the outpouring of the Holy Spirit, and the emergence of the church as signals that the last days were underway. Second, Luke believed many characteristics of the coming Realm of God were already at work in the present, initially through the ministry of Jesus but continuing under the power of the Spirit through the church. Indeed, the church was to embody qualities of the Realm while inviting others to prepare for its final arrival. Third,

Luke believed that the apocalypse was delayed. One purpose of the Gospel and Acts is to urge the community to continue their witness during the delay by assuring them that the Holy Spirit continued to empower them even in the face of conflict.

At one time, many preachers and scholars thought Luke-Acts was a political apologetic, a document designed to persuade the Romans that the church had no plans for sedition. Few scholars today follow this line of interpretation. In fact, Luke views the Roman Empire with a jaundiced theological eye: God will destroy Rome at the apocalypse. At the same time, however, Luke mentions individual Romans soldiers and officials who serve the purposes of the Realm. In the same way God used Cyrus the Persian to liberate Israel's leaders from exile in Babylon (for example, Isa. 44:24-28; 45:1-17), so Luke believed God used aspects of Roman machinery to protect Paul long enough for Paul to carry the gospel to Rome.

What Was Happening in the Congregation to which Luke Wrote?

The preacher wants to know what was happening in the congregation to which Luke wrote as well as how Luke sought to address those dynamics. The preacher can then find fitting analogies and points of difference between the ancient and contemporary contexts, and Luke's purposes in them, and can decide whether Luke's purposes are appropriate for today. Here is a simplified summary of major dynamics in Luke's situation.

- The delay in the apocalypse generated doubts and dissipated the congregation's witness. Luke wants the congregation to witness through the delay with confidence and energy.
- Luke's church was in tension with many Jewish people. Luke wants the church to recognize its own roots in Judaism while believing its Jewish critics are not faithful to their own tradition.
- Some gentiles treat Jewish people disrespectfully. Luke reminds gentiles of the Jewish origins of the movement toward the Realm and urges gentiles to respect Judaism.
- The congregation contained both Jewish and gentile members who were themselves in tension. Luke wants both groups to live together in the love, peace, and mutual support of the restored world. The life of the church should prefigure the life of the Realm.
- The wealthy were slow to share their resources with the poor. God seeks to use the sharing of material resources as God's means for

providing for the poor and freeing the rich from the idolatry of
  wealth. God wants all to experience security.
- The congregation was divided regarding the role of women in
  leadership. Luke-Acts does not portray women as having equal
  standing with men, but this literature does contain impulses toward
  liberation.
- The congregation perceived itself as harassed or in danger of being
  harassed. Luke uses the martyrdoms of Jesus, Stephen, James, Paul,
  Jesus's teaching that the disciples would take up their crosses daily,
  and the suffering of the church to urge the community to continue
  faithful witness even in the face of threat.
- Luke's community was uncertain how to relate to the Empire and its
  representatives. Luke wants his congregation to critique the idolatry,
  injustice, and violence of the Empire while making its way through
  the world dominated by the Empire, recognizing that individual
  Romans and even Roman systems can serve the purposes of the
  Realm.
- Underlying these concerns was a question that vexes the church to
  the present: authority. Where does the church turn for resources in
  discerning God's presence and purposes? Luke grounds the story of
  Jesus and the church in the Septuagint and uses the story of Jesus in
  the Gospel as authorizing the mission of the church in Acts. The
  apostles are the authorizing body for the church. The Holy Spirit
  aligns Jesus, the apostles, and the church with the purposes of God.

We may say generally, then, that the congregation was disheartened in faith and dissipated in mission. The congregation's internal life was conflicted, and the congregation's external witness was dissipated. Luke told the story of the church in Acts to stir the congregation in his day to the level of faithfulness exhibited by the community in Acts.

Continuing the Story of Israel but in Tension with Some Jewish People

Christians have often seen the story of Israel and the stories of Jesus and the church as discontinuous. Indeed, many members of the church regard the religion of Israel and the Old Testament as old, out-of-date, legalistic, repressive, judgmental, and teaching works-righteousness. Those same folk see the religion of Jesus and the New Testament as new, improved, liberating, and based on love and grace. Many in the church believe that Judaism is no longer valid and that Jesus, the New Testament, and the church have replaced the Old

Testament and Judaism. Indeed, in this paradigm, Jesus liberates his followers from Judaism!

A widespread movement in biblical and theological scholarship now regards the preceding paradigm as a horrendous mistake. In its worst forms, it feeds anti-Judaism and anti-Semitism. It contributed directly to the murder of six million Jewish people by the Nazis during World War II. Less virulently, it leads to subtle forms of anti-Semitism as well as to Christian smugness. In the last thirty years, however, many Christian scholars and preachers call for Christianity and Judaism to respect the integrity of the other and to express elements of shared identity, values, ethics, and mission.

Luke sees the stories of Jesus and the church growing out of the deeper story of Israel. Indeed, one of Luke's purposes is to explain how a movement centered in Jewish end-time expectation (Jesus) became a movement welcoming both Jewish and gentile peoples and pointing to the renewal of the entire cosmos.

For Luke—as for many of the authors of the Torah, Prophets, and Writings—God intended to bless all peoples through the life of Israel. According to Luke, God used the ministry of Jesus to signal that history was in its final days. Through the church, God welcomed gentiles into the movement toward the Realm. The mission of Jesus and the church, then, are a continuation of the mission of Israel. The church's outreach to gentiles is not a rejection of Judaism but an expression of God's intent to bless gentiles in the last days. For Luke the church is not a separate religion (Christianity) from Judaism but an extension of Judaism. The leading figures—such as Jesus, Peter, and Paul—are almost always faithfully Jewish.

At the same time, Luke-Acts reports considerable conflict between Jesus (and the church) and Jewish people. Scholars agree that the Gospel and Acts are not anti-Semitic (systematic hatred of all things Jewish). Luke-Acts does, however, articulate a bias against many Jewish people. The Gospel and Acts do not reject Judaism as such, but they harshly criticize Jewish people who do not endorse the validity of the mission of Jesus and the church. Indeed, the Gospel and Acts imply that Jewish and gentile people who do not respect the movement to the Realm will be condemned at the apocalypse.

Many scholars today think that the caricatures of Jewish people in Luke-Acts reflect tensions between Luke's congregation and some Jewish leaders of Luke's own time. What prompted this conflict? It was likely not a conflict between legalistic Judaism and liberating Christianity but was a conflict regarding what it meant to be faithfully Jewish. Many Jewish people in Luke's day who were not in the church believed they were living in the last days.

They wanted to be prepared to be saved, that is, welcomed into the Realm. The primary point of tension was the degree to which gentiles needed to be initiated into Judaism to be saved at the last day. Luke agreed with prevailing Jewish opinion that gentiles needed to believe in the one living God, to repent, and to adopt core Jewish attitudes and behaviors (see Acts 15:22-29). With history soon to end, however, Luke did not think that gentiles needed to be fully initiated into Judaism by following the dietary practices and circumcision.

When working with the Gospel and Acts, the preacher needs to handle carefully images of Jewish people and Judaism. A preacher's instinct is often to contrast negative Judaism with positive Jesus, Christianity and church. Instead, the preacher can explain the circumstances that gave rise to the negative caricature of Judaism. The preacher may need to say that Luke was theologically and/or ethically mistaken in regard to elements of some texts. I name these points in the commentary. Indeed, such reflection might help the congregation recognize and repent of its own anti-Judaism. If a preacher cannot find positive points of contact in the text itself, the preacher can nearly always do so in the conversation sparked by the text, a reading of passages that reinforces negative perceptions of Judaism today. By criticizing select texts, the preacher can help today's church break the cycle of anti-Judaism that has been self-perpetuating for two millennia.

Strategies for Moving from Then to Now

The first responsibility of the preacher is to explain what a text in Acts asked its readers to believe and do in antiquity. The second is to help the congregation today consider what it believes and what to do in response.

One of the most common means of moving from then to now is the hermeneutic of analogy. The preacher recognizes differences in culture and world view between antiquity and today, while also identifying similarities in experience. The preacher bridges these differences by making analogies in similar experiences then and now. I often use the language of surface and deeper meanings in this regard: a text has a surface meaning that may or may not be at home in the world view today, while also having a deeper meaning, that is, a significance not limited by the surface meaning but connecting to deeper realms of experience that we share with people in antiquity.

For example, the story of the ascension (Acts 1:1-11) pictures Jesus ascending from the earth to heaven where Jesus is at the right hand of God. At the surface level, Luke presupposes a three story universe (an underworld, the earth, and heaven above), so that Jesus could literally ascend from earth to heaven. The point of the text is that Jesus is sovereign over all other rulers, authorities, dominions, and powers (including Satan, demons, and Caesar). Today, science tells us we live in an ever-expanding universe in which talk of a three-story universe is out of date. However, from an analogical perspective, the preacher today can affirm the deeper point that God through Jesus has authority over all other forces and powers.

While the hermeneutic of analogy often makes it possible for the sermon to move from then to now in a clear and compelling way, the preacher needs to use theological caution when considering this hermeneutic. Some texts contain elements that are theologically or ethically inappropriate. In such cases, the hermeneutic of analogy would actually misrepresent God's purposes.

For instance, in Acts 5:1-11, Ananias and Sapphira claim to have given the entire price of a piece of property to the church's common treasury. However, when they lied, God struck them dead. This text implies that God is a murderer. To be sure, the deeper function of this passage is to impress upon the congregation the double importance of telling the truth and of contributing to the welfare of the community through sharing goods. But this point comes with what I believe is a misrepresentation of God. In my view, God is a God of unconditional love who wills for all people to live in relationships of love. Such a God would not murder Ananias and Sapphira.

The preacher is called to name the theological difficulties in such a text. Indeed, at times a minister must preach against a text. In the case of Acts 5:1-11, to fail to make such a critique is to leave the impression that God engages in murder. A congregant could then conclude that God sanctions murder in certain settings today.

The most common texts in Acts that raise theological difficulties for the preacher are those that caricature Jewish people. This issue is discussed above in connection with tensions between the church and Judaism.

Rather than think of a simple movement from then to now, I prefer to think of the sermon as a conversation with two parts. (1) The preacher identifies what a text from Acts invited the congregation in antiquity to believe and do. (2) The preacher explores how conversation with the text helps the congregation today clarify what we can believe and do. Our encounter with the text pushes us to clarify our own beliefs and to identify appropriate actions, even when the text itself contains problematic elements. For instance, considering God as murderer in Acts 5:1-11 pushes me to recognize that I do not believe God acts that way. I would not preach the text, but I would preach good news from God arising from conversation with the text.

CAUTIONS ABOUT ANACHRONISM

The first rule of biblical exegesis is to respect the integrity and otherness of a text by considering what it asked people to believe and do in its own historical, literary, and theological contexts. However, preachers sometimes bypass this practice and engage in anachronism. Anachronism occurs when preacher and congregation read today's issues, beliefs, assumptions, values and behaviors into the biblical text when those things were not found in the ancient world. We make the text into our own image by treating it as a mirror of our own lives and world.

Preachers and commentators like to think that our own theological and ethical values are confirmed in the Bible because we can then claim to stand on the authority of the Bible when advocating our views and values. However, anachronism greatly reduces the power of our encounter with the otherness of the text. When we read the text as reflections of ourselves, we reduce the power of the passage to offer us fresh ways of thinking about (and responding to) God.

For example, many people in the progressive Christian circles in which I move long for multicultural community. Many Christians believe that God values all cultures and that a central feature of the Realm of God is multiple cultures living alongside one another in mutual respect. I frequently hear preachers read this agenda into Acts. But the church in Acts is not a straightforward prototype of the kind of respect for different cultures that progressives and others hope to find in today's schools, work places, and neighborhoods in which people of different racial and ethnic groups, genders, religions, and sexual orientations live together in mutual respect while celebrating many of their differences. I share this hope for community today. But the community of the church in Acts is constituted by repentance, baptism in the name of Jesus, and by gentiles and Jews living together in covenantal commitment even as gentiles take on select Jewish values and practices. In a conversational mode, a preacher may make theological moves to get from Luke's picture of the church in Acts to the kind of multicultural community described above as one of God's purposes for today. But the preacher does violence to Acts by reading today's hope for multicultural community into the ancient text.

The Book of Acts in the Lectionary

The Revised Common Lectionary assigns readings from Acts each year on the Baptism of Jesus, on the Sundays after Easter, and on Pentecost. These are important Sundays that give Acts a place of honor.

In other respects, however, the Book of Acts is disadvantaged in the lectionary. The Revised Common Lectionary assigns only twenty-four texts from Acts in the entire three-year table of readings. Moreover, the congregation never hears the entire story of Acts in a continuous telling in the way that the congregation hears most of the Gospels and the Epistles. The last reading from Acts in the lectionary is from Acts 19. The congregation never hears Acts 20–28—the story of Paul's arrest, arraignment, and the journey to Rome that reveal Luke's ultimate purpose in the Gospel and Acts. Furthermore, the readings from Acts are always subservient to the readings from the Gospel. Acts never speaks in its own voice, except when the preacher chooses to make Acts the lead text in the sermon.

Beyond these things, Acts is involved in one of the most unfortunate theological moves in the lectionary. On the seven Sundays after Easter, the lectionary excises the main reading from the Torah, Prophets, and Writings and inserts instead a passage from Acts. At the climactic season of the Christian Year—when the church contemplates the demonstration of the Realm through the resurrection—the lectionary leans in an anti-Jewish direction by removing the Torah, Prophets, and Writings, implying they are not necessary to the church's identity and witness. When preparing for worship after Easter, the preacher and worship planners are encouraged to add a reading from the Torah, Prophets, and Writings that coordinates with the other lections. If a passage must be dropped, let it be the Letter or the Gospel.

In my view, the lectionary is to serve the witness to the Realm through church; the church is not called to serve the lectionary. The lectionary sometimes fails to yield a meaningful, mutual, critical correlation between the assigned readings and the local context. When that occurs—and correlation does exist between a non-lectionary reading from Acts and the local situation—ministers should feel free to depart from the lectionary and to preach from the text from Acts. Outside the lectionary, a preacher could develop a series of sermons from Acts. Appendix 3 outlines three same sample sermon series—on key passages, on leading characters, and on themes.

Outside of the service of worship, a minister or other Bible teacher can lead a Bible study series on Acts. Ideally the class could follow the entire narrative of Acts. If time does not permit such an extensive study, the leaders might do part of the book (say, the missionary journeys of Paul). The preacher could broaden the impact of such a study by using the same texts in the pulpit on Sunday as the study groups are using during the week.

Theological Perspectives of Luke and the Writer of this Commentary

Recent emphasis on preachers becoming aware of our own social locations includes the importance of naming our own theological convictions. By so doing, we can better avoid anachronism by being able to compare and contrast our theological perspectives with those of the biblical text and with other theological voices.

The purpose of this commentary is to point to possibilities for preaching from Acts and not to push my own theological perspective as the norm for moving from text to sermon. But in the commentary I occasionally use my theology as an example of moving from text to sermon.

Influenced by process (relational) theology, my own deepest theological conviction is that God is unconditional love. Indeed, God seeks for all people and all things to live together in love. I believe that while God is more influential than any other entity, God does not have the absolute power to do anything God wants. In my view, God is present in each and every moment to offer all entities—people as well as elements of creation—the optimum experience of love available to them in the circumstances of that moment. God cannot unilaterally change difficult contexts, but God is present as we make our way through them.

I do not believe, as Luke does, that God has divided history into two discontinuous ages or that God is going to (or can) end the present era in a single moment to bring about the Realm. God works in the world through lure rather than through coercion. God's power is limited to what God can accomplish through lure as human beings and other elements of creation choose (consciously or unconsciously) to cooperate with God's purposes of love, peace, justice, and abundance. We can embrace those purposes and facilitate them, or we turn away from God's purposes and frustrate them.

I do not believe that God intentionally causes pain or harm. Hence, I do not endorse Luke's view that God sentences people to temporary or everlasting punishment. Nevertheless, we do sometimes make decisions that go against God's purposes. By doing so, we invite circumstances that bring judgment on ourselves. God does not cause us to suffer, but we suffer the consequences of our own mistakes.

In the broad sense, I regard encounters with passages from the Book of Acts as occasions on which to consider how God seeks to lure us into ever-deeper relationships of love with God and other people. I believe God, through the Holy Spirit, is present with the preacher in the study, with the preacher and the congregation in the moment of preaching, and in the afterglow of the sermon to intensify our experiences of love and our responses of loving God and one another.

In the strict sense, we cannot know what the future holds. But I have experienced enough love and grace in this life to believe that we can trust God to be ever present, luring us toward a world in which unconditional love is all in all.

1

The Coming of the Realm of God: The Main Theme of the Book of Acts

Acts 1:1—2:13

Acts 1:8 sets out the basic movement of the plot of the Book of Acts (and the overarching structure of this commentary): the story will move from Jerusalem and Judea through Samaria to the ends of the earth. While Acts 1:1—2:13 takes place in Jerusalem, this commentary discusses this section because of its distinctive functions in the Book of Acts. Acts 1:1—2:13 reminds the reader that the story in Acts continues the story told in the Gospel of Luke. The main theme of the Gospel of Luke is that God is using the ministry of Jesus to signal that the transition is underway from the present Roman world to the Realm of God—a new cosmos of love, peace, justice, and abundance—is underway. In addition to inviting people to repent and to join the movement toward the Realm, the ministry of Jesus embodied the qualities of the Realm. Acts 1:1—2:13 reminds the reading community not only that the coming of the Realm of God is the main theme of the Book of Acts. Furthermore, God not only restored the community of Jesus' followers but filled them with the Holy Spirit to empower them to continue the ministry of Jesus but also promises to empower the congregation to whom Luke wrote so continue Jesus in their own time and place.

The Coming of the Realm of God: The Ascension Confirms the Coming of the Realm (Acts 1:1-11)

In many writings in antiquity the first and last scenes involving a major character are often keys to understanding the identity of that character, as well as the purpose of the story. That phenomenon is true of Jesus (and other characters) in the Gospel and Acts. From this point of view the narrative of the words and events leading to the ascension and the ascension itself are important because the ascension is both the last scene in which Jesus appears in the Gospel and the first scene in Acts. The birth, ministry, death, and resurrection of Jesus climax in the Gospel in the ascension. In Acts, the ascension is the defining moment out of which comes the story of the church.

Acts 1:1-5 introduces the reader to the Book of Acts and prepares the reader for the story of the ascension in 1:6-11. Luke addresses Acts to Theophilus. As noted in the Introduction, the name Theophilus may refer to an individual, or it may refer to all who love God or who are beloved by God. Whatever that case, Luke assumes the community was familiar with the story although Luke wants them to understand it from the perspective of Acts.

Today's congregation may be in a similar position to that of the people to whom Luke wrote. Multiple interpretations of the story of Jesus are afloat in the Bible, in the church and in today's culture. Paul, Mark, Matthew Luke, and John offer their own renditions of Jesus, as do historical figures such as Augustine, Anselm and Abelard, not to mention contemporary preachers as diverse as Howard Thurman, Paul Tillich, John Howard Yoder, Elizabeth Schüssler Fiorenza, the Jesus Seminar, Jacqueline Grant, John Dominic Crossan, Joel Olsteen, and Creflo Dollar. Many congregations today are familiar with such representations of Jesus and the church, but do not understand the sacred stories from Luke's point of view, nor with how Luke's perception might compare, contrast, and contribute to the congregation's own systematic understanding of Jesus and the church. A sermon on Christology might bring Luke's perception into dialogue with others while helping the congregation with theological integration.

Acts 1:3 summarizes the purpose of Jesus: to alert people to the presence and final (and complete) coming of the Realm of God. The church is to continue the ministry of Jesus by announcing the Realm and inviting people to repent and to become a part of the church—a community living toward the Realm in the present while anticipating its final consummation.

The Lukan Jesus intended for the church to invite gentiles into the community awaiting the Realm (Luke 24:47). Luke writes Acts not simply to report the history of an institution but to imply a program for the church. This mission has the double foci of embodying the Realm in the church's internal life and witnessing to the Realm in the external world.

According to Acts 1:4-5, Jesus promised the disciples they would receive the Holy Spirit in a special way to empower them in the end-time (Luke 3:15-17). Acts 1:4-5 indicates that one purpose of the Book of Acts is to give a narrative picture of Spirit-filled life and witness, a notion of the Spirit developed more fully in Acts 2:1-36. The Spirit enables the church in Acts to continue the spirit-filled, Realm-witnessing ministry of Jesus, and to extend it into the gentile world.

CONNECTION TO THE LECTIONARY

The Revised Common Lectionary assigns both Acts 1:6-11 and Luke 24:44-53 on Ascension Day in all three years of the lectionary. While Ascension Day does not fall on Sunday, the lectionary offers the ascension readings as alternatives for the Seventh Sunday after Easter. Since the ascension has a key place in Christian faith, the minister should occasionally preach on the readings for Ascension Day on the Seventh Sunday after Easter. However, preaching on the ascension only from Luke's perspective may leave the church with the impression that Luke's interpretation is normative whereas other writers in the Second Testament picture the ascended Jesus with their own theological nuances (for example, Matt. 22:44; Mark 12:36; 14:62; Rom. 8:34; Eph. 1:20; Col. 1:20; Heb. 1:3, 13; 8:1; 10:12; 12:2; 1 Pet. 3:22; cf. Luke 20:42; 22:69). From time to time, a pastor could help the church recognize the diversity of interpretations by departing from the lectionary and preaching from one of these other texts, or by bringing other passages into dialogue with Acts.

ACTS 1:6-11. THE ASCENSION CONFIRMS THAT GOD RULES

While Luke often uses the figures of the apostles to represent authority in community, Luke sometimes portrays these figures as imperceptive and in need of instruction, as when they ask in Acts 1:6. "Is this the time when you will restore the Realm to Israel?" The apostles want to know when God will restore Israel's political independence. This question indicates their understanding of the Realm is too limited. Jesus announces the Realm—social and cosmic restoration—not simply a restoration of Israel's political fortunes. Does the congregation today perceive God's aims in similarly limited ways?

While Luke may not know exactly when the final consummation will take place (Acts 1:7), Luke is confident that God gives the disciples a special outpouring of the Holy Spirit to witness, beginning in Jerusalem and Judea, moving through Samaria to the ends of the earth (Acts 1:8).

The geographical references in Acts 1:8 are important theological symbols with three levels of meaning. (1) These references articulate the broad narrative structure of Acts: the story moves from Jerusalem and Judea (Acts 2:1-8:30) through Samaria (Acts 8:4-25) to the ends of the earth (Acts 8:26-28:31). (2) When the narrative of Acts unfolds geographically as Jesus predicts, the reader has confidence in Luke's interpretation of the story. If we can believe Jesus (and Luke) about this geographical sequence, then we can be confident of the broader movement of history toward the final consummation. (3) The movement from Jerusalem to the ends of the earth shows the nature of the Realm. That witness is to become ever more inclusive: initially it includes Jewish people (in Jerusalem and Judea), Samaritans (people who are Jewish in origin but who distance themselves from Judaism) and gentiles (to the ends of the earth).

The core of this passage is Acts 1:9-10. God lifted Jesus into heaven at God's right hand (Acts 2:33-35, 5:31; 7:55-56). Jesus is thus God's representative who ultimately has power over all other rulers, including Satan, the demons, Caesar, and the Roman Empire. The ascension shows not only that God approves of the ministry of Jesus but that God wills for this ministry to continue through those who repent, embrace Jesus's message about the Realm, and receive the Spirit. Here, as in the Gospel, the focus is not upon the person of Jesus but upon the Realm. Jesus is God's representative in confirming and extending the Realm.

Luke here draws on two ancient assumptions. First, many people in antiquity imagined the universe as similar to a three-story house with God dwelling in the upper story (heaven), earth as the middle level, and an underworld beneath. According to the story of the ascension, God elevated Jesus from the earth (the second level) to God's right hand in heaven (the upper level). Second, many people in antiquity regarded the right hand of God as the more powerful hand (for example, Exod. 15:6; Ps. 16:11; 20:6; 110:1 Isa. 48:13; 62:8). Moreover, the ascended Jesus will be present with God for the final judgment (for example, Acts 10:42; 17:31).The ascended Jesus operates with the power from God's right hand.

The preacher could develop a sermon around the implication that all other powers are ultimately subject to the Realm of God. The preacher who uses media in the sermon (such as PowerPoint) could project pictures that depict the three story universe. To be sure, many people today are troubled by the ancient picture of the three story universe. What sense does it make in our scientific age to say that Jesus *ascended* to heaven? However, many thoughtful contemporary Christians (including me) believe that the deeper point of the text is not tied to Luke's outmoded cosmology. The lasting message is that God's authority and purposes transcend all others and that all authorities and powers are accountable to God. The text communicates this idea in the vivid first century image of a three-story universe, but the point is not tied to that picture.

The sermon could identify forces in the present that work against the purposes of God. These forces range from those that beset the individual to those that disfigure the congregation, the nation, and the world, including such things as personal addictions, diseases, the church's preoccupation with itself, racism, and international economic havoc wreaked by transnational corporations. The ascension gives the congregation the confidence to continue to witness to a more Realm-like world even in the face of resistance. No matter how powerful the Caesars we face—in the political realm, in community life, in the congregation, in personal affairs—the picture of Jesus at the right hand of God is one of ultimate sovereignty.

CHIASTIC PARALLELS. ACTS 1:1-11 AND LUKE 24:43-55

The chiastic parallel between Acts 1:1-11 and Luke 24:44-53 is unique in the great chiasmus of Luke-Acts in that these passages combine to form the central element. Indeed, these two elements not only interpret the same event but make the same point. Everything in the Gospel of Luke flows *toward* the ascension. Everything in the Book of Acts flows *from* the ascension. For the Gospel, the ascension is the climax of the story of Jesus. For Acts, the ascension is the charter for the church. The themes that surface in these two passages are central to Luke-Acts: the continuity of the story of Jesus and church with the story of Judaism, the suffering of Jesus (and the implied suffering of his followers), repentance, the Holy Spirit, and the vocation of the community to witness to all nations.

In the spirit of honest theological conversation, the preacher should acknowledge the difficulties with this viewpoint. While the text asserts the final authority of God, our immediate experience is often the rule of Caesar. The Realm may seem defeated as often as it makes headway. The ascension assures us that God will never give up offering opportunities to help the world become more Realm-like. One of my teachers said, "Death may win in every individual case, but ultimately life prevails."

The ascension has political dimensions. Caesar ruled the Roman Empire. If God through Christ rules over all, then the values and practices of the Realm ultimately take priority over those of Caesar. The preacher could reflect on how religious views can help shape our positions on public policy. At one level, this task is easy: Christians should stand for values that are consistent with those of the Realm. On the other hand, this task is complicated in a democracy claiming to separate church and state. Within the church, the preacher can claim that God's values should prevail because they are God's values. But in the pluralistic public square, on what authority can the preacher use the vision of the Realm of God as a basis for recommending public policy?

Congregations today often develop mission statements. Acts 1:4 and 8, combined with Luke 24:46 and Acts 2:38, is a shorthand version of Luke's understanding of mission. Luke's community is to witness to the Realm of God and to invite people to become a part of the movement toward the Realm through repentance, baptism, receiving the Holy Spirit, and witnessing through the life of the community. The sermon could lead the congregation in comparing and contrasting its own formal or informal understandings of mission with those of Luke-Acts. The sermon could help the congregation identify specific ways it can more fully carry out its mission.

One aspect of the witness moving from Jerusalem and Judea through Samaria to the ends of the earth suggests a norm that preacher and congregation can use to gauge the adequacy of their own witness to the Realm. By portraying the movement from Jerusalem and Judea through Samaria to the ends of the earth, Luke indicates that the faithful witness enlarges community. The witnessing church becomes ever more inclusive. The witness of the church today, then, is in continuity with Acts when it also extends the boundaries of community.

As Jesus ascends, his followers simply stare upward at the place where Jesus went. Two figures from heaven ask a question to the disciples that the preacher might ask the congregation. "Why do you [do nothing more than] stand looking up toward heaven?" (Acts 1:11). In other words, "Now that you have the confidence that Jesus is at the right hand of God, why are you not engaging in the mission Jesus gives you?"

The Coming of the Reign of God: Preparing the Community to Represent the Realm (Acts 1:12-26)

In Luke 24:40 and Acts 1:4-5, the risen Jesus instructs the community to wait in Jerusalem for the Holy Spirit, the power that comes from on high. Acts 1:12-26 depicts the community faithfully doing what Jesus commanded: they wait. Their waiting, however, is not passive. They pray. They support one another. They wrestle theologically with the death of Judas. They work with God to elect Matthias as the twelfth living apostle. Their wait is one in which they prepare to represent the Realm.

Acts 1:12-26 is a miniature of the situation of Luke's congregation. The congregation is in a delay between the ascension and the return of Jesus. They wait. Yet their wait is not to be passive, but is to be a season in which they witness actively to the possibilities offered by the Realm. The time between the ascension and Pentecost is a paradigm for the time between Pentecost and the second coming. After Pentecost, the congregation awaits the second coming by assertively engaging in mission.

We see in the larger context of this passage an instance of a larger pattern important in the Gospel and Acts. An authoritative figure, such as Jesus or an apostle makes a prediction or gives an instruction. The prediction comes to pass. The community follows the instructions, and finds that the instructions are true (or the community disobeys the instructions and suffers destructive consequences). In the present case, Jesus's promise of Luke 24:40 and Acts 1:4-5 comes true in Acts 2:1-4. This turn of events reinforces the congregation's confidence in the reliability of Acts as a guide for how live as they await the return of Jesus.

In antiquity, identity was more communal than in cultures of European origin today in which identity is often individualistic. Many Eurocentric people think of identity as something we achieve as individuals. Indeed, some folk glorify personal achievement even when it takes place at the expense of other people. By contrast, Acts 1:12-14 points toward a theme fundamental to Luke: participants in the movement toward the Realm are genuine *community*. They are together in identity, mutual support, and mission. The preacher could encourage the church today toward understanding itself as such a community. From the perspective of common identity, the individual is complete only when actively involved in the whole, and the community is represented in the individual.

Luke underscores the fact that the community of the Realm includes both men (v. 13) and women (v. 14). Unfortunately, Luke does not present the church in Acts as an altogether egalitarian community. The apostles, for instance, are all men, and they maintain the major roles of leadership. Nevertheless, in this passage we see evidence of Luke's belief that in the Realm God seeks to restore the relationship of women and men to the mutuality and equality of Genesis 1-2. The preacher could reflect on the degree to which relationships among women and men in the congregation and in the larger social world point toward the Realm.

Chiastic Parallel. Luke 24:36-44 and Acts 1:12-14

Luke 24:36-44 and Acts 1:12-24 present different responses to the risen Jesus. In Luke 24:36-44, the disciples are together, but when the resurrected Jesus comes into their sight, they do not recognize him and become afraid and immobilized. However, Jesus reveals he is present. In Acts 1:12-14 the community is together. Jesus has gone out of their sight (by ascending), but God assured them of the continuing validity of Jesus's ministry (through Jesus eating the fish in Luke 24:36-44 and through the ascension in Acts 1:6-11). The preacher could explore ways the congregation fails to recognize Jesus and the Realm and becomes fearful and immobilized (Luke 24:36-44) yet how the risen Jesus is present to assure them and to revitalize their common life (Acts 1:12-14).

The motif of prayer (v. 14) permeates both the Gospel and Acts. For Luke, prayer is the intentional opening of self and community to the coming of the Realm (Luke 11:2-4). By praying the congregation not only asks God to regenerate the present but indicates its willingness to join God in the movement toward the Realm. To pray is thus to seek social transformation that brings the world more into harmony with the values and practices of the Realm. This part of the passage could inspire a sermon on the doctrine of prayer. The preacher might survey the congregation's current attitudes and practices of prayer, bringing out similarities and differences with Luke's perceptions and with the church's systematic theological understanding of prayer. Can the preacher identify points at which Luke's notion of prayer could help enlarge the congregation's understanding and practice?

Connections to the Lectionary

The lectionary offers the congregation a choice of readings from Acts for the Seventh Sunday after Easter for each lectionary year. The minister may preach from the readings for Ascension Day (Acts 1:6-11 and Luke 24:44-53) or may follow the readings assigned for the Seventh Sunday after Easter: Acts 1:6-14 appears in Year A while Acts 1:15-16, 21-26 appears in Year B. Acts 16:19-34 is given for Year C. If the congregation does not have a service of worship on Ascension Day in Year A, then on the Seventh Sunday after Easter, the preacher could expose the congregation to the ascension via Acts 1:6-14. If the congregation does not have a service on Ascension Day in Years B and C, worship leaders can judge whether the congregation would be most helped on the Seventh Sunday of Easter by Ascension readings, by readings assigned for

The Coming of the Realm of God: The Main Theme of the Book of Acts

the Seventh Sunday, or by one of the other texts that depict Christ at the right hand of God (see "Connections to the Lectionary" for Acts 1:1-11). In Year B, if worship planners opt for the assigned texts, the reading should include all of Acts 1:15-26 to maintain the theological and literary unity of the passage.

ACTS 1:15-20. THE DEATH OF JUDAS

Many Christians are puzzled by Judas. Why did he betray Jesus? At one end of the spectrum of possible answers is Judas as a selfish person who wanted to profit from the sale of Jesus. At the other end of the spectrum is Judas as a person who wanted Jesus to bring the Realm and who thought that selling Jesus to the authorities would facilitate that process. From this point of view, Judas had a good intention but was misdirected. That both Matthew 27:3-10 and Acts 1:15-20 explain the death of Judas suggests that many in the ancient churches wondered how to understand Judas. The appearance of Judas in this text gives the preacher an opportunity to introduce the congregation to Luke's interpretation of Judas and to bring Luke's perspective into dialogue with opinions in the wider church.

When we first hear about the Lukan Judas, he is one of the Twelve (Luke 6:16). However, Satan took control of Judas (Luke 22:3). Judas betrays Jesus as part of Satan's attempt to put Jesus to death to prevent Jesus from continuing the movement toward the Realm (Luke 22:47-48). Satan thought that by murdering Jesus, the possibility of the Realm would go away. In Luke-Acts, the death of Jesus is not primarily salvific but is mainly a martyr's death; the crucifixion demonstrates the power of old age and the lengths to which the rulers of the old age to resist the Realm and to maintain their own privilege. With the prophet of the Realm dead, Satan's power would be intact.

Judas's presence in Jesus's inner circle might prompt today's preacher to ponder whether there are Judas-like people and values inside the church today. Are old-age values and behaviors still present in the church?

Matthew and Luke interpret the death of Judas differently. In Matthew 27:3-10, Judas repents and takes his own life. In Acts, Judas shows no regret. Instead, God puts Judas to death as punishment for being complicit in the death of Jesus (Acts 1:18). Luke joined many other Jewish writers in antiquity that God punished the disobedient in ways appropriate to their disobedience (cf. Acts 5:1-11; 12:20-23). Since Judas was complicit in bringing Jesus to a horrible death, God would cause Judas to die in a horrible way: "He burst open in the middle and all his bowels gushed out."

This text presents a significant theological challenge to many Christians today with its assumption that God punishes people in accordance with their disobedience. Because I believe God is unconditional love, I cannot affirm that God visits pain and suffering upon people, much less that God carries out capital punishment (as in the case of Judas). However, as presaged in the Introduction, I do believe that unfaithful attitudes set in motion values and behaviors that are self-destructive. A preacher might use Judas as a warning that when we resist the Realm, we create circumstances that bring collapse upon ourselves. Do we, like Judas, betray Jesus? If so, how? What consequences can we expect? And what can we do to avoid this fate?

ACTS 1:21-26. COMPLETING THE CIRCLE OF THE TWELVE

In the Gospel of Luke, as in the other gospels, Jesus gathers a group of twelve close followers. Luke reserves the term "apostles" for these twelve. The number twelve recollects the twelve tribes of Israel and in Jewish life represents community as God intends. The covenantal life of the twelve tribes was to be a light for all other peoples (for example, Isa. 42:6). For Luke, the twelve apostles indicate that the church continues the mission of Israel by representing the community of the Realm (Luke 22:28-30). The church of the apostles is to represent completeness of community in the Realm.

In Acts 1:15-20, the death of Judas reduced the number of active apostles to eleven, thus making incomplete the circle representing the Realm. In Acts 1:21-26, God reconstitutes the community of twelve. According to Acts 1:21-22, the criteria for an apostle is being with Jesus throughout Jesus's ministry, including being a witness to the resurrection. The congregation puts forward two such candidates—Joseph Barsabbas and Matthias. Matthias was chosen by casting lots. Ancient people did not regard casting lots as a mechanism of chance or luck but as a medium through which God revealed God's choice. Thus, God selected Matthias.

The twelve play an important role in Luke-Acts. Jesus is the model for the twelve, and the twelve are models for the church. In Acts the twelve are an authoritative body for the church. Luke often uses the figures of the twelve to authorize (or to partly authorize) significant developments in the witness of the church. Consequently, it was imperative for the number of active apostles to represent completeness of community.

CHIASTIC PARALLEL. LUKE 24:13-35 AND ACTS 1:15-26

These parallel elements in the Gospel and in Acts highlight the contrast Jesus and Judas and the possibilities they offer the community. In Luke 24:13-35 the disciples on the road are disheartened (Luke 24:13-24), but the risen Jesus appears as a definitive sign of the presence of the Realm (Luke 24:25-32). By the end of the story, the travelers join other disciples in witness (Luke 24:33-35). In Acts 1:15-20, the death of Judas exemplifies the old age and its resistance to the Realm. When Satan entered Judas, the community of the twelve was disrupted. Nevertheless, through the selection of Matthias, the twelve were restored so that the community could continue its witness to the Realm (Acts 1:21-26). A sermon might contrast the two possibilities for life represented by Jesus and Judas. Jesus creates the community of the Realm whereas Judas leads to destruction and death. In which force field does the congregation want to live—that of Jesus or Judas?

At the risk of making an interpretive move that Luke did not intend, the preacher might play on the fact that the community of the Realm was incomplete when there were only eleven apostles by asking, "Who is missing from the church today? Who needs to be included for the church adequately to represent the Realm?"

Most congregations in North America operate through the democratic process. For example, we elect officers. We vote on major directions, decisions, and expenditures. In seminary, we offer classes in church leadership and administration. The preacher might ponder similarities and differences between making decisions by means of casting lots and by means of democratic process. On the one hand, what confidence can a congregation have that casting lots is divinely guided? On the other hand, can a congregation be confident that every vote reflects God's highest purposes? The voice of the people is not inherently the voice of God. Indeed, I have witnessed some decisions made by the democratic process that seemed to contradict God's highest aims. In such situations, the preacher might meditate with the congregation on and develop methods and criteria to attempt to discern God's purposes in particular settings. The preacher could also help a person or group ponder what to do when the person or the group concludes that a congregation has made decisions that go against God's purposes. In these cases, difficult decisions need to be made. Do we leave? Do we stay and work for change? If the latter, to what degree do we need to confront, and to what degree do we need to take more indirect approaches?

The particular situation in this text raises a broader issue for preacher and congregation. Few churches today cast lots. The apostles are no longer with us to provide direct guidance in the way Luke pictures them in Acts. In any event, they did not consider many issues that are before the church today. Hence, the church can seldom appeal directly to apostolic authority.

The preacher could help the church ponder the sources on which the church draws when moving toward decision. Most ecclesial bodies implicitly or explicitly draw on the Bible, tradition, experience, and reason (or what makes sense). Of course, each of these sources is itself diverse. Moreover, different people and different churches give different weights to these different sources. Here self-awareness and honesty are important. For example, some churches say they rely almost solely on the Bible and do not recognize that they claim the authority of the Bible through the lens of their own theological tradition that developed much later than the Bible. Other churches claim to get back to what the Bible really says when they actually interpret the Bible through the lens of their contemporary experience without taking into account differences between the contemporary and ancient worlds. Interpreters need to be as self-aware as possible so they can reflect critically on their own theological moves and conclusions.

THE COMING OF THE REALM OF GOD: THE SPIRIT EMPOWERS THE COMMUNITY TO WITNESS TO THE REALM (ACTS 2:1-13)

The Torah, Prophets and Writings present the Holy Spirit as one of God's closest agents who operates in five related ways. (1) The Spirit was present with God at creation. (2) God sustains the world through the ever-present Spirit. (3) God fills people through the Spirit, that is, gives them an experiential awareness that God is with them. (4) God anoints people through the Spirit for special tasks. (5) In the end-times, God would pour out the Spirit even more generously to empower communities to endure the last days and to witness boldly. The outpouring of the Spirit is itself a sign of the coming Realm.

John the Baptist announced that Jesus would baptize his followers with the Spirit expected in the last days (Luke 3:15-17). Jesus received an eschatological apportionment of the Spirit (Luke 3:21-22) and promised the disciples they would be empowered similarly (Luke 24:44-49; Acts 1:4-5, 8). Acts 2:1-13 describes the event in which the promise of Jesus comes true: the disciples are filled with the Spirit to continue Jesus's ministry.

Given the many ways the Spirit is understood in the Bible and in the church, it is important note that that for Luke the primary purposes of the Spirit are to assure the beleaguered followers of Jesus they are following a faithful path, to strengthen them to witness, including manifesting signs of the Realm. The infilling of the Spirit empowers the church to extend the witness to the Realm to gentiles.

ACTS 2:1-4. THE SPIRIT FALLS ON JEWISH BELIEVERS

Pentecost was a Jewish holy day. Exodus 23:16 describes it as "the festival of the harvest of the first fruits," the beginning of the wheat harvest (Exod. 23:14-17; 34:18-24; Deut. 16:16; cf. Jub. 6:1-21, 22:1). By setting this event on Pentecost, Luke implies that the outpouring of the Spirit is part of the harvest of the end-times. Luke joins other Jewish end-time theologians in speaking figuratively of the coming of the Realm as a harvest (for example, Luke 3:16-17; 8:4-8, 11-15; 10:1-12).

By saying "They were all together in one place," Luke emphasizes that the outpouring of the Spirit is an event in community. As the narrative unfolds, we see that the Spirit forms community.

The coming of the Spirit sounds "like the rush of a violent wind." Some parishioners may be surprised with the description of the wind as "violent." However, the Greek word "violent" (*biaias*) typically refers to the use of force, often violently. This expression is consistent with the idea that the coming of the Spirit is part of the end-time. For that period was to include conflict between the forces of God and Satan. As in the temptation of Jesus (Luke 4:1-13), the Spirit strengthens the community in that tense time and aggressively leads the community to witness.

Luke pictures tongues, as of fire, coming down from heaven, with a tongue resting on each person. Luke here draws on fire as a Jewish symbol with multiple levels of meaning. Fire is often associated with manifestations of the divine presence (for example, Exod. 19:16-25; 1 Kgs. 19:11-12). The prophets use the vocabulary of fire to speak of judgment (Jer. 4:4; Isa. 66:24; Dan. 7:11; 1 Enoch 18:11). Even more to the point for Luke-Acts, the prophetic vocation is itself sometimes compared to being filled with fire (Jer. 5:14; Sir. 48:1; cf. Jer. 20:9). In this tradition, John the Baptist, an end-time prophet, promises that the disciples will be baptized with the Holy Spirit and with fire (Luke 3:16): God empowers them with the Holy Spirit to continue the prophetic vocation (cf. Luke 3:9; 9:54; 17:20; Acts 2:19). In the full exercise of the prophetic vocation, the prophet and the prophetic community announce both judgment and salvation, and invite listeners to repent. For Luke, the prophetic witness points to the present and coming Realm. The presence of the fire in this narrative identifies Luke's congregation as such a prophetic community.

Acts 2:5-13 develops the notion of what it means to speak in other languages. I discuss that phenomenon in the next section.

Chiastic Parallel. Acts 2:1-4 and Luke 24:1-12

These parallels bring the resurrection and the Spirit into interpretive relationship. For Luke, the resurrection is the definitive sign that the ministry of Jesus points toward the Realm. In Acts 2:1-4, then, the coming of the Spirit means that the power that resurrected Jesus—the power that brings the Realm—is still at work in the world. This chiastic connection gives the preacher a powerful opportunity to help the congregation grasp the Lukan understanding of the gift of the Spirit. Those who receive Spirit (per Acts 2:38-39) not only look forward to being resurrected at the last day but already operate with Realm power.

This passage gives the preacher a point of departure into both Luke's particular perception of the Spirit and the church's broader theological reflection on the doctrine of the Holy Spirit. On the one hand, many Christians in the historic Eurocentric congregations have little understanding of the Spirit. On the other hand, some Christians have truncated views—seeing the infilling of the Spirit in individualistic terms and not recognizing its community-forming power or its Realm-witnessing intent.

The preacher who uses media in the sermon could project paintings that depict Pentecost, or could broadcast the sound of rushing wind and the tongues. Furthermore, dancers could portray the dynamics at Pentecost.

Connection to the Lectionary

In the Revised Common Lectionary, Acts 2:1-21 could be read on Pentecost in Years A, B, and C. The boundaries of this passage capture the event of Pentecost itself (Acts 2:1-4), the manifestation and initial response (vv. 5-13), and the beginning of Peter's sermon (vv. 14-21). A passage of 21 verses is about as long as many congregations can pay attention given the typical matter-of-fact style of reading from the Bible in public worship. Nevertheless, by ending the reading at v. 21, the lectionary interrupts Peter's sermon. To capture more of Luke's purposes in this sermon, the lector should summarize vv. 22-36 and read Acts 2:37-39, which reveal Luke's purpose in the Pentecost drama: to impress upon the listeners that they are an *eschatological community empowered by the*

Spirit. Through repentance, baptism and the gift of the Spirit, God prepares them to witness to the Realm.

By using Acts' title for this day, "Pentecost," the Christian Year leaves the subtle impression that the Lukan account is the normative interpretation of the nature and work of the Spirit. This impression is reinforced when Acts 2:1-21 is read in each lectionary year. Of course, the Gospels and Letters contain several interpretations, and the preacher should help the congregation become aware of this range of perspective. The lectionary itself helps the preacher in Year A by appointing John 20:19-23 and 1 Corinthians 12:3b-13. The sermon could compare and contrast the Spirit in Luke-Acts, John, and Paul. Yet in Years B and C, the lectionary limits the congregation's exposure to Spirit theologies by again providing readings from Paul. To expose the congregation to more of the spectrum of the Spirit in the Bible, the preacher could supplement the lectionary texts with other passages.

ACTS 2:5-13. THE MANIFESTATION OF THE SPIRIT AND INITIAL RESPONSE

The story of the tower of Babel in Genesis 11:1-9 is part of the background for Acts 2:5-13. Genesis 11:1-9 recalls a time when everyone on earth spoke one language. The population worked together to create tower (a ziggurat) with its top in the heavens so they could "make a name for themselves," an inappropriate role for creatures. In response, God scattered the peoples and gave them different languages so they would not be able to understand one another, and, hence, could not repeat the error. From that time forward, human communities in the old age were contentious. Many end-time theologians—Luke among them—looked forward to a great reunion of the human family in the Realm.

Acts 2:5-13 pictures the Spirit demonstrating on Pentecost that the reunion of the scattered human family is beginning to take place. In Acts 2, the reunion is partial because it involves only people of Jewish origin and proselytes. Gentiles become a part of the reunion in Acts 10.

The first work of the Spirit is to create mutual understanding and community among Jewish people from many nations who were in Jerusalem for the Pentecost festival (Acts 2:5-11). In vv. 9-11 Luke illustrates the remarkable diversity present by listing residents from fifteen nationalities involved in the Pentecost experience. A preacher with a penchant for PowerPoint could project a map showing these different nations in relationship to one another.

Luke underscores the universal nature of this event and offers an indirect criticism of the Roman Empire by including peoples who lived outside the Roman Empire (for example, Parthians). Within the Empire, Rome could maintain quiet (the Pax Romana) by the sword. But the Empire could not achieve universal rule. Indeed, Rome was often suspicious and often afraid of Parthia. Yet, God through the Spirit brings together in community people from these enemy nations.

At Pentecost people from different cultures who spoke different languages understood one another. This phenomenon empowered them to work together in the Realm. Indeed, their mutual understanding was itself a manifestation of the Realm.

Under the power of the Spirit, these Jewish people from different nations, cultures and languages understand one another and become a community of mutual support without losing their particular cultural identities. They do not give up being Parthians, Medes and Elamites. They share a common purpose and many common values without becoming culturally the same.

An essential work of the sermon is to show where similar Realm-like community-building is happening today. My impression is that multicultural understanding is taking place more outside the church than in it. Despite many congregations becoming more diverse today than in the past, most are still dominated by one culture whose values and practices are the informal norms. To be sure, the preacher wants to celebrate points at which expressions of the church are moving toward Realm-like community today. But the pastor may need to help the church name points at which the congregation can learn from outside cultural movements how better to become a multicultural community.

Some nonbelievers who were present at Pentecost did not understand what was happening. Some bystanders sneered that the believers were drunk (Acts 1:12-13). These bystanders were creatures of the old age whose structures of awareness were not prepared to recognize the community of the Realm. The sermon could help the congregation identify ways that individuals and groups today fail to recognize the emerging community of the Realm. Eurocentric people particularly resist the multicultural dimension of the Realm. They continue to see people and cultures of European origin as the norm. Indeed, some people today sneer at the multicultural respect and solidarity emerging in increasingly pluralistic North America. To such folk, Luke offers a pastoral word: the Holy Spirit is the force behind such efforts. Those who join the Spirit experience Pentecost afresh. Those who resist the Spirit continue to try to build the tower of Babel.

Chiastic Parallels. Acts 2:5-13 and Luke 23:26-56

Luke 23:26-56 recounts the death and burial of Jesus whereas Acts 2:5-13 depicts people from different nations speaking about God's deeds of power in community. This chiastic pair illustrates two possibilities for life by showing two different spheres of influence—one shaped by the old age and the other shaped by the Spirit. Luke 23:26-56 is a snapshot of the old world: the rulers of that age crucify Jesus in an attempt to maintain their rigid and exploitative control of community. Indeed, as this part of the story closes, the body of the primary prophet of the Realm, Jesus, is in the tomb, and the immediate possibility of the Realm seems to be finished (Luke 23:50-56). The old age appears to be the only possibility for existence. But after the resurrection and the ascension, the possibility of the Realm is very much in evidence as the Spirit brings together people from different nations in a community of mutual understanding (Acts 2:5-13).

In the passages leading to Luke 23:26-56, different kinds of people cooperated to put Jesus to death, whereas in Acts 2:5-23 different kinds of people understand one another and engage in mutual support. The preacher could use these two scenes to ask the congregation whether we want to orient ourselves toward the old age (ultimately leading to death) or to the Spirit-empowered new world in which people live together in mutual understanding and support.

For the public reading of scripture during the service of worship, many congregations have several lectors read the story of Pentecost simultaneously, each in a different language. This custom captures the mood of the Pentecost event, but does not fully capture the mutual understanding that Luke pictures.

The preacher could help Christians today distinguish between people speaking and hearing in other languages at Pentecost and the glossalalia Paul reports in 1 Corinthians 12-14 (cf. Romans 8:12-17, 26-27). The latter—sometimes called "unknown tongues"—is ecstatic sound prompted by the Spirit but not organized into words and grammar. At a crucial point Luke and Paul agree. For Luke, the purpose of understanding at Pentecost was to build up community. For Paul, the purpose of glossalalia is to build up the believer who can then build up the community. When glossalalia is interpreted, the community is built up directly (1 Cor. 14:1-12).

2

You Will Be My Witness in Jerusalem and in all Judea
Acts 2:14—8:3

Jerusalem is powerful theological symbol for Luke as it is a definitive place of revelation. Luke exposes the intensity of hostility to the Realm of God when the powers of the present broken age put Jesus. At the same time, God raises Jesus from the dead in Jerusalem, thus assuring the reading community in the most dramatic way that the power of God transcends the power of all other rulers and authorities. Acts 2:14 begins the witness of the church to those outside the church. While the church in Acts continues the witness of Jesus to the coming of the Realm, the church quickly faces hostility similar to that faced by Jesus, yet the church responds as Jesus did by faithfully continuing the witness. In moments of difficulty, the Holy Spirit infuses the community with the power of the resurrection so that the church can be confident and faithful in witness even when threatened. Luke, of course, wants his later congregation to recognize that while they, too, face hostility, they can also count on the presence and activity of the Spirit to strengthen them.

You Will Be My Witnesses in Jerusalem and All Judea: The Community Interprets the Spirit and Embodies the Realm (Acts 2:14-47)

In Acts 1:8, Jesus says to the disciples, "You will be my witnesses in Jerusalem and all Judea and Samaria, and to the ends of the earth." In Acts 2:14, the community begins to witness in Jerusalem.

In Acts 2:12, participants at Pentecost raise a question important to Luke's community and to congregants today; "What does this mean?" This question points to one of the most important purposes of preaching: to help people understand the meaning of life and how to respond appropriately. From that perspective, Acts 2:1-47 is a case study in what should happen in the preaching event: something calls the attention of the congregation to the need for interpretation (Acts 2:1-13); the preacher theologically interprets (2:14-36); the congregation responds appropriately (2:37-43).

ACTS 2:14-36. PETER INTERPRETS THE OUTPOURING OF THE SPIRIT

Most scholars think the speeches in Acts express Luke's theology more than recollect the actual words of historical figures. In Acts 2:14-36 Luke theologically interprets the believers' dramatic behavior on Pentecost and summarizes core theology for Acts.

Like many preachers, Peter interprets the Pentecost experience through a passage of Scripture, a modified version Joel 2:28-32. Luke uses this quote to indicate several things. (1) The outpouring the Spirit is a sign that the last days are here (v. 17a). (2) The Spirit will fall on all flesh (both Jews and gentiles) (v. 17a). (3) The Spirit-filled community will be inclusive—women, men, young, old, slave, and free (vv. 17b-18a). (4) The community shares the vocation of Jesus as end-time prophet (vv. 17b-18). (5) God will signal the immediate coming of the apocalypse through dramatic changes in nature (vv. 19-20; cf. Luke 21:5-11, 25-28). (6) God will save all who call upon God's name; they will become a part of the Realm (see Acts 2:38) (v. 21).

Luke further uses Acts 2:22-36 to explain that Jesus is God's representative in facilitating the apocalypse. Jesus's actions demonstrated the Realm (v. 22). God raised Jesus from the dead (vv. 23-24). David—an authority in Judaism—recognized Jesus as arbiter of the Realm (vv. 25-31, 34-35). While David is dead, Jesus is at the right hand of God (v. 33). These things should convince listeners and readers that God made Jesus Sovereign and Messiah (v. 36).

Acts 2:22-36 is a first-century apologetic. One purpose of apologetics is to give insiders (Luke's congregation) confidence in what they believe. Another purpose is to answer the objections of outsiders. For Luke, the resurrection and ascension are evidence the Realm is present and coming. For many people in today's world, however, the resurrection and the ascension are themselves problematic. Nevertheless, Luke's apologetic effort poses a possibility for the sermon. What evidence would today's congregation find convincing that God is attempting to refashion the world?

Luke makes a move with Joel that could spark a sermon. Luke alters the wording of the passage. In the Septuagint, Joel 2:28 begins "Afterward" but

Luke changes that expression to "In the last days" (Acts 2:17a), thus reinforcing the idea that Luke's church is in the end times. In Acts 2:18c, Luke adds "and they shall prophesy" to Joel 2:29, thereby reinforcing the idea that Luke's congregation is a community of prophets. Luke thus violates today's exegetical axiom of honoring the otherness of the text by recasting the text to serve Luke's agenda. The preacher could wrestle with the congregation regarding respectful attitudes toward the biblical text. Has Luke gone too far in rewording the text itself to serve his own theology?

CONNECTION TO THE LECTIONARY

The lectionary has some of its better and worse moments in its use of Acts in connection with Acts 2. On the better side, the congregation hears almost the whole of Acts 2:14-47 on three successive Sundays in Year A: Acts 2:14-1, 22-32 for the Second Sunday after Easter, Acts 2:14a, 36-41 for the Third Sunday after Easter, and Acts 2:42-47 for the Fourth Sunday after Easter. The preacher can use these readings to consider possibilities made possible by the resurrection. Moreover, lectionary brings the entirety of Acts 2 into the consciousness of the congregation by appointing Acts 2:1-13 on Pentecost Day.

However, Acts 2:14-47 is read in the lectionary cycle *before* Acts 2:1-13. This placement can be confusing. Moreover, the message of Acts 2:14-47 is made possible not simply by the resurrection (as implied by current placement in the lectionary) but by the ascension and the outpouring of the Spirit.

One way to honor the literary and theological unity of Acts 2 would be for the lectionary preacher to re-arrange the Sundays on which the congregation considers the four parts of Acts 2. The congregation could read Acts 2:1-13 on Pentecost Day, Acts 2:14-36 on the First Sunday after Pentecost (Trinity Sunday), Acts 2:37-41 on Proper 4 [9], and Acts 2:42-47 on Proper 5 [10]. The congregation would thus hear the story of Acts 2 in its natural literary and theological sequence and in size-bites that are about right for one Sunday.

Luke presents the preacher a similar opportunity by referring to David as the author of the psalms quoted here (Ps. 16:8-11; 16:10; 110:1) and writes as if David had Jesus in mind. Few biblical scholars in the historic denominations today think the historical David wrote these Psalms or that the Psalmist had Jesus in mind. On this point, Luke would likely get a bad grade in an exegesis class in seminary today. Nevertheless, the preacher could help the congregation recognize that we do not have to adopt Luke's methods to understand that Luke employed interpretive principles, typical of the time. Luke's deep point is that the ministry of Jesus and the coming of the Realm are continuous with the life and hope of Israel.

This text introduces a negative portrayal of many Jewish people. Peter indicts the Jewish listeners with conspiring with gentiles to put Jesus to death (Acts 2:23, cf. 36b). This statement is part of Luke's polemic against many Jewish leaders (see pp. 7–9). For now it is important to encourage the preacher avoid anti-Judaism and anti-Semitism.

Chiastic Parallel. Luke 22:47—23:25 and Acts 2:14-36

Luke 22:47-23:25 tells of a number of Jewish leaders conspiring with gentiles to put Jesus to death. Their behavior exemplifies the brokenness of the old age. By contrast, in Acts 2:14-36, Peter asserts that while some misguided people put Jesus to death, God worked through their conniving to raise Jesus from the dead, to elevate Jesus to God's right hand, and to pour out the Holy Spirit. The outpouring of the Spirit brings people together as a demonstration of life in the Realm.

These two passages contrast the old age with the Realm. The preacher could sketch these two fields of influence and urge the congregation to consider whether it would rather live in a world whose values and behavior put Jesus to death, or a world in which God makes it possible for people to live together in the mutual support demonstrated at Pentecost.

Acts 2:37-42. Response to Peter's Preaching about the Realm

Luke now summarizes how he hopes people will respond to the Realm. Peter's audience gets to the heart of the matter by asking, "What should we do?" (Acts 2:37). How do we respond when we believe we are living in the end times and we would like to be part of the community moving toward the Realm?

In Acts, a full-bodied response is to repent, to be baptized, and to receive the Holy Spirit (Acts 2:38). To repent is to turn away from the old age Acts 2:40), and to turn toward God and the coming of the Realm. Baptism (immersion) assures people that God has forgiven their sins. For Luke, sin is complicity with the old age; forgiveness, means that one is no longer determined by that age. Baptism initiates the believer into the community of the Realm. On the Holy Spirit see Acts 2:1-36.

Luke points out that God's promise is not only for Jewish people but is also "for those who are far away" (gentiles) (Acts 2:39). Many congregations today need this reminder: the church is to embrace those who are "far away," both literally and symbolically.

Acts 2:42 calls attention to four qualities of the church. (1) The community follows the apostles' teaching (Luke's interpretation of the story of Jesus in the Gospel and of the church in Acts). (2) The church engages in fellowship, *koinonia*, which includes mutual uplift and which may also include financial support. (3) They break the bread, that is, they continue to partake of the eschatological banquet (see Luke 22:7-22). (4) They pray for the coming of the Realm (see Luke 11:2-4).

Since Luke writes to an established congregation, this material is designed to help the congregation reflect on its own life. Is the congregation living in a way that befits repentance? Is the congregation living as baptized community? Is the congregation living in the Spirit? Is the congregation communicating the promise to those who are far away? These questions could outline a sermon.

Many congregations in the long established denominations know how to recruit new members from people who are already Christian. However, few such congregations know how to evangelize people who have never been a part of the church. The preacher could use Luke's notions of repentance, baptism, and the Spirit as a place to start thinking about how to offer these opportunities to those who have never done so.

Peter speaks to a Jewish audience. Luke does not urge Jewish people to leave one religion (Judaism) and convert to another (Christianity). At the time of Luke, Christianity had not separated from Judaism as a distinct religion. For Luke, the church does not replace Judaism but is a community with Jewish roots and a distinct Jewish end-time perception. Peter invites these Jewish listeners to join a community whose witness is Jewish (from Luke's point of view).

For Luke baptism takes place only in the name of Jesus and not in the name of the Father, Son and Holy Spirit (Matt. 28:16-20). This pluralism could prompt a sermon on diversity in the church. These two, different formulae for baptism raise the questions of where such diversity originates, how it is helpful (or not), and whether there are (or should be) limits to diversity.

CHIASTIC PARALLEL. LUKE 22:39-46 AND ACTS 2:37-42

In Luke 22:39-46, Jesus admonishes the disciples to pray they will not come into the time of trial. The time of trial is the conflict between the forces of the old age of the new when suffering increases as the apocalypse draws near (cf.

Luke 21:5-24). In Acts 2:37-42, Peter, under the Spirit, does not yield to the time of trial but tells others about the opportunity to avoid the time of trial. By following this path, believers can make their way through the immediate conflicts that beset the church (Acts 3:1-4:31ff.) and the final tribulation (Luke 21:5-24).

Many Christians today are like the disciples: aware of conflict between the ages and in need of strength to witness. A homily might recall situations in which believers feel the tension between the old world and the new, and remind the congregation that through repentance, baptism, and the gift of the Spirit, God empowers them to faithful witness. They can then not only "save themselves" from being overwhelmed by "this corrupt generation" but can help transform that generation.

ACTS 2:43-47. THE COMMON LIFE OF THE COMMUNITY EMBODIES THE REALM

This is one of the most well known pictures of the early church. However, most scholars think that this picture derives more from Luke's ideal memory than from historical occurrence. Many groups in antiquity described their origins as a golden age. Nevertheless, for Luke this passage sets out a powerful picture of how people can live together as a community of the Realm. The preacher could use it as a vision toward which today's church can aspire. Many of these themes recur in Acts 4:32-37 where they are discussed more fully.

The apostles continue the ministry of Jesus by performing miracles (Acts 2:43), a topic discussed at Acts 3:1-10. They were "all together" (2:44), that is, they felt themselves constituted as genuine community prefiguring the life of the Realm.

Today's listeners are often fascinated by (and nervous about) Luke's statement they had all things in common (Acts 2:44b-45). Believers did not claim private ownership, but sold what they had (for example, land, houses) and put the proceeds into the common treasury (Acts 4:32-37). They distributed resources from this fund so that there were no needy among them. For Luke, God used this common sharing as a means for extending providential care for those in need.

I still occasionally hear Christians contrast the spiritual and the material in such a way as to downplay the importance of material resources. Acts 2:44b-45 affirms that God seeks for people to live in material security. Indeed, the Realm is a new *world* in which all experience abundance.

Many listeners today ask, "Do *I* need to sell everything?" I answer that question, "No." Many people in Luke's time believed that the world would end soon. Consequently, they did not foresee a long-term need for material resources. By contrast we need to plan for the long term.

The Jewish orientation of this community is revealed in their worship in the temple (Acts 2:46a) while also partaking of the sacred meal when they worshipped in homes (Acts 2:46b). The tone of the community is revealed in their "glad and generous hearts."

Luke says that they have "the goodwill of all the people" (Acts 2:46). We should not, however, take positive public recognition as a criterion by which to gauge the success of a church's witness. At this point the narrative of Acts has only pointed to the positive dimensions of the community. In the next passage, the witnesses come into conflict with some of the local leaders.

A preacher could develop a sermon on the life of the church structured around the qualities of the community Luke mentions here: signs and wonders, being together, sharing all things, breaking bread, praising God, and enjoying the good will of the larger world.

CHIASTIC PARALLEL. LUKE 22:35-38 AND ACTS 2:43-47

When Jesus sent the disciples on missions in the Gospel, Jesus advised them not to take provisions. It was customary in that time for local communities to provide food, housing, and other forms of hospitality to itinerant charismatic missionaries such as the disciples (cf. Luke 9:1-5; 10:1-12). Such welcome was an expression of community approval. By Luke 22, however, this approval is waning. Jesus is about to be crucified, and the disciples come under suspicion (for example, Luke 22:54-62). In Luke 22:35-38 Jesus instructs the disciples to prepare with material resources for their coming mission. For the time being, they must prepare for their own survival.

By comparison, in Acts 2:43-47, we find a church under the Spirit modeling the community of the Realm in which God provides for material needs through the sharing of the community. No one is anxious about their day to day survival. The common life of the church is the means whereby God provides.

The preacher should alert the congregation to differences in cultural expectations between then and now around these issues. Many people today think that missionary trips are irresponsible when travelers presume others will take care of them. Most Eurocentric people, operating out of an individualistic worldview, assume we should be responsible for our own food and housing.

Luke's deeper point reframes both perspectives. For Luke God provides for the faithful (cf. Luke 12): the shared life of the community is the means through which God provides. A sermon could explore how the congregation could become a more vibrant community of the sharing of material resources, and how such a community could be a sign to the wider world of the providence God intends for all.

You Will Be My Witnesses in Jerusalem and all Judea: A Healing at the Beautiful Gate Demonstrates the Realm (Acts 3:1-26)

In Luke-Acts, the ministry of Jesus is the paradigm for the ministry of the church. In the power of the Spirit, Jesus announced the coming of the Realm, interpreted its implications through teaching, revealed its presence through miracles, and confronted the rulers of the old age. In the power of the Spirit, the church in Acts carries out a similar ministry. At the Beautiful Gate, Peter and John demonstrate the Realm by being the instruments through whom God healed a person who could not walk (Acts 3:1-10). Peter interprets the significance (Acts 3:11-26).

The miracle stories in Luke-Acts—healings, exorcisms, nature miracles, raisings from the dead—perform multiple functions. The key to interpreting them is Luke 4:16-19. The ability to perform miracles confirms that both Jesus and the church represent God and the presence and character of the Realm (Luke 4:18). What happens in the miracle is a miniature of the restoration occurring in the Realm. Miraculous events sometimes become occasions for conflict when the dialogue prompted by the miracle is as important as the miracle itself. All of these considerations come into play in Acts 3:1-4:31.

Acts 3:1-10. A Healing at the Beautiful Gate

As faithful Jewish people, Peter and John pass through the Beautiful Gate (probably the bronze Nicanor Gate) in the temple on the way to pray at the customary time of 3:00 p.m. They encounter a person whom we often call a "crippled beggar." However, linguists rightly note that such designations suggest that his identity was being lame and begging. Properly speaking, these qualities are not the core of who he is; they are only things he does. We should refer to this figure—and others in similar situations—as a person who was unable to walk and who made his income by asking for alms.

Peter and John did not set out to be agents of healing. They encountered the person who needed healing on their way. This perspective could become a lens for the homily. Who do we encounter along the everyday paths of life who need healing?

The person at the gate asks only for alms. From the end-time point of view, alms were a survival tactic in the old age. While alms enable survival, they do little more. Going beyond alms, Peter heals the person, thereby demonstrating the presence of the Realm.

This miracle story, along with many others in Acts, gives the preacher a chance to think about how important it is to believe that miracles of the kind reported in Acts 3:1-10 happened in the past, whether we can expect them today, and alternative possibilities. This concern weighs on the minds of some congregants, especially when they wonder whether they can pray for miraculous healings today. Here is a point at which the distinction between the surface and deeper perspectives (pp. 9–10) is helpful. The scientific world view makes such events seem unlikely in either the past or the present.) Further, it seems to me that if God has the power to heal as posed by this text but does not do so, then God is not fully loving and not fully just. To encourage people to pray for such healing seems to me to set the stage for disappointment and, ultimately for distrust in God and in the church. However, the deeper concern is to point to the presence of God working to make the world more Realm-like.

When preaching from the deeper point of view the preacher might be able to make analogies between then and now by asking, "How are we in situations similar to that of the person at the gate? Figuratively speaking, how are we unable to walk? How do we beg? How are dependent? What do we need to be able to walk? The preacher can ask such questions of individuals and communities. The key to such a sermon is to help the congregation recognize where and how people today encounter the healing power of the Realm represented in by Peter and John.

A preacher could take a more holistic Lukan approach, which could provide the structure for the sermon. The preacher could (1) describe a manifestation of the realm (vv. 1-10), (2) offer an interpretation of that manifestation (vv. 11-26), and (3) explore how the Realm brings witnesses into conflict with the rulers of the old age (Acts 4:1-22).

This passage inspired the scripture song, "Silver and gold have I none."[1] If the service includes a moment for children, the preacher could teach this song.

CHIASTIC PARALLEL: LUKE 22:31-34 AND ACTS 3:1-10

These chiastic parallels focus on Peter before and after the resurrection/ ascension/ coming of the Spirit. In Luke 22:31-34, Jesus predicts that Peter will deny Jesus. Jesus prayed for Peter to be a source of strength for the community. Peter claims to be ready "to go with you [Jesus] to prison and to death," but Jesus knows that Peter will deny him. When confronted by a servant-girl outside the hall where Jesus was on trial, Peter states, "I do not even know [Jesus]" (Luke 23:47). In Acts 3:1-10, after the resurrection/ascension/ outpouring of the Spirit, Peter leads in healing the person at the Beautiful Gate. Peter claims not only to know Jesus but to act in Jesus's name (Acts 3:6). Even more, in Acts 4:1-31, while Peter does not go to prison, he is taken into custody and questioned. Peter fulfills the hope that Jesus has for him in Luke 22:32.

These parallels offer the preacher an opportunity to consider what happens when, like Peter in Luke 22:31-34, we intend to be faithful and even to make a dynamic witness, but run aground. Peter was strengthened by witnessing the resurrected Jesus, the ascension, and the outpouring of the Spirit. Today's congregation does not witness those things directly, but the preacher could help the life of the community itself become a source of strength for those who want to be faithful but struggle to do so.

ACTS 3:11-26. PETER INTERPRETS THE MEANING OF THE HEALING

The occurrence in Acts 3:1-10 becomes something like a newspaper headline or a breaking news report in electronic media as people nearby, astonished, gather in Solomon's Portico, a large porch on the east side of the temple whose roof was likely supported by double columns, where people discussed religious matters (Acts 3:11). Taking advantage of the moment, Peter addresses the group. In this sermon, Luke seeks to show that responding favorably to the ministry of Jesus and the church is faithfully Jewish. This perspective both reinforces the Jewish identity of the Jewish members of Luke's community and urges gentile members to respect the Jewish members.

Peter underscores the fact that the God of Israel is the power behind Jesus in whose name Peter performed the healing (Acts 3:12-13a, 16). Yet, Peter asserts that Jewish people were the moving force in putting Jesus to death. Pilate had decided to release Jesus but they preferred the murderer to Barabbas (Luke 23:18-19).

The Jewish people who contributed to the death of Jesus did so out of ignorance (Acts 3:17). In doing so, they participated in the plan of God (Acts 3:18). Consequently, God offers them the opportunity to repent. Indeed, Acts

3:19-21 is an exceptionally clear and compelling picture of repentance and its effects. Repentance is to turn away from sin (collusion with the old age) and to turn toward God and the Realm. When that happens: (a) God will "wipe out" their sins; (b) they will be refreshed in the present; (c) they become part of the "universal restoration," that is, the post-apocalypse Realm when God will restore all relationships to the way they were in Eden.

The notion of acting wrongly because of ignorance resonates with many parishioners today. When I served a congregation, parishioners often confessed, "I just didn't know any better." This phenomenon is true of communities. For example, many Eurocentric congregations today are not conscious of their participation in racism, even assuming that the early twenty-first century is a post-racial society. In fact, Eurocentric racism today is merely less flagrant than previously. The preacher can help individuals and communities become cognizant of the things for which we need to repent, emphasizing that repentance includes not only turning away from sin but becoming an active agent of restoration.

CONNECTION TO THE LECTIONARY: ACTS 3:12-19

The lectionary appoints Acts 3:12-19 for the Third Sunday after Easter, Year B. This passage is placed here for the same reason that other texts from Acts appear after Easter: to illustrate the effects of the resurrection. The reading ends with a winsome invitation to the congregation to repent so that their sins will be wiped out (3:19). This invitation is one of the driving purposes of the passage and could become the purpose of the sermon.

Unfortunately, the beginning of the reading, v. 12, does not give listeners the context of Peter's address. The reading inexplicably ends in the middle of a sentence, thereby missing one of Luke's most provocative reasons to repent: to be included in "the time of universal restoration." The reading should be lengthened to vv. 11-21, and worship leaders should introduce the reading by recalling the context in Acts 3:1-10.

The preacher could make slight substitutions so readings from Acts in Year B correspond with the movement of the gospel in Acts 1:8: from Jerusalem and Judea (using the current readings for the Second and Third Sundays of Easter) through Samaria (making Acts 8:4-13 the reading for Fourth Sunday), to the ends of the Earth (using the current readings for the Fifth and Six Sundays of Easter). A PowerPoint map could show the places associated with these readings: Jerusalem, Samaria, the road to Gaza, and Azotus (Ashdod), and Caesarea.

Acts 3:22-26 directly describes the ministry of Jesus and the church as that of end-time prophet and end-time prophetic community. Peter's listeners should pay attention because Jesus is the prophet of whom Moses spoke in Deuteronomy 18:15-20 (Acts 3:22-23). Those who do not respond appropriately "will be rooted out of the people" (Acts 3:23a). Samuel and other prophets articulated the same ideas (Acts 3:24). Peter reminds listeners (a) they "are the descendents of the prophets and of the covenant" (b) through whom "all the families of the earth will be blessed" (Gen. 22:18; cf. Gen. 12:1-3). They are thoroughly Jewish (heirs of Moses, Samuel and the prophets); their vocation is to be a conduit of God's eschatological blessing for all people (Genesis 22:18). That blessing is now being mediated through Jesus. This prophetic motif opens the door for the preacher to consider about what it means to be a prophetic community calling attention to the presence and coming of the Realm. While such a community must warn the world that its complicity brings about condemnation (Acts 3:23b), its major work is to point the way to universal restoration.

Some Jewish members of Luke's congregation doubted whether they were truly Jewish since they participated in the church. Identity is at issue. Amid the welter of today's denominations, movements, and competing theological and ethical claims, some Christians have similar questions. "Is our congregation truly Christian?" The preacher could use this passage as an entrée.

In the background is the question of whether Luke believes (and whether we should believe) that Jewish people must become followers of Jesus to be included in the Realm. This difficult question comes up at Acts 4:12.

CHIASTIC PARALLELS. LUKE 22:7-23 AND ACTS 3:11-26

Suffering while awaiting the coming of the Realm is a central theme in these parallels. Luke 22:7-23 is a Passover meal remembering the event when God liberated the Hebrews from slavery. For some apocalyptic theologians, the Passover became the prototype for the eschatological Passover, that is, for the day when God would fully release the old age from slavery. But this event was accompanied by the slaughter of the Passover lambs and the deaths of the Egyptian first-born.

Jesus willingly suffers as part of the movement toward the Realm. For Luke, Jesus's death is not so much redemptive in itself as a demonstration of the brutality of the old age. Jesus subjected himself to the old age so God could demonstrate the Realm by raising Jesus from the dead. In Acts, Peter asserts that his audience handed Jesus over to suffering and death, thereby revealing their alliance with the old age. Nevertheless, God wants the audience to repent and to join the "universal restoration." Peter is taken into custody as a result of his witness, thus sharing in the suffering of Jesus. Yet, like Jesus, Peter presses ahead with witness (Acts 4:29-30).

The preacher might help the congregation search for ways they might identify with Peter's audience and/or with Peter and Jesus. Although we do not literally put Jesus to death, are we complicit with attempts to quash the Realm? Though we may not suffer as Pete and James did, must we face or give up ways of benefitting from the old age? In Acts, the breaking of the bread instituted in Luke 22:14-23 is a source of strength for the witnessing community as it faces such tensions. It continues to be such source.

You Will Be My Witnesses in Jerusalem and All Judea: The Witness to the Realm Provokes Confrontation with Authorities (Acts 4:1-31)

At the Beautiful Gate, God healed the person who could not walk, after which Peter preached a powerful sermon interpreting the resurrection as the definitive sign of the presence and future coming of the Realm (Acts 3:1-26). The events immediately in Acts 4:1-31 are important in their own right, and also because they introduce a pattern prominent in Acts: representatives of the movement toward the Realm make a bold witness to which some Jewish leaders object. This pattern comes with a detrimental effect: reinforcing a negative picture of Judaism.

This pattern reminds congregations both in antiquity and today that witnessing to the Realm can bring the community into conflict with the power structures of the old age. If the congregation today is in tension with those who represent the old age, the preacher could move from Acts 4:1-31 to pastoral support by pointing out that such acrimony is as old as the Bible. God gives us the Holy Spirit in the same way God gave the Spirit to the disciples so we may witness as boldly in our time as they did in theirs.

However, many Eurocentric congregations have been co-opted by the old age. Not only do such communities not confront the authorities, but actually support them by speaking and acting as if God is the power behind old age attitudes and behaviors. Such congregations are effectively chaplains of the old age. They even provide theological support for people, groups, and systems that engage in cruelty. In such a situation the preacher's task is to help the congregation recognize its situation, repent, and open itself to the Spirit.

The preacher might ponder with the people the degree to which the congregation's witness is bold enough. Indeed, with regard for what is required for such witness in a given context, a preacher might use the degree of conflict between the congregation and the culture as an index of the degree to which the community is faithful. The pastor can then gauge the appropriate mix of support and challenge for preaching.

ACTS 4:1-12. PETER AND JOHN ARE ARRESTED AND SPEAK BOLDLY BEFORE THE AUTHORITIES

A group of Sadducees and temple authorities are greatly disturbed because the apostles preach that "in Jesus there is the resurrection of the dead" (Acts 4:1-3). The Sadducees, a wealthy social group, did not believe in the resurrection of the dead. The priests controlled the temple bank. The Sadducees and priests were often intertwined. For Luke, these leaders are not simply "annoyed" (as the NRSV renders the verb *diapeneomai*) but are "greatly disturbed" because the occurrence of a resurrection threatens their theology as well as their social and economic power.

The Jewish authorities arrest the disciples and put them in custody until the next day when, following Jewish legal protocol, they could be examined in the day light. Luke's description of the examiners (Acts 4:5-6), later named explicitly as the council (Acts 4:15), heightens the contrast between the social and political prestige of the council and the lower social standing of the Peter and John (Acts 4:13).

The council wants to know the name by whom the apostles healed the person who could not previously walk (Acts 3:1-10). In antiquity the speaking of a name invoked the force-field associated with that name. Mighty deeds could be done in the name of the devil (for example, Luke 11:14-23, esp. v. 15). If the council can show that the apostles acted in this name, their social power is secure. However, Peter reply that the apostles acted in the name of Jesus, whom God raised from the dead. The resurrection of Jesus not only confirms the doctrine of the resurrection (against the Sadducees) but reveals the presence of the Realm, now further confirmed by the healing at the Beautiful Gate.

An irony. The Jewish authorities put the apostles on trial. But from the reader's point of view the Jewish authorities are on trial. The people have already rendered the right verdict (Acts 4:4). The reader thinks that God has passed judgment on the Sadducees and temple leaders because the temple had been destroyed (in 70 CE) by the time Luke's congregation read these words (80-90 CE; cf. Luke 13:31-35; 19:41-44; 21:20-24).

In Acts 4:12, Luke uses a double entendre: the language for "saved" (*sōdzō*) refers both to the healing and to being included in the Realm. Yet, many standard exegetical commentaries avoid a concern that is the first to come to the mind of many parishioners regarding Acts 4:12, namely whether all people must become followers of Jesus to be saved. A sermon considering these issues would find a welcome audience in many quarters. To be sure, the preacher should help the congregation recognize that Luke did not think about these matters in the same terms as early twenty-first century systematic theologians or people puzzling over whether to invite their Jewish, Muslim, and Buddhist neighbors to become Christian.

Acts 4:12 raises two issues central to a sermon. One is whether *Luke* means that one must become a follower of Jesus to be saved. Luke sees salvation in Jesus as certain (for example, Luke 9:24; Acts 2:37, 47; 15:11; 16:31; 17:30) while keeping open the possibility of other ways of salvation (for example, Luke 8:28-29; 19:10; Acts 15:1). The other issue is broader: regardless of what Luke believed, should *the church today* insist that people become Christian to be saved? Or, can the church acknowledge other ways to salvation, and even the possibility of universal salvation?[2] The preacher can answer these questions only by drawing from the preacher's deepest convictions about God's nature and purposes.

The sermon could take account of Luke's deeper use of v. 12, namely to assure members of the ancient congregation that they would be saved. Many Jewish and gentile members of Luke's congregation would have questions about whether they were included. Many people in congregations today have similar concerns. What does it mean to be saved? Am I in that company?

CHIASTIC PARALLELS. LUKE 22:1-6 AND ACTS 4:1-12

Here we see a contrast between what happens when Satan enters a person and what happens when the Holy Spirit does so. In Luke 22:1-2, a small group of leaders seeks to put Jesus to death because they feared losing their own privilege and power. Judas received money (though not the famous thirty pieces of silver of Matthew 26:15) thus intending to profit from the death of Jesus. By noting that Satan entered Judas, one of the twelve, Luke warns that evil can penetrate even the tightest circle of the faithful. In comparison, Peter and John boldly witness to God's work in Acts 4:1-12. Whereas Judas conspired in secret with evil people to benefit himself, these apostles witness public, putting themselves at risk of arrest to offer the Realm to the crowd.

A homily might consider whether some in the congregation (or in groups or institutions in the larger world) conspire in secret, like Judas, to maintain their own privilege, and to disrupt the witness to the Realm. By contrast, where does the preacher see the Spirit attempting to move toward the openness of Peter and John and toward testifying to those who, like Judas and the group with whom he conspired, would maintain the structures of the old age?

This passage opens the door for a doctrinal sermon on questions that perplex many Christians. "Will everyone be saved or will only some people be saved? And if only some will be saved, on what grounds?" While such a sermon would consider Luke's particular contribution to the topic, it would necessarily have to go beyond Luke to the deepest points of the theology of the preacher and the church.

Connection to the Lectionary

Acts 4:5-12 is appointed for the Fourth Sunday of Easter in Year B. As already pointed out in connection with both Acts 3 and 4, the real literary and theological unit is Acts 3:1-4:31, a sequence too long for public reading. Yet Acts 4:5-12 requires a sense of context. The reader (whether the preacher or a lay lector) could supply background in a teaching moment before the reading.

Acts 4:13-31. The Disciples Experience Distress at the Hands of the Authorities

The council cannot deny the evidence of the person who had been cured standing before them. The power that healed at the Beautiful Gate can also raise the dead and will bring the Realm. However, the council tries to limit the damage caused by this revelation. To protect their power and to preserve their own safety from a popular uprising, the council does not actively punish the apostles, but does attempt to silence them (Acts 4:13-18, 21). In a line preachers love, the apostles retort they "cannot keep from speaking of what we have seen and heard."

Taking into account the dangers of asking the congregation to identify with Jewish leaders, a preacher might point out that Luke identifies one of the most potent ways that authorities in the old age seek to maintain their own power: by enforcing silence on others. The preacher could help the congregation recognize way how the church itself has attempted to silence individuals and groups.

A question such a sermon must face is how those who are silenced find the courage to speak. The title of an important book puts the matter provocatively: *Saved from Silence*.[3] The sermon could encourage voice in those who are silenced. One way forward is to listen to those who have come to voice in *Saved from Silence* and also for the preacher to interview people in the community who had been silenced but who now have voice.

When the apostles are released, they gather with the community and pray for boldness in the face of both the Gentile inclination to violence and the Jewish participation in the same (Acts 4:25-29). God sent a tremor anticipating the apocalypse, and answered their prayer by empowering with boldness (Acts 4:31). Acts 4:23-31 thus assures Luke's congregation that God will fill them in a similar way with the Spirit so that in their later time, they, too, can witness boldly.

The preacher might explore with the congregation what it would take for the congregation to pray for such boldness. What stands in the way? What inclinations toward such prayer are already evident? The preacher or worship leader can lead the congregation in such a prayer. To be honest, I both yearn for such boldness and yet I fear it.

Chiastic Parallels. Luke 21:5-37 and Acts 4:13-31

Luke 21:5-37 is Jesus's most sustained discussion of the last days. Two elements are central. (1) Social distress will increase in the last days, especially for the witnesses to the Realm (Luke 21:7-24, esp. 9-19). Though Luke wrote about 80-90 CE, Luke has Jesus speak as if the destruction of the temple (70 CE), a sign of the end times, is in the future (21:5-6, 20-24). Since Luke's congregation lived after that destruction, Luke used this literary device to signal the congregation that they were nearing the end. (2) The congregation can make its way through the distress by anticipating the apocalypse and being ready (21:29-38). In Acts 4:13-31, we see this apocalyptic distress in the disciples as they are in custody and silenced (4:13-22). The violence against Jesus is a sign of the end (4:23-28) Nevertheless, the Spirit emboldens the disciples to preach and to heal, that is, to point people toward the coming apocalypse (4:29-31).

A sermon could focus on God's ultimate purposes. Many congregations, especially in the historic denominations, struggle with the tension of whether to believe in the second coming or in a more realized eschatology. Regardless of where the congregation lands on this issue, a preacher could come to this salient

Lukan point. Acts 4:29-31 leaves no doubt as to what it means to be faithful while moving toward eschatological fulfillment: it is to preach boldly and to work the signs of the Realm. For Luke, learning the lesson of the fig tree and being alert (Luke 21:29-38) should not lead to passive waiting but to the bold witness of Acts 4:29-31.

A preacher needs to handle carefully the negative portrayal of the Jewish leaders in this text, and throughout Acts. The sermon could unwittingly contribute to anti-Judaism and even anti-Semitism if the preacher uncritically repeats Luke's caricatures, especially if the sermon uncritically invites the congregation to identify with Jewish leaders. For while Christians may see ourselves committing misdeeds similar to those of Jewish leaders, we can easily drift into negative associations with Judaism. A preacher needs to help the congregation develop a critical consciousness recognizing that Luke uses the characters in Acts to represent select aspects of the Jewish community with whom Luke's congregation is in tension. We should take Acts' earlier advice and repent of such caricatures.

You Will Be My Witnesses in Jerusalem and All Judea: Sharing Possessions Faithfully and Unfaithfully (Acts 4:32—5:11)

Luke-Acts is permeated by the deep Jewish conviction material resources should benefit everyone in covenantal community. Everyone in the community should live in peace and security. God does not want anyone to be anxious about survival. When individuals and groups are free from survival-anxiety, they are likely to be less absorbed by their own immediate concerns and are more available to serve God's wider purposes of love, mutual support, justice, peace, and abundance.

The Realm of God is an age in which all inhabitants live in material abundance.[4] While the final and full coming of the Realm will occur only with the return of Jesus, aspects of the physical provision of the Realm begin in the present through the life of the community. The practical means through which God provides material security is people sharing material resources. The distinction between the old and the new ages is not that the old world is material and the new world is not, but that people with an old age mentality use material goods inappropriately (for example, for self-serving purposes to the neglect of the community) whereas people on the way to the Realm use material goods to support community.

For Luke, the use of material resources has both material and symbolic dimensions. At the material level, the sharing of goods makes it possible for members of the community to be relieved of anxiety about material goods. At the symbolic level, the willingness or unwillingness to share one's physical substance with the community represents one's level of response to the Realm.

ACTS 4:32-37. COMMON LIFE FLOURISHES AS COMMUNITY MEMBERS HOLD ALL IN COMMON

Many communities in antiquity depicted the time that they originated as a golden age (for example, the Garden of Eden). These stories articulate an ideal memory of core values. Even though community life changed over the years, the memory of the golden age provided a base line by which to gauge whether the later community was consistent with the originating vision. Both Acts 2:43-47 and Acts 4:32-37 function this way. These passages put forward the same general picture. When Luke reiterates essentially the same motif more than once, Luke's intent is to impress its importance. In Acts 2:43-46 and 4:32-36, Luke underlines the centrality of the sharing of material goods as part of the identity of the community. While the mode of sharing changed from the commonism of these early vignettes to members maintaining control over their own goods, the principle of sharing for the common good endured.

The community is "of one heart and soul:" at the deepest levels they are a community of common purpose. Although different in national origin and culture, they understand themselves inherently connected.

In this idyllic stage of the church's life, no one claimed private ownership, but "everything they owned was held in common." The description in vv. 32 and 34-35 suggests that the people sold their possessions and put them in a common treasury. A few scholars think the believers retained private ownership and sold their goods as need arose in the community. Either way, the result was that the members regarded their material goods as resources to serve Realm purposes.

The members of the community do not simply make contributions to the congregation. They enter into economic solidarity with one another. Their mutual support is itself an anticipation of the material dimension of the Realm.

Acts 4:36-37 gives the example of Joseph, a Levite from Cyprus, who sold a field and put the proceeds into the treasury. This reference to Joseph puts a specific face on people selling their land as part of the movement toward the Realm. By mentioning Joseph was a Levite from Cyprus, Luke makes the subtle point that (a) some leaders within the priestly world and (b) some immigrants recognize the movement toward the Realm. The apostles give Joseph a new moniker, "Barnabas," which Luke interprets to mean "child of encouragement." This name is given in the context of a discussion of material resources: Joseph's first act of encouragement is to be in economic solidarity with the community.

While the picture of the community sharing all things in common is prominent in Acts 2:42-47 and in Acts 4:32-37, this motif disappears as the narrative of Acts unfolds. In the later chapters of Acts, believers appear to retain private ownership but regard their goods as in the service of the community.

The sharing of material resources in Luke-Acts blesses both the poor and the rich. The blessing for the poor is immediate as they are relieved of the enervation of finding provision. For Luke, the rich face the temptations of greed and making an idol of wealth. At the final judgment, such wealthy people would be condemned. However, the rich have an opportunity to join the movement toward the Realm through sharing their resources. When participating in the community of the Realm, the rich no longer need to be anxious about material provisions for themselves; they have the joy of being in solidarity with a community in which all are secure.

The preacher cannot escape the fact that this text calls for the congregation to go beyond a charity mentality in which individuals to contribute to the needs of the poor, but instead to enter into economic solidarity and to call for systemic reform of the economic structures that reinforce so much poverty and that justify the ever growing gaps between the wealthy and the poor.

A sermon that calls for economic reform can be threatening. As a strategy the preacher today might follow Luke's approach in 4:32-37. Luke first offers a vivid picture of the community anticipating the Realm (vv. 32-35), then introduces a particular person and shows how Barnabas participates in the new reality. After painting a world shaped by dynamics similar to those of vv. 32-35, the preacher might name particular people, groups or forces actively trying to reconfigure our economic life in ways that more fully embody the values and practices of the Realm.

Given that Luke sometimes polemicizes against temple leadership, the fact that Luke turns to Joseph, the Levite from Cyprus as an example to be emulated, reminds preacher and congregation not to regard others as stereotypes but to be alert to kindred spirits even among those with whom we disagree. We can make mutual commitment with all who share the values of the Realm.

While moving from Cyprus to Jerusalem did not have the same political dimensions as aspects of immigration today, Luke uses an immigrant as a role model. The preacher might listen to those—like immigrants—who are outside the main stream of our economic system for clues from their experience that can expose how the present economic system abuses and exploits, and how the witness the church might witness for Realm-like reform.

Chiastic Parallels. Luke 21:1-4 and Acts 4:32—5:11

In these parallel sections, we see the church in Acts continue an important practice of Judaism. In Luke 21:1-4, a widow places all that she has—two of the smallest coins then minted—in the temple treasury, thus making herself destitute. However, one of the several purposes of the temple treasury was to provide for needs of the poor. Thus, by offering her last financial resource to God through the temple, she expresses her trust that God will use the distribution for the poor through the temple to sustain her. In Acts 4:32-37, the church continues God's care for the poor through community members holding everything in common so "there was not a needy person among them." Luke assures those who commit their physical resources to God that God will provide for them as God provided for the widow.

Acts 5:1-10 contrasts the faithful widow with Ananias and Sapphira. The widow trusted God to support her through the temple. Ananias and Sapphira sold property and gave most of the sale price to the community but kept some for themselves. They did not fully trust that God would support the community. Whereas Jesus praises the widow, God punishes Ananias and Sapphira. In the sermon, the preacher could invite the congregation to consider the characters with which they most want to identify: the widow, or Ananias and Sapphira.

Preachers today often use the widow in Luke 21:1-4 as a model of selfless giving, especially when the congregation campaigns to underwrite the budget. However, few preachers make the connection between the woman giving sacrificially and her confidence that God would provide for her through the temple. When preaching on Luke 21:1-4, the preacher could (a) encourage listeners to move toward the same level of confidence as the woman while (b) helping the congregation recognize that such confidence is increased when the congregation is in real solidarity with one another and with the widows of the world. When preaching on Acts 4:32-5:10, the preacher might use the widow as a model of the faithful use of material resources.

ACTS 5:1-10. GOD JUDGES ANANIAS AND SAPPHIRA FOR CHEATING THE COMMUNITY OF THE REALM

This story vividly illustrates the consequences of not fully sharing one's resources with the community. Ananias and Sapphira sold a piece of property. The couple apparently acted as if they committed all of their proceeds to the community when, instead, they put only some of the money in the common treasury while retaining a bundle for their private use. They cheated the community and lied. By saying that Satan had filled their hearts, Luke explicitly indicates that Ananias and Sapphira behaved as people still living according to the values of the old age. They did not trust that God could work through the community to supply their needs.

Peter first confronted Ananias with a straightforward indictment. Ananias immediately fell dead. Peter gave Sapphira the opportunity to tell the truth. Not knowing that her spouse was dead, she also lied, and was immediately struck.

This story and others like it raise a haunting theological issue. Do preacher and congregation believe that God straightforwardly puts people to death for lying, for misuse of funds, and for other violations of the common good?

The deeper purpose can be important to the church and world today. This story is a cautionary tale. When we are dishonest, and when we do not use our material resources for the common good, we become part of a chain of values and behaviors that eventually collapse.. Lying creates distrustful relationships. Failing to share destroys true community. Ananias and Sapphira could not survive in such a setting. While this story focuses on individuals, it extends to groups and nations. When groups engage in deceit and hoard resources, they create climates of distrust and hostility that eventually lead to downfall. This text comes to a bracing point: what we do with our possessions is a matter of life and death.

CONNECTIONS TO THE LECTIONARY

The Revised Common Lectionary appoints Acts 4:32-35 for the Second Sunday of Easter in Year B as part of the lectionary's strategy to help today's congregation ponder appropriate responses to the resurrection. While 4:32-35 can stand alone as a literary unit, the preacher could widen the focus to Acts 4:32-5:10 since Luke intends the larger unit to communicate one message from two points of view: those who share and those who do not.

The lectionary makes a bold move with a Lukan quality by placing Acts 4:32-35 on the first Sunday following Easter. This placement suggests that the resurrection reshapes believers' attitudes toward material possession. Indeed, one of the implications of the resurrection is to reconfigure the economic structures of support for human community from the old age model in which individuals and households must provide for themselves to one based in community. Acts 4:32-5:10 puts forward a Realm model in which the total supply of money and goods is a common fund out of which everyone lives. In Spirit, the community partially realizes this aspect of the Realm. For Luke, what we do with our possessions signals our commitments, and, as we see in Acts 4:32-5:10, has direct consequences.

Preachers sometimes hear or read that Luke has a bias in favor of the poor and against the rich. One could get this impression by looking at individual texts in isolation from their overall context in Luke-Acts. However, in Acts, Luke often matter-of-factly reports the wealthy retaining immediate control of their resources but using those resources to support the life of the community. The issue is not simply the possession of wealth but whether one regards one's resources as self-serving or community-serving.

You Will Be My Witnesses in Jerusalem and All Judea: God Delivers Faithful Witnesses from Prison (Acts 5:12-42)

This section is the next installment in the pattern introduced at Acts 4:1-31 in which faithful witnesses come into conflict with authorities. Acts 5:12-42 reminds the congregation to which Luke wrote to expect resistance to their witness, which can provoke harsh consequences. Acts 5:12-42 offers the courage, testimony and behavior of the apostles as a model for those seasons when Luke's congregation faces immediate hostility. In their own later time and place, they need to say, "We must obey God rather than human authorities" (Acts 5:27-32). They need to assess critically responses others make to their witness, and to be on the lookout for unexpectedly sympathetic voices (5:33-42).

Acts 5: 12-16. Faithful Witness Overflows

This passage plays two important roles in Acts. First, it creates the impression that many people not connected with the council responded positively to the church's testimony. The witness was so successful that Solomon's Portico could not contain the crowd so the crowd placed the sick where Peter's shadow could fall on them. Secondly, the passage provides the occasion for the high priest and the Sadducees to imprison the apostles (Acts 5:17)

The preacher might raise the question of why the witness of the community was so magnetic in antiquity in contrast to the tepid witness in so many historic congregations today. The witness in antiquity obviously correlated with the felt need of many people. How might the church today better correlate our witness with the needs that people feel today? As people respond, the congregation could help them explore deeper dimensions of discipleship.

The reference to Peter's shadow could might generate a sermon exploring the role of such things in the church (cf. Luke 8:44; Acts 19:12). Preachers are sometimes tempted to make fun of such things. "Magic!" one of my colleagues says. However, one could take the view that while such phenomena have no power in themselves, they can function as symbols that can evoke Realm-related responses.

Chiastic Parallels. Luke 20:27-44 and Acts 5:12-32

These parallels share a common structure: controversy sparked by the Sadducees, response (by Jesus in Luke and the apostles in Acts). In the Gospel, the Sadducees put forward an erroneous understand of the resurrection. Jesus corrects the Sadducees' theology (Luke 20:34-44). In Acts the controversy centers on why the apostles did not obey the council's injunction to silence (Acts 5:17, 27-28). The apostles correct the council (Acts 5:29-32).

In Luke 20:41-44, Jesus points out that David—a leader respected in the Jewish community—declared that the Christ is not David's child but is sovereign over David. God appointed Christ (not David) to be at God's right hand. God has already exalted Jesus to God's right hand (Acts 5:29-30)

Luke's congregation—reading this material after the destruction of the temple—knows that the Sadducees, the high priest, and the council had faded from power. By contrast, Jesus was resurrected from the dead and the church was flourishing, thus proving the Sadducees and their allies wrong, and vindicating Jesus and the church.

Possibilities for preaching go beyond the specific issues of (a) resurrection from the dead, (b) what it means to obey God, and (c) whether Jesus is superior to David. Luke portrays Jesus and the apostles as better interpreters of Judaism. The congregation today faces a similar situation within the church. Given conflicting ways of interpreting the Bible, doctrine, and Christian witness today, what are the most reliable interpretations? This issue goes beyond the church. For example, what are the most reliable interpretations of the constitution of the United States? Ministers need to nuance discussions of the Jewish leaders so as not to reinforce anti-Judaism and anti-Semitism.

ACTS 5:17-26. GOD RELEASES THE WITNESSES FROM PRISON

The high priest and the Sadducees are jealous of the popular welcome of the apostolic witness, so they react by jailing the apostles (Acts 5:17-18). An angel, however, opens the prison doors and commands the people to continue their witness (Acts 5:19-21). The work of the angel assures the readers of God's providence in the midst of threats: the witness to the gospel cannot be contained within prison walls.

The high priestly entourage sends for the apostles only to discover the jail is empty. While the high priest and those with him were perplexed about the missing prisoners, the reader is fully aware that divine guidance is at work.

The hermeneutic of analogy could lead the preacher to identify similarities between the imprisonment of the apostles and various ways people are imprisoned today both literally and figuratively. This preacher must describe the prisons in which people are constrained and help the congregation discern where they encounter God's liberating work. In this text, God works through an angel. What instruments—people, movements, agencies—is God using to open prison doors today?

The preacher could alert the congregation to people who are physically imprisoned because of their witness today. How can the congregation stand in solidarity?

A sermon sparked by interaction with the text could suggest prison ministry to the congregation. How can the congregation bring the witness to the Realm to people who are incarcerated and for whom an angel is not likely to open the prison gate?

ACTS 5:27-32. PETER: WITNESSES MUST OBEY GOD RATHER THAN HUMAN AUTHORITIES

When the temple police bring the apostles to the council, the high priest correctly points out that the apostles violated the command of the council not to teach (Acts 4:18). Peter makes one of the most famous statements in Acts: "We must obey God rather than any human authority." Here "human authority" refers to the values and behaviors of the old age. According to Peter, the council acted against God by hanging Jesus on a tree. Yet, God exalted Jesus to God's right hand, and offers repentance and forgiveness of sins to the people who crucified Jesus.

The purpose of this passage is to encourage Luke's congregation to obey God (i.e. to live and witness as pictured in Acts) rather than to diminish their witness in response to harassment from human authorities. This call can easily become the central focus of a sermon: the church today needs to obey God and not human authorities. The preacher could identify issues on which the congregation should take a similar stand: we must witness to God's purposes (even if such a witness is unpopular) rather than yield to prejudice and other old age behaviors.

The church needs criteria by which to attempt to distinguish the things of God from those of human authority. Preachers and churches sometimes uncritically identify their own images, biases, and self-serving interpretations of the Bible and Christian tradition with the values and practices of God whereas Luke implies that the vision of the Realm is the norm which the church can gauge the things of God.

Peter sets out a stark choice: a person serves God or human authorities. In real life, the choice is sometimes that clear but not always. Matters are often more ambiguous such that the preacher should more honestly speak of choices that *lean more* toward God than to the old world. A recent study of people who listen to sermons found that congregants are more likely to engage sermons when the preacher honestly acknowledges such complexity when the preacher paints an oversimplified dichotomy.[5]

CONNECTIONS TO THE LECTIONARY

The church reads Acts 5:27-32 on the Second Sunday of Easter Year C. I surmise that the lectionary appoints this passage to encourage the church to take the resurrection as the ground on which to make the witness of v. 29 in today's context: "We must obey God rather than any human authority." However, while lection captures central elements of Luke's theological conviction, the tone is as weighted toward blaming the council for Jesus's crucifixion as it is toward announcing the resurrection. The preacher thus needs to lift up the positive theological assertion ("We must obey God") while critiquing Luke's caricature of the council.

Furthermore, the readings for the Second Sunday of Easter, Year C, are from three different theological perspectives: the fourth gospel (John 20:19-31),

Revelation (1:4-8) and Acts (5:27-32). Each interprets the resurrection with different theological nuances and in different historical contexts. The preacher could use these distinctions as entries into a discussion of theological pluralism. Such a sermon should go beyond recognizing diversity to helping the congregation articulate a coherent understanding of the resurrection for today.

ACTS 5:33-42. DIFFERENT RESPONSES TO PETER'S ASSERTION— THE COUNCIL AND GAMALIEL

The council is enraged and wants to put the apostles to death. However the respected Pharisee Gamaliel proposes that the council permit the witness to continue so the council can see whether it moves in fruitful directions or disappears (in the manner of the movements that grew up around Theudas and Judas). Says Gamaliel, "If this . . . undertaking is of human origin, it will fail; but if it is of God, you will not be able to overthrow them—in that case you may even be found fighting against God" (Acts 5:38-39).

The principle that Luke articulates here—that longevity is a standard by which to gauge whether a movement is of God—could become the subject of a sermon. This criterion is only partly useful to today's church. The fact that a movement survives does not necessarily mean it is of God. Slavery persisted in North America for more than 200 years. However, the message can ponder whether enduring movements measure up to the criteria of the Realm.

In Acts, Luke pictures the Pharisees less harshly than other Jewish groups. Perhaps by the time Luke wrote (80-90 CE), other Jewish groups had lost power in the wake of the collapse of the temple (70 CE). By Luke's time, the Pharisees, with their emphasis on Judaism as a people of Torah, had begun to emerge as the primary group that would carry Judaism into the future. While Luke is critical of the Pharisees in the Gospel, Luke also knows that his congregation must co-exist with synagogues that are Pharisaic in spirit. Moreover, the Pharisees and the Lucan community share a common belief in the resurrection of the dead (Acts 23:6-10). In Acts 5:33-42, Luke depicts Gamaliel as a voice of reason in an enraged council. Luke's pictures of Gamaliel and the Pharisees in Acts 23:6-10 implies that the congregation should respect Pharisees who give the Christian movement a chance.

Some Christians today dismiss those who are not on the same page as themselves—not only the Pharisees but other historic and contemporary groups. The preacher might urge the congregation not to stereotype such groups but to respect the particularity of individuals and communities. By doing so, we might find points of positive contact and shared mission.

A Pharisee could look at Gamaliel and think, "If Gamaliel found possibility in this movement, perhaps I could, too." A church seeking to engage others from outside Christian circles might consider Luke's style. Luke tells a story within which Pharisees could find themselves in a positive way. The church could similarly present the church and the Christian message in ways in which people outside the church could find themselves.

CHIASTIC PARALLELS. LUKE 20:45-46 AND ACTS 5:33-42

These parallels contrast two types of Jewish leaders. The Gospel excoriates the scribes for being self-impressed and for devouring the houses of widows (Luke 20:45-46). This statement is part of Luke's polemic against the scribes. By contrast, Acts creates a sympathetic picture of a Pharisee in Gamaliel (Acts 20:45-47).

By Luke's time the Pharisees were emerging as the group that could carry Judaism into the future. Gamaliel reminds the Lukan congregation that some within the Pharisaic world have an open mind as to whether the church's witness is of God. The church needs to respect such folk.

On the one hand, the sermon could invite the congregation to consider whether their current attitudes and practices are more like the scribes or Gamaliel. If the former, what changes can the congregation make to embody more of the spirit of Gamaliel? On what issues might the congregation maintain an open mind while they play out? On the other hand, the preacher needs to be careful not to use Luke's caricature of the scribes in a way that reinforces anti-Judaism and anti-Semitism.

Gamaliel articulates a perspective that could be a helpful approach to leadership. Gamaliel wants to let the mission of the church go on, and then evaluate it. Many clergy, congregational leaders, and even entire congregations, act as if every initiative in leadership must be an immediate success. While Luke did not intend to suggest a philosophy of leadership, the preacher might meditate with the congregation on Gamaliel as modeling a promising approach to leadership: try something, see what happens, and evaluate.

You Will Be My Witnesses in Jerusalem and All Judea: The Community in Solidarity with Widows: The Realm Provides for All (Acts 6:1-7)

Christians today accustomed to thinking of the church in institutional terms often read Acts 6:1-7 as if it establishes an office in an formal ecclesial structure. Instead, we find here a development in a dynamic community at a point at which its internal life did not embody the central concern of the Realm for all people to live together in mutual support. The congregation acts to embody the care of the Realm for all. The seven people on whom the community lays hands in Acts 6:1-7 are less officers of an ecclesial organization and more mission team leaders.

As in Acts 6:1-7, leadership positions in churches over the centuries often initially emerged to serve the mission of the church in particular contexts. However, ossification sometimes sets in so that leadership roles lose their missional dynamism and focus on maintaining the institution as institution. Indeed, churches today—upper and middle judicatories, congregations—sometimes develop elaborate leadership structures that delineate lines of authority so that officeholders maintain their domains of power. In such settings, Acts 6:1-7 is a generative model of leadership whose purpose is to help the church embody the Realm.

Acts 6:1-7. The Community Appoints Seven to Be in Solidarity with Widows

By focusing on care for both the Hellenist and Hebrew widows, this passage expresses Acts' concern for all in community to live in material security (Acts 2:43-47 and 4:32-5:10) as well as for people from different ethnic backgrounds to live in mutual support. Widows were vulnerable. Judaism provided guidance through which the community could be in solidarity for security for them (for example, Deut. 10:17-18, 14:28-29; 24:19-22; Isa. 1:16-17; Jer. 7:5-7).

While Acts 2:43-47 and 4:32-5:10 set out ideal pictures of the common life, Acts 6:1-7 portrays this ideal quickly giving way to the factionalism of the old age. The Hellenist widows, complained that they did not receive an adequate amount in the daily distribution whereas the Hebrew widows received plenty (Acts 6:1). While the English reads that the Hellenists were neglected in the daily distribution *of food*," the Greek lacks the actual words "of food. The distribution likely included a fuller range of material resources.

The Hellenists were Jewish women who did not speak Aramaic—the everyday language of Jewish people in Palestine. They spoke Greek and may have originally lived in settings in which Greek and Roman culture were influential. The Hebrew widows were Jewish women who did speak Aramaic and evidently had largely lived in Palestine in cultural settings in which Jewish values were more prominent. The conflict implies that Hebrew widows were more privileged than Hellenists.

The twelve—authorities for the community—indicate they have the particular ministry to teach and pray. Someone must be in practical solidarity with the widows around the daily distribution. However, for the twelve to do so would diminish what they do best—lead through teaching and prayer (Acts 6:2). Consequently, the community selects seven people who represent the values of the Realm to serve the widows.

The twelve describe the ministry of the seven as "waiting on tables" or "keeping accounts" (as in making sure that all widows receive equally from the distribution) (Acts 6:2). Both are possible translations of the verb *diakoneō* in this context. The importance and meaning of this service is revealed in the fact that Jesus describes his own ministry in the same language (Luke 22:26-27). The seven are agents of the Realm in relationship with the widows.

The apostles ordain the seven by means of the rite of the laying on of hands (Acts 6:6). In antiquity, many people believed that laying on hands transferred power from one person to another, rather like electricity passing through a cable. Through the laying on of hands, the Holy Spirit gives the seven the power they need to serve. Further, this act commissions the seven to represent the community. They do not simply act on their own.

Chiastic Parallels. Luke 20:20-26 and Acts 6:1-7

These parallel elements contrast two modes of leadership—one according to the old age (Luke 20:20-26) and the other according to the Realm (Acts 6:1-7). Instead of responding directly to the trick question of Luke 20:22, Jesus shows the questioners a denarius, a coin on which the image of Caesar was stamped, and asks them who appears on the coin (Luke 20:24). When Jesus asks, "Whose head . . . does [the denarius] bear," he uses the Greek word *eikōn*, here rendered "head" but better translated "image;" this word calls to mind Genesis 1:26 and human beings made in the image of God. This image means that human beings are to do in our limited spheres what God does in the cosmic sphere—help all things live together in true community. Jesus then reconfigures the issue from what the people owe Caesar to what belongs to God (Luke 20:25). A thoughtful Jewish listener would immediately recognize: (a) all things belong to God (and not Caesar) and (b) Caesar does not fulfill what it means to bear the image of

God but is an idolater whose rule intensifies the slavery, poverty, injustice, and violence of the old age.

By contrast, in Acts 6:1-7, the deacons serve the needs of all in the community. Whereas the emperor serves his own power, the deacons reveal that, in the Realm, leadership is service in behalf of all. While this passage does not use language related to the image of God, it depicts the deacons engaging in the deepest purposes of bearing that image: helping the members of the community live in mutual support. Although Acts 6:1-7 does not address government per se, the passage models the kind of leadership required of public servants: to create structures that embody the values of the Realm.

The preacher could ponder where the congregation encounters these two kinds of leadership both in the larger world and in the church. Where are little Caesars in our world, and how can the preacher expose them? Where are leaders representing the diaconal spirit of Acts 6, and how can the congregation join them? The preacher needs to take a careful look within the church itself: ecclesial leaders sometimes function as little Caesars,

The church sometimes uses Luke 20:20-26 to legitimate paying taxes as if the domains of God and government are separate. However, the text assumes that the domain of God is over all and that government is intended to serve the purposes of the Realm. From the perspective of Luke's apocalyptic theology, Caesarism is condemned. These texts doe not urge readers to refrain from paying taxes. Presumably Luke's congregation paid taxes as a survival strategy as they awaited the end of the present age. Luke 20:20-26 reminds readers not to idolize government and to gauge the success of government by the degree to which it promotes the aims of the Realm. Nevertheless, given the fact that many Christians today do not expect the world to end soon, the preacher might explore whether not paying taxes might be an appropriate form of witness today. In the early twenty-first century we witness popular revolts effecting massive change (for example, in Tunisia and Egypt). Perhaps a Christian taxpayer revolt in the U.S. could bring the government toward policies more in the spirit of the care for widows in Acts 6:1-6.

At the most basic level, this text concerns material resources that widows need to live a Realm-like life. The preacher could ask, "Do the widows in our church have enough to eat . . . enough material resources to live securely . . . enough emotional support to live in the security of the Realm?" If not, what can the congregation do? The sermon could range beyond the congregation to widows in the neighborhood and the larger world.

At another level, the widows in this text might also represent other people whose quality of life is threatened. The homily could identify people in situations comparable to that of the widows in antiquity—ignored, in danger, and vulnerable. The preacher could ask such folk what the congregation could do to enter into solidarity with them.

The text raises an issue that could be sensitive. Do some members of the community receive more attention than others from the minister and other leaders in ways that damage the community?

In the early twenty-first century we are increasingly aware that middle and upper class heterosexual males of European origin, like the Hebrew widows, have access to disproportionate resources. The preacher might help listeners consider how such males could divest themselves of power and move toward truly sharing power among all community members. The preacher could further lead the congregation to think about encouraging the larger world to move beyond privileging Eurocentric males into egalitarian distribution of material resources and power.

In this passage the early church adapts its organization and strategies for mission to the situation between widows. A pastor whose congregation clings to modes of congregational life that worked in an earlier period but that no longer serve the Realm could use the situation in Acts 6:1-7 as a case study from which to ponder how the congregation might create fresh forms of congregational life for a postmodern world. Indeed, multi-ethnic ministry (as in the text) is increasingly important in congregations in North America.

Although the passage does not use the noun "deacon," many churches look to this passage as formative for that office (along with 1 Tim. 3:8-13; cf. Rom. 16:1; Phil. 1:1). The preacher might inform the congregation about the different ways in which the office of deacon is understood in representative churches—for example, Baptist, Episcopal, United Methodist, and United Presbyterian Church in the U.S.A. and then compare and contrast the service of the seven in Acts 6:1-7 with the ministry of deacons in the church today. In my own movement, the Christian Church (Disciples of Christ), the ministry of the deacons in most congregations has been reduced to little more than serving the bread and the cup. While this act is a powerful symbol of the core ministry of the seven, the actual ministry of the deacons seldom goes beyond, thus becoming a shadow of the ministry of the deacons in Acts. In such cases, a sermon on Acts 6:1-7 could help the congregation imagine how the ministry of the deacons could more fully witness to the Realm.

You Will Be My Witnesses in Jerusalem and All Judea: Stephen Is the First Person Martyred for Witnessing to the Realm (Acts 6:8—8:3)

This long narrative tells a simple story with a savage climax. Stephen is falsely arrested (Acts 6:8-15) and makes a defense by interpreting the history of Israel so as to suggest that many Jewish people have been stiff-necked (Acts 7:1-53). The crowd violates their own Jewish legal system by vigilante action—stoning the disciple. Stephen dies in the manner of Jesus (Acts 7:54-55). Saul was present for the stoning (Acts 7:58, 8:1-3).

What is Luke's purpose in this story? While Luke's congregation did not face martyrdom, Luke wants to strengthen the congregation's resolve when it confronts hostility. As in Acts 2:37-43 and Acts 4:32-5:10, Luke gives the congregation a memory of the their heritage as a model they can adapt for their later circumstance.

This long story has two sides. On one, the story drops Luke's caricature of Jewish leadership to a new low: the crowd reacts against Stephen as the crowd reacted against Jesus at his trial. The story thus helps explain to Luke's congregation why they encounter hostility from many Jewish people in their later time: many Jewish people are stiff-necked and persecute the prophets. A homilist today is called to help the congregation recognize the polemical nature of this account and to urge the congregation away from letting this negative picture reinforce anti-Judaism and anti-Semitism.

On the other side, Stephen is a model for Luke's community. When confronted with a false accusation, Stephen makes a thoughtful defense. When the mob turns to violence, Stephen forgives the killers. When confronted with controversy in their own day, the text implies that Luke's congregation can have Stephen's courage, theological acuity, confidence in God, and pastoral concern for those who oppose them. The homilist could use Stephen as an exemplar for the congregation that faces hostility today.

Acts 6:8-15. Stephen Is Arrested

After participating in public debate (a common practice at the time of Acts) with Stephen and losing the arguments, freed slaves from Cyrene, Alexandria and other places, secretly agree to bring false charges to the council against the disciple. This motif repeats one from the Gospel in which Jewish leaders misconstrue Jesus's ministry to have him put to death (Luke 22:66-23:5; 23:18-25). The reader knows Stephen is not guilty of blasphemy against Moses, God (v. 11) the temple, or Torah (v. 14). Neither Jesus in the Gospel nor the disciples in Acts claim that *Jesus* will destroy the temple (God will do that) nor do they completely negate "the customs that Moses handed down" to the Jewish community (v. 15). This passage thus depicts the Jewish leaders violating one of the fundamental tenants of Judaism: "You shall not bear false witness against your neighbor" (Exod. 20:16; cf. Deut. 5:20). Thereby, they invite judgment on themselves.

The preacher today might help the congregation identify situations in business, in education, in government, and in the wider world in which individuals and groups deliberately misrepresent other people or situations so that the first individual or group can maintain their own power. The preacher could pick up on the sad irony that the former slaves, once abused, now abuse Stephen. Such behavior undermines the movement toward the Realm.

As we have noted frequently, Luke bears false witness against many Jewish people in a way similar the former slaves misrepresenting Stephen. The preacher needs to ponder whether false witness is taking place in the congregation and in the broader movement toward the Realm. If so, Luke's own prescription applies: repent.

CHIASTIC PARALLELS. LUKE 20:9-18 AND ACTS 6:8—8:3

In Luke 20:9-18, Jesus tells a parable whose prediction points toward the behavior in Acts 6:8-8:3. The parable verges on allegory as it depicts an absentee landowner (like God) who sends messengers (like prophets) and the heir (Jesus) to the tenants (Jewish leaders) of a vineyard (the community whose purpose is to witness to God; Isa. 5:1-7). The tenants beat up the messengers and kill the heir (Luke 20:10-15). The landowner vows to destroy the tenants and to give the vineyard to others (Luke 20:16-18).

Acts 6:8—7:60 depict certain Jewish people acting like the tenants of the parable by killing Stephen, a representative of the heir (Jesus). Luke thus implies that the removal Jewish leadership depicted in Luke 20:16-18 is already underway (see Luke 13:31-35; 19:11-27, esp. 47, and 19:41-44; 21:5-6). Indeed, for Luke, the fall of the temple demonstrates that God is actively shifting the vineyard (witnessing to God's deepest purposes) to others (the church). The vigilantes in Acts 6:8-7:60 may have killed Stephen, but God is now removing them from power.

The negative attitude toward Jewish leaders in both elements presents the preacher with an opportunity for a conversation whose focus is on how to understand Luke's negative attitude toward Jewish leaders in historical context and how we might respond to it theologically today. While the texts functioned as part of a family fight in antiquity, the preacher can help the congregation see why we need not bring that fight to our own time.

ACTS 7:1-53. STEPHEN INTERPRETS MANY IN ISRAEL AS STIFF-NECKED

In accord with Jewish legal practice, the defendant, Stephen, has an opportunity to make a defense. The disciple offers an interpretation of the story of Israel that concludes by reversing the charges: Jewish people who resist the Holy Spirit and persecute the prophets are the guilty ones.

Stephen begins by recounting God's call to Sarah and Abraham, (Acts 7:1-8). While Stephen emphasizes God's promises, the only direct words of God that Stephen quotes are: "I will judge the nation that they serve" (v. 7). God condemns those who oppose God's movement. Stephen recalls God's providential care for the children of Sarah and Abraham through Joseph (Acts 7:9-19).

When the disciple adds Moses to the epic, the point is to establish the centrality of the office of prophet in Israel (Acts 7:20-38, esp. 37-38). The prophet is important to Luke since Luke pictures Jesus as the definitive end-time prophet and the church as a prophetic community. However, the ancestors of Stephen and the council did not obey Moses but besought Aaron to make the golden calf, setting in motion a pattern of infidelity that led to God to turn away from them and to the exile (Acts 7:39-43).

Although the people had the tent of testimony in the wilderness and the temple that Solomon built, they did not remain faithful. Stephen climaxes his charges by invoking Jeremiah 7:1-4, Deuteronomy 10:16 and Isaiah 63:10 to declare that many Jewish people are "stiff-necked, uncircumcised in heart and ears," as well as "forever opposing the Holy Spirit," and killing the prophets who anticipated the coming of Jesus (Acts 7:51-52). At this point, Stephen does not need to make explicit a point that is implied; God judges those who resist the work of Holy Spirit through Jesus and the church even as God judged Egypt, those who made the golden calf, and the disobedience that led to exile.

Stephen does not negate Judaism as a religion centered in the promises of God. According to Stephen, many Jewish people violated fundamental values of their own tradition (Acts 7:53). The promises God made to Sarah and Abraham are now being eschatologically completed through the Righteous One, Jesus.

A natural sermonic tendency may be to ask who in the world and church today are similar to Stephen's picture of the stiff-necked Israelites. Indeed, the words "stiff-necked," "uncircumcised in heart," and "persecuting the prophets," describe a number of Christians, congregations and movements I have known.

A preacher taking this tack must work overtime to help the congregation recognize the polemical nature of Luke's selective retelling. Moreover, while unfaithfulness may set in motion actions that lead to collapse, God still waits with promise for those who are circumcised in heart and who respond positively to the Holy Spirit and the prophets.

As an alternative, preachers could develop a sermon around different ways the story of Israel can be told. Stephen represents one pole: the history of Israel as resisting God and persecuting the prophets. The preacher could help the congregation recognize other ways of telling the story of Israel that are more positive.

ACTS 7:55-60. VIGILANTES MURDER STEPHEN

This scene reaches its climax when Stephen finishes speaking, and the enraged crowd and rushes to drag Stephen out of the city for stoning. The ancient reader would condemn this action on three grounds. (1) Stephen has not been accorded a fair hearing. The reader knows that Stephen is innocent. The mob thus violates their own traditions. (2) The Romans alone had the power to put people to death. The mob risks Roman reprisal. (3) The mob murders a prophet, thereby demonstrating the truth of the claims of Stephen's address. This vigilante action reveals the worst of Jewish unfaithfulness and is a warning to Luke's congregation.

Luke describes Stephen as filled with the Holy Spirit, thus impressing upon readers that the Spirit will strengthen them in their most harrowing moments. Furthermore, Stephen sees Jesus at the right hand of God, a vision that assures the reader that the power of God is more powerful than the will of the mob.

We have earlier noted that Jesus in the Gospel is the pattern for the disciples in Acts, a fact that shapes Luke's picture of Stephen. The disciple dies in much the same way that Jesus died on the cross, yielding his spirit to God (Luke 23:46). Stephen's last words embody the practices of the Realm as the martyr asks God to forgive the mob.[6]

On the one hand, the preacher can point out that Stephen's behavior exemplifies the courage needed by Christians from Luke's time to our own. Indeed, communities of witness in some parts of the world face persecution and martyrdom. Even in congregations in North America in which persecution and martyrdom are not typical, Christians sometimes find themselves in need of the courage of Stephen when a witness is necessary but social or psychological threats are high.

When individuals and communities disappoint or harass me, many of us are inclined to try to respond in kind. A preacher might suggest that instead of engaging in reprisal, further fracturing human community, we take a cue from Stephen and forgive, thereby attempting to help human community today be more like that of the Realm.

On the other hand, the preacher does not want to speak about Stephen's acceptance of his death in a way that encourages passivity when confronted by evil. Stephen does not just give in, but uses the occasion of martyrdom to make a witness. Furthermore, the preacher should discourage cheap forgiveness, that is, excusing disruptive behavior as if it really does not matter. At its best, forgiveness brings both perpetrators and victims into mutual awareness.

Connections to the Lectionary: Acts 7:55-60

The lectionary handles Acts pretty well on the Sundays after Easter in Year A. On the Second, Third and Fourth Sundays of Easter, the readings follow Acts 2 seriatim. Acts 2:15a, 22-32 (Second Sunday) interprets the relationship of the Spirit to the community of the Realm; Acts 2:14a, 36-42 (Third Sunday) identifies what is necessary to be a part of that community; Acts 2:14a, 4:43-47 (Fourth Sunday) portrays the life of the community as an anticipation of the Realm. Against that inviting picture, Acts 7:54-60 sets out a sober reminder that those who become a part of the movement to the Realm face challenges from those outside.

Before the public reading of the lection for today, or in the sermon itself, the worship leader or preacher could help the congregation hear Acts 7:54-60 in the context of the overarching story of Luke's second volume by recollecting the passage from Acts 2 from the previous Sundays. Even more importantly, the lector or preacher should summarize the events of Acts 6:8-15 and Stephen's defense in Acts 7: 1-53.

Acts 8:1-3. Saul Persecutes the Church

The function of this passage in Acts, along with 7:58, is to introduce Saul to the reader by associating Saul with the violence against Stephen. Indeed, Luke says that Saul ravaged the church "by entering house after house; dragging off both men and women, [Saul] committed them to prison" (Acts 8:3). When we encounter Saul again in Acts 9 his name sends a chill down our spines.

Acts 7:58—8:3 is probably not a preaching text in its own right. However, when developing a sermon on Acts 9, the preacher wants to invoke Acts 6:8-8:3 background within which to hear the call of Saul. The savagery with which Luke characterizes persecutor then enlarges our wonder at the transformation from persecutor to preacher in Acts 9.

Notes

1. For the lyrics, one source is: http://www.hymnlyrics.org/hymns_children/silver_and_gold_have_i_none.php.

2. In technical theological discourse, the expression "universal salvation" means that everyone will be saved and not simply that everyone has the opportunity to be saved. The contrast to universal salvation is limited or exclusive salvation.

3. Mary Donovan Turner and Mary Linn Hudson, *Saved from Silence: Finding Women's Voice in Preaching* (Saint Louis: Chalice, 1998).

4. A more detailed consideration of this theme can be found in Allen, *Preaching Luke-Acts*, 123–40.

5. Mary Alice Mulligan and Ronald J. Allen, *Make the Word Come Alive: Lessons from Laity* (Saint Louis: Chalice Press, 2005), 83–92.

6. Many ancient manuscripts picture Jesus forgiving those who crucified him (Luke 23:34). Scholars disagree as to whether Jesus's word of forgiveness belongs to the oldest form of the Gospel. A scribe may have read the sentiment of Acts 7:60 into Luke 23:34. In either event, the sentiment in Luke 23:34 is Lukan in tone.

3

You Will Be My Witnesses in Samaria
Acts 8:4-25

In Acts 1:8, Jesus commissions the disciples to witness first in Jerusalem (the symbolic heart of Judaism), then in Judea (largely Jewish environs), and then in Samaria. Samaritans shared some beliefs and practices with the Jewish people, but developed their own culture. Samaria is on the border between the Jewish world and "the ends of the earth" (Acts 1:8).

The Samaritans worshipped a God in the same general tradition as the Jewish people. The Samaritan canon centers in their own version of Pentateuch, which teaches that worship should take place on Mount Gerizim (Exod. 20:17 as modified by Samaritans). The Samaritans believe that many biblical events took place near Mount Gerizim, including the Garden of Eden, Noah's ark coming to rest, and Abraham offering Isaac. The Samaritans believe Moses founded the Samaritan religion. They had their own priesthood and observances of Passover, Pentecost, and Booths. In short, Samaritanism is first cousin to Judaism. Some Samaritans are alive today near Mount Gerizim and near Tel Aviv.

Preachers sometimes speak of the relationship between Jewish and Samaritan communities as if the two communities were perpetually hostile. While there were tensions, there were also periods when the two groups lived in tolerance and even cooperation. In Acts 8:8:4-25, the disciples enter Samaritan territory and interact with its residents. This reception is consistent with Luke's earlier positive depictions of Samaritans (Luke 10:30-37; 11:11-19).[1]

A preacher using electronic media in the sermon could project a map showing Jerusalem, Judea, and Samaria. The projection could show Mount Gerizim and Jerusalem in relationship, and might project a parallel passage or from the Samaritan Pentateuch and the Jewish Bible with differences highlighted (for example, Exod. 20:17).

A preacher might explore who, from the perspective of the congregation, is similar to the Samaritans today. Where do we encounter individuals and communities whose beliefs and practices are similar to those of the church but are different enough for the differences to prompt wariness? Who is on the borders of the congregation's worlds?

Acts 8:4-13. Samaritans, Including a Magician, Welcome the Realm

According to Acts 8:4-8, Samaritans gladly receive the presence and coming of the Realm. In this story, Philip is the major figure carrying the witness to the Samaritans. Since Philip was one of the seven, his presence indicates the mission to Samaria was authenticated by the church. This point is underscored when Peter and John come from the apostolic circle to join Philip and the converts (Acts 8:14). Through Philip, God works signs that demonstrate the Realm, and Luke explicitly names Philip's preaching the news of the Realm (Acts 8:12). The preacher might call attention to this case as one in which the power structure of the church (represented by the apostles) is on the side of outreach. The preacher could use this text to help the congregation develop such a consciousness. But the sermon could also consider the question of what a congregation should do when the power structure resists faithful initiatives.

Simon is a widely heralded magician (Acts 8:10). Since the ancient meaning of magic is so different from the rabbit-coming-out-of-the-hat of today, pastors should explain that in antiquity, magic was a popular way to attempt to affect the forces that control life. Through incantations, formulas, ceremonies, and other means, magicians sought to manipulate supra-human forces. Many Jewish people believed that magic was either false, or that it was demonic (for example, Lev. 19:31; Deut. 18:1-12; Wis. 17:7; 18:13).

However when Philip preaches the news of the Realm, many respond positively, including Simon, and are baptized (Acts 8:12-13). The ethnic composition of the church expands. Hitherto, the community was altogether Jewish. Now the circle of disciples includes Samaritans. The preacher might help the congregation ask, "If Samaritans then, who next now?"

Chiastic Parallels. Luke 20:1-8 and Acts 8:4-13

Luke's congregation found itself on the boundary between cultures. Jewish in origin, tensions developed between the congregation and some traditional Jewish leaders While the congregation welcomed gentiles, it required gentiles to give up their gods, to worship the God of Israel, and to become more Jewish in their life-orientation (Acts 15:1-29). The congregation needed an authority to engender confidence that its luminal existence between cultures was of God

Luke 20:1-8 exposes the chief priests, scribes and elders as unreliable authorities: they do not understand the authority of Jesus or the baptism of John. The reader knows that God is the authority behind Jesus and John. Acts 8:4-13 assumes that magic, represented by Simon, had an authoritative place for many in Samaria. However, Philip's preaching of the Realm of God proves so much more trustworthy that Simon himself turns away from magic and seeks baptism. The Samaritan magician thus shows more insight than the leaders of Judaism.

Many congregations today are on the boundaries between cultures. The preacher could take the leaders from Luke 20:1-8, and Simon and magic from Acts 8:4-13, as representing inadequate theological and cultural forces that seek to shape the congregation. The sermon might then help the congregation name how Jesus and the Realm give authority to the church. For example, without casting aspersion on Judaism, the preacher might take the chief priests, scribes and elders as representatives of Christian leaders who do not understand Christian tradition or how God is at work today. Simon and the magic in Acts might represent secular forces that seek to shape the congregation.

While Luke reports that large numbers of Samaritans joined the movement toward the Realm, Luke does not say why. Perhaps Samaritans welcomed this news in view of the general brokenness of the world and the particular fractiousness of dealing with both the Roman Empire and with occasional animosity with the Jewish community. The church promises strength of community in resisting the Empire. In the congregation, tensions between Samaritans and Jews should be replaced by mutually supportive relationship. The preacher might ponder whether individuals and groups today are in life situations, similar to that of the Samaritans, that create a particular openness to the news of the Realm.

Few people today overtly practice magic in the ancient sense. Yet, a preacher might call the attention of the congregation to advertising promising that consumer products will bring about magical results. Business consultants sometimes promise that doing certain things will almost mystically improve efficiency. Even within the church, Christians sometimes act as if particular Christian formulas automatically cause certain things to happen.

The preacher could point out that magic seeks an easy way through the present world, but leaves the structures of this world intact. The news of the Realm promises a new and improved world, but only as the old dies so the renewed world can come. Moreover, those who want to be part of the new age must be prepared for struggle because many individuals, groups and systems who are tied to the present resist the great transformation.

CONNECTIONS TO THE LECTIONARY

Acts 8:14-17 appears on the Baptism of Jesus in Year C. This reading is well situated with the baptism of Jesus in Luke (Luke 3:15-17, 21-22). Luke believes that what happened to Jesus in baptism also happens to believers. Immersion confirms that the baptized are beloved of God, that they receive the Spirit, and that they join Isaiah and Jesus in prophetic community of witness, the latter emphasis emerging as Luke 3:22 evokes Isaiah 42:1-7, the prophet's first servant song. The lectionary appoints Isaiah 43:1-7 for this day, but the preacher would have an even better connection from Isaiah 42:1-6

The focus on the baptism of Jesus invites a sermon on Luke's understanding of baptism, including the fact that Luke sees baptism in the name of Jesus as normative (rather than God, Jesus and the Spirit). Or, the preacher might begin with baptism in Luke-Acts and move to the larger doctrine of baptism in the theology of the church.

ACTS 8:14-25. PETER AND JOHN LAY HANDS ON THE BAPTIZED, AFTER WHICH SIMON ATTEMPTS TO BUY THE POWER OF THE HOLY SPIRIT

Acts 8:14-18 introduces the relationship between water baptism and Spirit baptism. Peter and James come from the apostles in Jerusalem to lay hands on the newly baptized converts to impart the Spirit to the Samaritans. Some passages in the Gospel and Letters seem to indicate that baptism and the Spirit come together (for example, Matt. 28:16-28). That is true at the baptism of Jesus (Luke 3:21-22), but here, as frequently in Acts, the two phenomena sometimes occur at separate times (for example, 8:38; 10:44-48; 11:16-18; 19:1-6; cf. Luke 3:15-16; Acts 1:5; 11:16-18)[2]. The fact is that the Bible and church at large contain different viewpoints on the issue of whether water baptism and the manifestation of the Spirit are simultaneous or separate. However, nearly all churches would agree with. Luke's essential point: both baptism and the Spirit are necessary for a fully empowered Christian life. Clergy might help the congregation consider the degree to which they have an adequate appreciation for baptism and the degree to which they respond adequately to the Spirit.

Simon, practically still damp from the water of immersion, tries to buy the power of the Holy Spirit when he sees the apostles imparting the Spirit through laying on hands (Acts 8: 19). Simon wants to use the Spirit to enhance his own privilege. Peter immediately calls Simon to repent by threatening that otherwise the former magician and his fundage will perish.

While Simon had been baptized, he did not have an adequate understanding of the Realm. The preacher could help the congregation assess the theological and ethical maturity of the community as a whole as well as of individual constituents. A congregation-wide strategy for education may be needed to help the community mature in its understanding and practice of the Realm.

In the latter part of the text, a preacher might regard Simon as representative of people and groups who seek inappropriate power in the community. Occasional people may literally try to buy their way into power through financial gifts. But most who want the kind of privilege imaged by Simon will take more subtle routes. For example, they may ingratiate themselves with leaders. They may even threaten to withhold their gifts of money, leadership, talent, or presence. This text flashes an urgent warning: such behavior leads to social destruction (Simon would have perished had he not repented). A pastor could help the congregation as a whole become Realm-like community in which people do not need to grasp for power to feel they have an important and secure place.

CHIASTIC PARALLELS. LUKE 19:45-48 AND ACTS 8:14-25

Although Christian preaching has often interpreted Luke 19:45-48 as a cleansing of the temple, another interpretation is more likely. The money-changers (who changed Roman money into Jewish currency suitable for use in the temple) became functional robbers by charging exorbitant exchange rates. Such money was supposed to fund the temple, especially support for the poor. The phrase "den of robbers" calls to mind Jeremiah 7:8-15 in which the prophet anticipates the destruction of the temple if the people do not repent. Instead of repenting, the temple authorities sought to kill Jesus (Luke 19:47-48). By Luke's day, the temple was destroyed. God's judgment portended in Luke 19:46 had come true.

In Acts 8:14-25, Simon seeks to buy the power of the Spirit. In Acts, money is supposed to support community—especially the widows and poor (Acts 2:43-46; 4:32-5:10; 6:1-7). Simon, in effect, robs the congregation. Instead of being condemned, however, however, Simon repents (Acts 8:24). A sermon could reflect on the degree to which the congregation joins the money changers and temple authorities in misusing the real call of the church, or the degree to which they join Simon in repenting of their attempts to misuse the church for their own personal gain and ego.

Much of the area that people in Luke's day knew as Samaria is now in the West Bank, occupied by Palestinians. However, Jewish settlers are building homes and communities in that area under the claim that God has designated that land for Jewish habitation. Indeed, many settlers today continue to refer to the land as "Judea and Samaria." Acts, of course, knows nothing of this contemporary controversy. But a preacher could use the tensions between Jewish and Samaritan peoples in antiquity as a starting point for theological and ethical reflection on tensions between Israelis and Palestinians today. Some Christians in North America hold vastly oversimplified views. For example, some Christians operate with the equations Palestinians = good but Israelis = evil. Certain strains of premillenialism urge Christians to support Israel as a part of the scenario leading to Jesus's second coming. Many other Christians in North America are confused and would welcome thoughtful theological reflection on what they can do to be a part of processes moving toward Realm-like community in the Middle East.

If the sermon goes in this direction the preacher who uses electronic media in the sermon might project a map showing the relationship between ancient Samaria and the West Bank. I am surprised at how many North American Christians today lack basic geographical information about this aspect of the Middle East.

Notes

1. Luke 9:51-56 recounts an incident in which the Samaritans did not receive Jesus because "his face was set toward Jerusalem," that is, he was determined to press ahead. When James and John want to call down fire from heaven to consume the Samaritans, Jesus rebukes the disciples. Even though the Samaritans did not receive Jesus, the Lukan Jesus wants the Samaritans to be in a position to receive the disciples in Acts.

2. Luke does not mention the Spirit in connection with baptisms at 8:36-38; 16:15, 33; 18:8; 22:16). The relationship between the Spirit and baptism is unclear in 9:17-19.

4

You Will Be My Witnesses to the Ends of the Earth

Acts 8:26—28:29

This long section tells the story of the witness of the church in accord with Jesus' directive in Acts 1:8: the witness would makes way from Jerusalem and all Judea through Samaria to the ends of the earth. For Luke, the ends of the earth include not only general gentile communities outside of Jerusalem and Samaria but also the city of Rome, which for Luke represents the idolatrous Roman Empire. For Luke Rome represents the immediate rule of the present broken age, even as Jerusalem represents the presence and coming of the Realm of God. Acts 8:26—28:29 authorizes the movement of the witness into the gentile world by picturing God in charge of the events that take place in the story. God calls Paul to be missionary to the gentiles and confirms the gentile mission through Peter's encounter with Cornelius, When controversy arises in the church regarding whether gentile converts should be circumcised, an important meeting in Jerusalem, inspired by the Holy Spirit, places a stamp of approval on the mission. God is ever present with Paul and his companions when they are repeatedly threatened by danger from human beings, demons, and forces of nature. Nevertheless, Paul does what Luke wants his congregation to do; invite the gentiles to become part of the church—a community witnessing to the Realm and embodying qualities of the Realm while pointing to the second coming as the time when God would fulfill all of God's promises. The story of the gentile mission in Acts 8:26-28:29 is a model for the community to whom Luke writes. Luke intends for his congregation in its later time to continue the story told in Acts 8:26-28:29. Indeed, as the Introduction suggests, Luke wants the story of his congregation to be the 29th chapter of Acts.

You Will Be My Witnesses to the Ends of the Earth: An Ethiopian Eunuch Becomes Part of the Movement of the Realm (Acts 8:26-40)

After the witness to the Realm passes through Samaria in Acts 8:4-25, God guides the news a step further in Acts 8:26-40. The encounter between Philip and the eunuch on the wilderness road between Jerusalem and Gaza moves the witness to the Realm toward the ends of the earth with respect to geography, ethnicity, political power, and matters related to gender. In ways perhaps unanticipated by Luke, this story touches primal concerns for many people today.

Preachers sometimes take the Ethiopian eunuch as a poster child for exclusion and inclusion. Preachers are wont to say Judaism excluded the eunuch whereas the church welcomed the eunuch. The sermon calls the church to include people today who in situations similar to that of the eunuch. Unfortunately, this approach oversimplifies attitudes toward eunuchs in ancient Judaism while buttressing anti-Jewish sentiments. A preacher needs to respect the fullness of Judaism's concern around eunuchs and help the church recognize its own ambiguity and even unfaithfulness with respect to persons represented by the eunuch.

Acts 8:26-31. Philip Encounters an Ethiopian Eunuch

An angel guided Philip to a chariot on the wilderness road from Jerusalem to Gaza where the Spirit directs Philip's encounter with an Ethiopian eunuch reading from Isaiah. The presence of the chariot indicates that the eunuch is well supplied (as a high government official). The fact that he is reading is noteworthy since only three to ten percent of the population of antiquity was literate.

The Ethiopian was a eunuch, deprived of the gifts of sexuality, including children (who would have carried on his name, an important notion in antiquity). He was cut off in certain ways. He was likely a God-fearer (a gentile who was greatly attracted to Judaism but not a full convert). He had been in Jerusalem to worship, though, according to Leviticus 21:17-23 and Deuteronomy 23:1-8 the eunuch could not participate fully in temple worship.

However, Isaiah 56:3-6 looks forward to the day when God will give faithful eunuchs "a monument and a name, better than sons and daughters." Wisdom of Solomon 3:14 declares that a eunuch is blessed "whose hands have done no lawless deed." The events on the wilderness road are consistent with Jewish compassion for eunuchs.

A preacher could lead the congregation in identifying people or groups in today's setting who are in situations similar to that of the eunuch: limited in community (perhaps because of traits that make other people uncomfortable), no longer generative, and insecure. Who, today, is cut off?

While Luke did not intend for this story to address sexuality in the ways that communities think of such issues today, the appearance of the eunuch in this story could become a stepping stone into a sermon that deals with theological matters related to the multiple forms of gender identity in the contemporary world. The church has often been ambiguous, even repressive. The figure of the eunuch could prompt a preacher to ask, What is the nature of gender identity and from where does it come? What are God's purposes in sexuality? To embody the purposes of the Realm, how should the church relate to heterosexuality, same-gender orientations, bi-sexuality, trans-gender orientations, those who question their gender orientations, and asexuality?

The eunuch was from an area in Africa along the south of the Nile River, approximately where the nations of Ethiopia and Eritrea are today. Some ancient authors thought of Ethiopia as near the ends of the earth. Many lighter skinned people of Mediterranean origin regarded darker skinned people from Africa as beautiful or handsome. Taking account of these facts, a sermon on Acts 8:36-40 might be enhanced with a projection of a map locating the wilderness road, Azotus (Ashdod), and Ethiopia, as well as photographs from archeological artifacts depicting Ethiopians.

The African setting reminds congregations today that Africa plays an important role in the Bible. A minister could develop a series of sermons highlighting Africa or Africans). The preacher could project a map showing the areas of Africa that appear in the Bible.

Given the painful history of racial relationships in the United States the preacher should indicate that while people in antiquity recognized different ethnic communities, they did not have the modern concept of race. The European notion of race originated in the 1700s in connection with Eurocentric interest in exploiting people of color. Group prejudice in antiquity fell along lines of geography: from west (more valued) to east (less valued) or from within the Roman Empire (more valued) to outside the Empire (less valued).

Chiastic Parallels. Luke 19:41-44 and Acts 8:26-40

Many scholars think that Luke 19:41-44 is an instance of prophecy after the fact (*vaticinium ex eventu*): a writer pens a text after an event occurred using language that predicts the event (prophecy). Luke wrote as if Jesus in the past had predicted events that came true. The motif of prophecy after the fact adds to the authority of the document in which it appears since the readers knows that the prophecy has come to pass. Luke 19:41-44 obviously presumes the destruction of the temple, an event that occurred at least a decade before Luke wrote the Gospel and Acts. Luke gives a reason for the destruction of the temple: Jerusalem "did not recognize the time of [their] visitation," that is, Jerusalem did not recognize Jesus's witness to the Realm as the work of God.

The story of the eunuch assures the reader that while the temple has been destroyed, the visitation from God continues in the Spirit. Those who, like the eunuch, welcome that visitation become a part of the community of the Realm. From Luke's perspective this eunuch is more faithful than the leaders of Judaism whose behavior led to the destruction of the temple.

A sermon could put the congregation in the position of pondering whether the community today responds to possibilities for joining the movement toward the Realm more like leaders of Israel or like the Ethiopian. Do our visions ally us more with forces moving toward ecclesial and social chaos, or are we open to possibilities for renewal in the surprising qualities of the Ethiopian eunuch?

A preacher is theologically obligated to challenge Luke's assertion that God caused the temple to fall because Jerusalem did not embrace Jesus. Luke's statement is a bald evidence of the gospel writer's antipathy toward many leaders of traditional Judaism. We should respect Luke's voice as one contribution to the wide-ranging conversation of that time trying to find a theological reason for the fall of the temple. However, I find it unthinkable for a God of unconditional love to reduce a city to rubble because they did not welcome Jesus.

The Ethiopian was a treasurer to the Candace (a title for the queen of Ethiopia). Because they posed little sexual threat to women, eunuchs often served women of high standing, and thereby enjoyed prestige.

A preacher might focus on the eunuch's role as leader. "What circumstances might encourage today's leaders to develop an openness to the Realm like that of the Ethiopian?" What might the congregation do in the public square to attempt to awaken interest in Realm-like values on the part of public officials? Another sermon comes to mind. "Do people in the congregation's world sometimes make damaging changes in themselves and others—in the way that eunuchs were made—to gain access to power? At what costs to themselves and to others?"

ACTS 8:32-40. ISAIAH HOSTS A MEETING FOR THE EUNUCH AND THE REALM

The eunuch reads Isaiah 53:7-8, a passage describing the servant of God as a sheep led to the slaughter, silent and denied justice. The passage concludes "For his life is taken away from the earth." For Isaiah the servant was the community of Israel and the experience in the passage was the exile.

The eunuch wants to know of whom the passage from Isaiah speaks (Acts 8:34). The circumstances of the eunuch and that of Israel in Isaiah resonate: both were led to the shearer, both were denied justice, both lost certain dimensions of life. Perhaps the eunuch recognized his own story in that of the servant.

Long before the writing of Acts, the church recognized a correlation between the experience of Israel in Isaiah 52:12-53:12 and the death of Jesus Philips draws on this tradition as a starting point from which to explain the meaning of the ministry Jesus. Philip explained Jesus as the prophet through whom God would bring the Realm which would include the restoration of eunuchs (Isa. 56:1-8).

Luke's readers, hearing Isaiah 53:7-8, would remember the larger setting of Isaiah 52:12-53:12. Other nations had derided Israel because of their defeat and exile. Isaiah claims that Israel's suffering in exile gave Israel the opportunity to make a witness to the other nations by continuing to trust in God despite their circumstances God demonstrated sovereign power and trustworthiness by using the exile as discipline for Israel and by vindicating Israel by returning the community to their homeland in the sight of the nations that had derided them. Israel thus was a light to the nations.

CONNECTION TO THE LECTIONARY

The congregation reads Acts 8:26-40 on the Fifth Sunday of Easter, Year B. Although the lectionary eschews readings from the Torah, Prophets, and Writings on the Sundays of Easter, the worship leader should read Isaiah 53:7-8 and Isaiah 56:1-8 since Acts 8:26-40 directly quotes the first passage and presumes the second.

The events in the readings from Acts on the Second, Third and Fourth Sundays of Easter in Year B all take place in Jerusalem. The story in Acts 8:26-40 is the first to occur outside of Jerusalem on the way to the ends of the earth. This reading represents for the congregation both the geographical movement of the narrative (Acts 1:8) but also the mission of the church. Figuratively speaking, a congregation today might want to stay in the glow of the resurrection in Jerusalem—a familiar place. However, God does not leave the church in Jerusalem but guides the church onto wilderness roads to encounter Samaritans, eunuchs, and gentiles—some of whom create discomfort for relatively homogenous congregations—who enlarge the congregation's sense of the community of the Realm. Joining in solidarity with others not only helps others but also becomes a blessing to the church.

At the risk of offending liturgical scholars, I suggest that commitment to the Christian Year and the lectionary can sometimes become a liturgical Jerusalem—a way of worship with which we are familiar but which (for all its strengths) is still limiting. Worship planners, preachers, and congregations might explore wilderness roads in liturgy. For example, a congregation that only uses a pipe organ might worship for a season with a band. A preacher who only preaches from the lectionary might develop a series of topical messages.

The eunuch wants to be baptized and thereby become a part of the community awaiting the final restoration (Acts 8:36). Luke typically interprets baptism as representing the forgiveness of sins (for example, Luke 3:3-6, 15-17; Acts 2:38-39; 22:16). In end-time theology, sin is not simply personal transgression but is a power in the old age. Forgiveness of sin means release from ultimate domination by the powers of the old age. Baptism is also a mark of initiation into the community of the Realm: God assures the eunuch that the powers that broke him do not determine the ultimate significance of his life. Moreover, baptism assures the eunuch that he has a place in the Realm. In a certain sense, the community of the Realm becomes the eunuch's sons and daughters. Indeed, sexuality disappears after the apocalypse when the Realm is fully manifest (for example, Luke 20:34-36).

In antiquity, water was a potent symbol of life, fertility, and generativity. These associations were especially strong in semi-arid areas such as the wilderness road. Baptism, for the eunuch, means a return of generativity. A preacher could develop a sermon on baptism from this perspective. Through the water, God assures people who identify with the eunuch that they are not ultimately cut off, dried up, or infertile. Since baptism creates a community, this notion suggests that the church itself is to be a community whose generativity encourages generativity in its participants and in other communities in the world.

You Will Be My Witnesses to the Ends of the Earth: The Risen Jesus Calls Saul (Paul) (Acts 9:1-31)

With the call of Saul, the witness begins to turn toward gentiles as prescribed in Acts 1:8. While the first gentile (Cornelius) comes into the community of the Realm through Peter (Acts 10:1-48), Paul is soon the pioneering figure in that mission, which consumes most of the remainder of the narrative of Acts.

Although Christians often refer to the events on the road to Damascus as Paul's "conversion," a better phraseology is Paul's "call." The language of conversion implies leaving one religion (Judaism) and converting to another (Christianity). However, Christianity had not emerged as a religion distinct from Judaism in Luke's day. Instead, God called Paul to a particular mission in a way similar to God's calls to the prophets of Israel.

The preacher should comment on the relationship between Paul in Acts and the historical Paul (known through his letters). Many scholars agree that Luke shaped his picture of Paul more to serve Luke's theology than to recount information about the historical Paul. Ironically, many Christians today know more about the Lukan Paul than the historical Paul since Luke tells the story of Paul so vividly. A minister should not casually use the historical Paul to explain texts in Acts, or vice versa. Rather, the preacher should help the congregation compare and contrast the two pictures of Paul.

Acts 9:1-9. The Risen Jesus Encounters Saul on the Road Approaching Damascus

Acts earlier depicts Saul approving of the vigilante action against Stephen (Acts 7:58) and then gaining legal traction to imprison Christians (Acts 8:3). In Acts 9:1-2, Saul has letters from the high priest to bring disciples to Jerusalem. The Jewish establishment did not have the authority to put people to death, but the Romans allowed the council to discipline their own people. Persecution is no longer a vigilante action but is legally sanctioned harassment. (This narrative picture is another way Luke discredits Jewish leadership). While Acts does not specify the grounds for persecution, Luke presents Saul authorized by the high priests in league with other opponents of the Realm. Such folk sought to end the Jesus movement because it threatened their power.

Luke describes the community of the Realm as "The Way" in Acts 9:2. This title is continuous with Judaism which depicted the obedient life as a way (for example, Ps.1:1-4) while implying that Luke's own community was on the way to the Realm. A homily could remind the church that Christian life is not static but is a journey toward a more Realm-like world. The question is whether we are moving toward or away from the Realm.

Acts 9:3-6 is a Christophany (a dramatic manifestation of the risen Christ) similar to many theophanies (dramatic manifestations of the presence of God) in Jewish tradition. In the same way that God appeared to Sarai and Abram (Sarah and Abraham) (Gen. 12:1-3; 15:1-21; 18:1-15), Moses (Exod. 3:1-22), Elisha (2 Kgs. 2:2:1-17), Isaiah (6:1-13), Ezekiel (Ezek. 1:1-3:15) and others, the risen Christ now appears to Saul. The purpose of this manifestation is to communicate to Luke's' congregation that God fully authorized Saul's role in the gentile mission.

A preacher could perform pastoral service for Christians who lament they have not had a dramatic experience like Paul on the road to Damascus. Luke makes no suggestion that such a dramatic manifestation is a normative element in a call to leadership. The seven servants of Acts 6:1-6, for instance, were selected by the community in response to the leading of the Spirit. Luke describes Saul's call in this exceptional way to assure readers that God had indeed called this person who so ravaged the church.

While many believers today may be relieved to learn they are not spiritually second class because they have not had a Damascus road experience, the preacher needs to offer guidance in discerning how to trust calls to leadership. As a part of this process, the preacher might explain how the congregation's denomination interprets such things. How does the preacher's own theological method handle confirm or disconfirm call?

Witnesses confirm the veracity of the event (Acts 9:7). Saul is blinded so that what happens to him becomes evidence of the truth of Jesus's sermon at Nazareth: God offers "recovery of sight to the blind" (Luke 4:18e). Saul had been unable to perceive God's purposes through the Realm, but now comes to fresh understanding.

CHIASTIC PARALLELS. LUKE 19:28-40 AND ACTS 9:1-19A

In Luke 9:51 Jesus begins a journey to Jerusalem where significant revelatory events occur—Jesus's death, resurrection, and ascension. Luke 19:28-40 is a turning point as Jesus reaches Jerusalem where the climactic events of his ministry unfold. Similarly, the call of Paul is a turning point in Acts from Jerusalem to the Damascus road, and, thence to the gentile mission.

Many congregations in the long established churches are near turning points. For example, membership gets smaller year by year, members age, and questions of survival appear. Some congregations must decide whether to remain in their present locations in changing neighborhoods or to move to the suburbs. Some congregations must decide whether to change worship styles, or to ordain women and men who are oriented to people of the same gender. If a congregation does not perceive itself at a turning-point but it should do so, the preacher might use the sermon to help the congregation to such realization.

The preacher could use these chiastic parallels to lead the congregation to consider which options ahead are most promising for the community's witness. Both the texts portend struggle—Jesus's trial and crucifixion, and Paul's imprisonment, and death. But beyond the struggle is fuller witness to the Realm through resurrection and the ingathering of gentiles. Will the congregation join those who turn away from the Realm by betraying and crucifying Jesus, and by rejecting the outreach to gentiles? Or will the congregation continue the struggle to resurrection and Realm?

ACTS 9:10-19A. THE RISEN JESUS COMMISSIONS SAUL

God now communicates the contents of Saul's call through Ananias. By describing God speaking to Ananias in a vision, Luke indicates that Ananias did not act on his own but at God's behest. By calling attention to Ananias, Luke reminds readers of the role community can have in mediating call and in providing support for the called. The preacher might suggest how the congregation could become an Ananias-like community.

Ananias was skeptical that Saul had changed (Acts 9:10-14) We perceive Ananias in many people today: people who hear of others making positive contributions to life but who respond with skepticism. Sometimes people in Ananias's position build up their own sense of self-righteousness by feeling superior to the Sauls of the world. A pastor might help a congregation consider whether they sometimes use skepticism about others as a mask for the fear of losing their own sense of self-righteousness.

The heart of the passage is Acts 9:15-16. Saul is an "instrument whom I have chosen" to carry the news of the Realm before gentiles, political rulers, and the Jewish people (v. 15). This expression has a Septugintal feel and puts the weight of the Septuagint behind the call of Saul.

The preacher might compare Luke's vision of Paul's mission with that of Paul himself. Whereas Luke sees Saul preaching to both gentiles and Jewish people, Paul speaks only of being called to gentiles (Gal. 1:16). Paul echoes Isaiah 49:1 and Jeremiah 1:6 in Galatians 1:16, thereby indicating that his ministry is in the tradition of the prophets.

Furthermore, Saul will suffer as powers from the old age resist his testimony (Acts 9:16). For Luke, Saul is in the line of suffering prophets, including Jesus. Not only does Paul repeatedly encounter Jewish and gentile opposition, but also Luke later tells Saul's story so as to leave no doubt in the reader's mind that Saul was martyred in Rome (for example, Acts 21:11-14;

Luke shows that Saul is a participant in full standing in the community of the Realm. Saul is baptized. Scales fall from Saul's eyes. Ananias lays hands on Saul so that Saul receives the Holy Spirit. The type of ministry that Saul carries out is a prototype of one inspired by the Spirit. The preacher can ask, to whom is God sending the congregation in the way that God sent Saul?

Connections to the Lectionary

Acts 9:1-6 (7-20) is set for the Third Sunday of Easter in Year C. The actual reading should be Acts 9:1-20 since the point of this story is the call of Paul to carry the news of the Realm per Acts 9:15-16.

The events in the text from Acts on the Second Sunday of Easter take place in Jerusalem (Acts 5:27-32). Reading Acts 9:1-20 marks the turn from Jerusalem/Judea/Samaria to the ends of the earth (Acts 1:8). The readings from Acts on the Fourth, Fifth and Sixth Sundays of Easter in Year C fill out some of the effects of the gentile mission. On this Third Sunday of Easter, then, the preacher could clarify the relationship among the mission to the Jewish community in Acts 2-8 and the gentile mission (Acts 9-28).

The Gospel for this Third Sunday of Easter is John 21:1-19, climaxing with the commission to Peter to feed Jesus's sheep. By changing the reading from the Book of Revelation to 1:9-20 (the call of prophet John), each scripture text for the Third Sunday of Easter would focus on call and mission. The preacher could enrich the mix by adding Paul's own account of his call from Galatians 1:11-17. The preacher could then use these texts from different authors to help the congregation become explore both common and differing elements in their understandings of call and mission.

Acts 9:19b-30. Saul Sent to Safety: Over the Wall in a Basket and in Caesarea

After a few days with the disciples in Damascus, Paul begins his mission by preaching in the synagogues that "Jesus is the [Child] of God" (Acts 9:20). In the context of Luke-Acts, these words are not only a description about Jesus's person but are a statement that Jesus is God's representative in ending the present age and beginning the Realm.

In line with Jesus's prediction that Saul would suffer, Saul's preaching soon arouses opposition in the synagogues in Damascus. Intimating that many Jewish people violate both their own tradition and Roman law, Luke recounts that Jewish people sought to kill Saul (Acts 9:23-24). In an incident memorialized in pictures in children's Bibles, the faithful in Damascus lower Saul in a basket through an opening in the wall (Acts 9:25). Many congregants would have warm feelings if the preacher projected such a picture during the sermon.

When Saul travels to Jerusalem, the believers are hesitant to accept Saul (Acts 9:26; 9:13-14). Barnabas, however, brings Saul to the apostles—the central body of authority for the church—and testifies to Saul's trustworthiness. The apostles place their imprimatur on Saul, thus making Saul's authorization complete: Jesus/Spirit/baptism/apostles.

As in Damascus, Saul preaches powerfully but encounters opposition, this time from Hellenists (Greek speaking Jewish people) who attempt to murder him. In a mind-boggling touch pointing to future developments, the disciples in Jerusalem send Paul to safety in Caesarea. In Luke's day, Caesarea was a larger center of Roman power than Jerusalem. Luke's ironic point, sad in the way it casts aspersion on Jewish leaders, is that Caesarea is safer than Jerusalem for Paul the Jew.

CHIASTIC PARALLELS. LUKE 19:11-27 AND ACTS 9:19B-31

Luke 19:11 sets up the parable of the pounds to address a community that expects the apocalypse. The parable (Luke 19:12-27) is a soft allegory in which the situation of the Lukan community is similar to that of the slaves in the parable. The noble with royal power (Jesus) goes away (ascends). While the noble is away, the slaves manage the money the noble gave them (the congregation is to witness to the realm). When the noble returns, the slaves must give an accounting. The parable urges the community to witness to the Realm with the same energy and expansion that the first and second slaves displayed and thereby to avoid the fate of the third servant. The parable concludes with a warning that all who oppose the Realm will be condemned (Luke 19:27)

In the face of conflict, Luke's congregation is tempted to behave like the third servant by minimizing their witness to the Realm. Instead, Luke wants the community to witness in the manner of the first and second slaves by facilitating the mission to the gentiles in the way that the disciples do: risking their lives to save Saul (Acts 9:23-25), vouching for him as did Barnabas (Acts 9:27), sending him to safety in Caesarea (Acts 9:28) As gentiles flock into the church in response to Saul's ministry later in Acts, these leaders will see ten-fold and five-fold returns on their witness.

Many congregations today are tempted toward the behavior of the slave to whom the noble gave one pound. What are our pounds—our resources for witnessing to the gentiles —in the preacher's congregation? What can we do with our pounds to multiply our outreach to gentiles?

The last line of the parable, Luke 19:27, speaks directly to the Jewish leaders who seek to kill Saul (Acts 9:23, 29): you will face a similar fate at the apocalypse if you continue to resist the movement of the Realm. The preacher who avoids anti-Judaism could bring the congregation's attention to ways the church itself seeks to destroy movements toward the Realm. Luke's warning is stern: those who persist in such behavior invite a painful and public death.

The preceding incidents raise a question for preacher and congregation. When does faithfulness require that the a minister or congregation risk annihilation by confronting those who oppose it (such as the Jews who wish to kill Paul in Damascus and the Hellenists who seek to do so in Jerusalem)? And when is it prudent to slip over the wall in a basket or to slip away to Caesarea and thus live to witness another day? How can we tell the difference between practical wisdom and cowardice?

Christians sometimes say that the change of Saul's name from Saul to Paul in the book of Acts corresponds with his change from persecutor to preacher. Unfortunately, this perspective is unfounded. Saul and Paul are simply Hebrew and Greek forms of the same name. As the narrative of Acts moves away from Jerusalem and Judea (where the form Saul would have been commonplace) and into more gentile settings, the name Saul recedes.

While a preacher cannot use the change of names as itself indicating a new self-understanding, the structure of two understandings of identity could provide a germ for a sermon. The clue to Paul's new life is not a change in name but a change in mission. To what degree does the church think it continues to serve God's purposes when it is locked into dated paradigms that frustrate God's current aims? How can the church live into an identity appropriate for the early twenty-first century?

The name Saul may be freighted with theological symbolism: as Saul of ancient Israel was the first leader of the twelve tribes united in a new, single nation, so the later Saul (Paul) was a leader in a new initiative into the gentile mission field. The preacher can help the church identify new initiatives as fresh in our time as the formation of the monarchy and the emergence of the gentile mission.

You Will Be My Witnesses to the Ends of the Earth: The Healing of Aneas and Raising of Tabitha (Dorcas) Demonstrate the Realm (Acts 9:32-43)

These stories perform multiple functions in Acts. Their placement contributes to the geographical movement of the Realm forecast in Acts 1:8 by getting Peter from Jerusalem to Lydda (about 25 miles northwest of Jerusalem) and Joppa (about eight miles beyond Lydda), from which Peter will go to Caesarea (about 35 miles north of Joppa). These healings remind the reader that the power of the Realm is still at work after the threats to Paul in Damascus and Jerusalem (Acts 9:23, 29) and in anticipation of the conversion of Cornelius (Acts 10:1-48). While the focus in Acts 9:1-31 has been on Paul, Peter returns to center stage reminding readers that the apostolic circle is the central authority for the gentile mission.

Luke has a penchant for showing women and men alongside one another (for example, Luke 2:25-38; 4:24-27; 10:25-42; 15:3-10; 18:1-14; 24:1-11; Acts 2:17-18; 9:32-43; 18:1-4, 24-27). By pairing women and men, Luke subtly anticipates the confidence God will restore gender relationships to the mutuality of Genesis 1:26-28. Given the sexism continuing to privilege males in both the church and wider North America, a preacher could use this motif as doorway into a sermon calling for egalitarian gender relationships in church and culture.

Acts 9:32-35. The Restoration of Aeneas Demonstrates the Realm

In Lydda, Peter encounters Aenas, bedridden and paralyzed for eight years. The detail that Aenas was bedridden adds an element of pathos to the story. The reader can imagine both Aeanas and those around Aenas organizing their time around his care. Through Peter, ascended Jesus restores Aeneas's body. Aeneas immediately makes the bed, demonstrating the completeness of the restoration. This brief story embodies the power of the Realm at work through Peter and the community. Those who follow Peter can expect evidences of the Realm the kind of that took place in Lydda.

As noted in connection with the healing of the person at the Beautiful Gate, some congregations have questions about whether miracles like these occur today. The message could focus on this matter.

A preacher could take paralysis figuratively. I was once in a Bible study focusing on the story of a paralyzed person in which one of the participants told the story of being emotionally immobilized around a particular issue, but her Bible school class helped her regain the ability to move on that issue. A preacher might explore ways in which the congregation is paralyzed and ways the community can be restored.

When thinking about the relevance of the healing miracles to people who live with disabilities and to the church today, Kathy Black, who teaches preaching and worship at the Claremont School of Theology, offers a perspective with which a minister could develop a sermon that begins with Acts 9:32-35. Black distinguishes between cure and healing.[1] Cure is the end of the disabling condition. For example, a person who was paralyzed walks. A person who was blind sees. While the Bible pictures Aenas cured, few such cures take place among people with permanent disabilities today. By contrast, healing refers to the ability of people to accept their situations and to live meaningfully.

This perspective has important outcomes for both persons with disabilities and for the church. Those living with disabilities can see themselves as active agents who contribute to life. What would it mean for Aeneas to be healed? The church should recognize such people not just as objects of ministry but as vital contributors to the church. Indeed, the disability perspectives articulated in the church by people living with disabilities can help the church better imagine how it can become a healing community. How can the church call for changes in the larger culture so that persons who are differently-abled can live fully and freely? What would it mean for the congregation to have Aenas as such a member?

CHIASTIC PARALLELS. LUKE 19:1-10 AND ACTS 9:32-43

Luke 19:1-10 tells the story of Zacchaeus, a chief tax collector. In Palestine, the Romans employed Jewish people to collect taxes to reduce the offense of paying tariffs to Rome. Tax collectors had to pay a certain amount to their Roman bosses, but could then gouge the tax-paying population (Luke 3:12-13). The Jewish populous viewed tax collectors as collaborators with the Roman system. Since Jewish taxes funded the Roman armies and civil government that oppressed Palestine, Jewish people paid for their own oppression.

As a tax collector, Zacchaeus is essentially dead to the purposes of God, yet, when Zacchaeus encounters the Realm in the person of Jesus, Zacchaeus repents. According to Jewish custom, a thief made restitution by returning the amount of money stolen plus one-fifth (Lev. 5:16; 6:1-5; Num. 5:5-7).

Zacchaeus exceeds that expectation by paying back four times the amount he defrauded.

The characters in the parallel chiastic elements represent the social breadth the community of the Realm: Zacchaeus: a tax collector, a person confined to a bed, a woman who supported widows. These different characters give the preacher and opportunity to audit the congregation and the denomination or movement with which it is affiliated. Does the social spectrum of today's church reach from Zacchaeus to Aeneas to Dorcas? If not, how can preacher and congregation try to expand its embrace?

Furthermore, pairing Zacchaeus and Dorcas suggests that Zacchaeus had been in league with the power of death. He exploited others. But through repentance and restitution, God raised Zacchaeus to join Dorcas in living for others. These stories have a double edge for preaching. (1) The stories tell the tax collectors of the world that through repentance and restitution, they can be raised from collusion with the powers of death to life and to a place in the community of the Realm. (2) The stories urge the church to welcome tax collectors who repent. Congregations sometimes resist such folk, but such resistance is itself a form death.

Acts 9:32-43 demonstrates what can happen when the congregation follows Peter's example in leaving the security of Jerusalem and joining Aeneas and Dorcas. How can we connect with the Aeneases and Dorcases of our world?

Acts 9:36-43. The Raising of Tabitha (Dorcas)

When reading Acts 9:36-43, the congregation remembers that Elisa and Elijah performed similar miracles (1 Kgs. 17:17-24; 2 Kgs. 4:18-36). Jesus, likewise, raised a person from the dead (Luke 7:11-17). The reader is not surprised Peter continues this aspect of the ministry of Israel as refracted through Jesus to announce the presence of the Realm.

The name Dorcas is Greek while Tabitha is Aramaic, the everyday language, similar to Hebrew, spoken by Jewish people in the first century. Both names mean "a gazelle." I use the name Dorcas in these comments because I think it is more familiar to North Americans.

Acts 9:36 is the only passage in the Gospels and Letters to use the feminine noun *mathētria,* meaning "woman disciple." Indeed, Dorcas is a model: disciples are to do what she does. Dorcas epitomizes the faithful disciple by engaging in "good works and acts of charity." These expressions refer to actions whereby people share their resources (for example, Tob. 1:3; 1:16; 2:14; Sir. 31:11;

cf. Luke 11:42; 12:33; Acts 2:41-46; 4:32-5:11). Dorcas made clothing (for example, tunics) for the widows in Joppa.

Some scholars think Dorcas was a member of an order of widows, a group of widows in the church who committed themselves to remain single until Jesus returns so they could care for one another and for other needy persons (see 1 Tim. 5:3-16). Because ancient society lacked public social security, widows were vulnerable. Even if Luke does not assume a developed order of widows, Dorcas embodies women who care for one another a culture that could be uncaring and dismissive. Jewish tradition stresses that God intends to provide for widows through the actions of the community (for example, Exod. 22:22-24; Deut. 24:19-22). Dorcas was not simply a philanthropist, but was a means through whom God provided for widows. God raised her from the dead as a sign that this ministry is to continue until Jesus's return.

Dorcas was really dead: her body was washed (a common practice in antiquity). The raising of the dead woman confirms that the Realm is real. Through the Spirit, Peter has the same power to raise the dead that Jesus had. This power will appear again in a gentile context when God through Paul raises Eutychus (Acts 20:7-11).

The story of the raising of Dorcas is set in Joppa, the city from which Jonah embarked on his mission to invite the gentile sinners of Nineveh to repent (Jon. 1:3). In the immediately following material (Acts 10:1-11:18), Peter embarks from Joppa for the conversion of the first gentile, Cornelius. Coming immediately prior to Peter's journey to Joppa, the raising of Dorcas suggests that gentiles are not fully alive to the promises and purposes of the God of Israel, and that the gentile mission is itself a raising from the dead.

CONNECTIONS TO THE LECTIONARY

The congregation hears the story of Dorcas, Acts 9:36-43, on the Fourth Sunday of Easter, Year C. In the introduction to Acts 9:32-43, I proposed a sermon on the egalitarian relationships of women and men. Since the lectionary assigns few texts whose central character is a woman, the preacher could take advantage of Acts 9:36-43 as the starting point for a sermon with the raising of Dorcas as a lens through which to view God's liberating purposes specifically for women. This story could be the beginning point for a sermon that follows Luke's concern for women as a theme.

The preacher could otherwise build on passages from Acts on the Third, Fourth, and Fifth Sundays of Easter, Year C, moving seriatim through Acts

9:1-21, Acts 9:36-43, and Acts 11:1-18, to preach in the mode of *lectio continua* ("continuous reading") for three weeks. In this mode the homilist preaches through a body of scripture in sequence from start to finish. (The preacher taking this approach should add representative selections from Acts 10 to set the stage for Acts 11:1-18.)

A preacher could work from this text both figuratively and literally. At the figurative level, if Dorcas was a widow, she was one of the most vulnerable people in ancient society. Who is the vulnerable Dorcas today, in need of regeneration?

But Dorcas is more than a dead woman. She had been connected to a network of widows whose quality of life was threatened by her death. The preacher could look for people, movements, and circumstances whose circumstances today are similar to Dorcas and the widows: people and groups enmeshed in life-supporting community but who are threatened with death, such as organizations, agencies and movements that stand for life but whose existence is threatened by diminishing funding or political of cultural opposition. How might the congregation become a life support?

At the literal level, Dorcas worked with widows. In zeal to attract young couples with children, congregations sometimes overlook actual widows and widowers. In the larger world, the social safety net for such people is threatened, especially when money is tight. The church needs to stand with widows.

In an earlier generation, many congregations had a "Dorcas Circle," a group of women who met for Bible study, prayer, mutual support, and mission. The preacher might tell the story of that group (or a similar group) in the congregation, replete with pictures of beloved members, their classroom, and their mission projects. The sermon could observe that while the style of the Dorcas Circle belonged to a previous era, the mission represented by Dorcas in Acts 9:36-43—solidarity with widows and others who are vulnerable—is a cutting edge concern as more people in North America are in threatening situations. Dorcas could lend her name and inspiration to a new generation of women who relate and organize appropriately for our time as they witness to the Realm as Dorcas did in her time.

You Will Be My Witnesses to the Ends of the Earth: God Welcomes the First Gentiles into the Movement (Acts 10:1—11:18)

Cornelius is the first gentile in Acts to convert. To show this development was properly authorized, Luke highlights the role of Peter as God's instrument in walking with Cornelius to conversion (Acts 10:1-33). Peter both presides over the "gentile Pentecost," the coming of the eschatological Spirit upon a number of Gentiles (Acts 10:34-48) and interprets the gentile mission to the congregation in Jerusalem (11:1-18).

Preachers sometimes draw lines between Jewish and gentile cultures as if the two communities never interacted and as if Jews hated gentiles. This picture is an oversimplification. Jews and gentiles often lived alongside one another. One purpose of Judaism was to point gentiles to the path to blessing (pp. 24–25). By Luke's day, many Jewish people regarded idolatry as the core gentile problem. Worshipping false gods led to misperceptions and fractiousness, promiscuity, injustice, exploitation, violence, and death (for example, Ps. 115:4-8, Wis. 13:10-14:31). Luke shares such views (for example, Acts 4:24-28).

Nevertheless, several end-time theologians believed that God would welcome gentiles to into the Realm. Luke believed that a great reunion was underway among God, gentiles and the Jewish community. Acts 10:1-11:18 provides narrative assurance that this movement is of God. Gentiles must repent and be baptized. Acts 10:1-11:18 is Luke's version of the first embrace in that great reunion.

Most of the readers of this book are gentiles. As my colleague Clark Williamson often says in conversation, "If it were not for Jesus Christ who leads us gentiles to the God of Israel, our gentile religion would include painting our bodies blue and baying at the moon" (as certain gentile groups did in antiquity). Acts 10:1-11:18 is *our* spiritual autobiography.

Acts 10:1-33. Peter Is God's Agent in Leading Cornelius to the Realm

This passage makes use of a double-vision, a literary device in which two characters have individual visions that bring the characters together for a common purpose. The double vision motif confirms that God is present leading the events.

Cornelius is not only a gentile but a centurion, an officer in charge of 100 Roman soldiers. Cornelius is a God-fearer, a gentile attracted to the God of Israel who does not fully convert to Judaism. Cornelius prays and gives alms.

Peter is a leader among the apostles. While full apostolic sanction for the gentile mission does not occur until Acts 15, Luke invokes apostolic authority through Peter.

In the first vision, an angel tells Cornelius to send for Peter (Simon) from Joppa (Acts 10:3-6). In the second vision, Peter receives a vision of a smorgasbord of animals (so to speak), some of which are unclean (Acts 10:10-15). Three times a voice instructs Peter to kill and eat, whereupon Peter protests that he has never eaten anything profane or unclean. Ancient writers sometimes invoke the principle of three to show that something is important and reliable.

Christians often misconstrue the distinction between clean and unclean in Judaism. While this separation had multiple levels, one dimension is important for Acts 10:1-31. The categories of reminded the Jewish community of their distinct identity and mission. By not eating all the foods that gentiles eat, every meal reminded the Jewish community that God chose the to show the path to blessing to gentiles. The notions of clean and unclean are thus not repressive legalisms but are boundary markers to maintain a strong witnessing community.

Luke's end-time theology illuminates why Luke believed that this distinction was no longer necessary. God is drawing this age to a close: the faithful do not need the full set of boundary markers that had sustained Judaism during the old age. The apostolic council draws upon these categories when prescribing how faithful gentiles should live (Acts 15:28-29).

In Acts 10:19-22, the Spirit gives Peter another vision of messengers coming from Cornelius and then guides Peter to the gate where the messengers explain their mission: to bring Peter to Cornelius. When Peter arrives at Cornelius's house, he joins a group. Peter says it is unlawful for a Jewish person to associate with gentiles (Acts 10:23b-28). This last statement is not correct. While complications sometimes arose around eating together, Jewish and gentile peoples associated every day. Luke evidently makes use of dramatic overstatement to underscore the importance of Peter's visit.

Cornelius asks Peter to interpret these events (Acts 10:33). Thus far in the narrative, Luke has done two things. First, he reminds Jewish members of his community that the gentile mission is of God. Second, he reminds gentile members of the congregation that the good news that comes to them is of Jewish origin.

CHIASTIC PARALLELS: LUKE 18:35-43 AND ACTS 10:1-33

Both Luke 18:34-43 and Acts 10:1-33 use elements related to sight as figures for understanding. In the Gospel, Jesus heals a person near Jericho who was blind. In antiquity blindness was a serious physical condition often resulting in poverty. Many Jewish writers also used the language of blindness as a metaphor for not perceiving the purposes of God (for example, Isa. 42:18-19; 43:8) .The opening of the eyes of people who are blind both physically and metaphorically is a sign of the Realm.

Both Cornelius and Peter have visions they do not understand. However, as in Luke 18:35-43, God opens their figurative eyes to perceive the gentile mission. Both Luke 18:35-43 and Acts 10:1-33 promise readers that God opens the eyes of the community of the Realm to God's intention for them to welcome Others.

Individuals and congregations sometimes fail to understand God's similar purposes today. Does the congregation not perceive such things (as in the story in Luke). Does the congregation have some inklings about such things, but not know how to fully interpret them (as in Acts)? How does becoming aware of the Realm help the community come to understanding?

The preacher can help today's gentile congregation give thanks to the God of Israel for making it possible for us to join Cornelius as part of the movement toward the Realm. Christians today could seek solidarity with our Jewish neighbors.

The church continues to have a mission to gentiles. Many qualities of life today are similar to gentile existence in antiquity. What values, practices, communities or systems function as idols? Where do we find fractiousness, injustice, exploitation, violence, and death? In the tradition of Peter visiting Cornelius, how can the church bring the renewing word of the Realm to such settings?

A sermon could evolve around what to make of people who claim that God speaks to them in dreams and visions today. Does the preacher believe that God does so? If so, by what criteria does a congregation conclude that a dream or a vision may be of God? If not, a preacher could draw on the difference between surface and deeper dimensions of a text to respond to this issue. The double vision was a means of establishing authority. The preacher might help the congregation identify things that function authoritatively for them. How might such things support the call to the congregation's particular mission to gentiles?

ACTS 10:34-43. PETER INTERPRETS THE SIGNIFICANCE OF THE COMING OF THE REALM FOR GENTILES

Peter interprets what is happening by stating a principle still quoted in Christian circles: "God shows no partiality"[2] (Acts 10:34). Christians today often use this statement as justification for including a wide range of people in the purview of God's concern, but omit the second part of the statement: "But in every nation anyone who fears [God] and does what is right is acceptable to God."

The notion that God does not exhibit partiality was long established in Judaism. In matters of justice, God judges alike those at the top and the bottom of the social pyramid (Lev. 19:15; Deut. 10:17-18; Sir. 35:14-26, esp. 15c-16a). In Acts 10:34-35 Luke draws on this principle to show that God responds to gentiles who show reverence for God ("who fear God") and who live in God's ethical ways ("do what is right").

In Acts, this principle is limited in scope. It assures gentile converts that God is not biased against them. However, the principle does not extend to nonconverted gentiles. The limited scope of this principle will not be theologically satisfying to those Christians today who believe that a God of unconditional love is by definition impartial in responding to all human beings, not just to those who repent.

CHIASTIC PARALLELS. LUKE 18:31-35 AND ACTS 10:34-43

In Luke 18:31-35, Jesus predicts his death and resurrection for the third time (cf. Luke 9:21-2; 43b-45). In the ancient world, the number three sometimes signified completeness, especially in stories that employed the principle of three. The three repetitions of Jesus's death and resurrection confirm that God controls these events and that they are essential to the coming of the Realm. However, despite having three opportunities to get the message, the disciples did not understand the significance (Luke 18:35).

In Acts 10:34-43, Peter helps the audience grasp the significance of Jesus's death and resurrection as important to the Realm in the context of interpreting the double visions of Acts 10:1-33. The death and resurrection of Jesus are important milestones on the way to the Realm, a central element of which is the gentile mission.

The message God sent to Israel through Jesus is the presence and coming of the Realm of God. In Luke's context in which the reader cannot forget that Cornelius is a centurion in the army that represses the Mediterranean world, Luke emphasizes that the story of Jesus and the Realm leads to peace. Jesus, not Caesar, is "[ruler] of all" (Acts 10:36).

Peter traces several of the main lines in Luke's story of Jesus. John the Baptist announced that God would anoint Jesus with the Holy Spirit and power (Acts 10:37). In a phrase much loved by preachers, Peter says that Jesus "went about doing good," and casting out demons. Jesus thus embodied the presence of the Realm (Acts 10:38). The congregation at Cornelius's house can trust this report because Peter and other apostles witnessed the things that Peter describes (Acts 10:39a)

In the presence of gentiles, Peter diplomatically uses the ambiguous "they" to describe those who put Jesus to death when the reader knows that while Jewish leaders were complicit in the death of Jesus, gentiles alone had the power of capital punishment. The apostles further witnessed Jesus risen from the dead, the definitive sign that the ministry of Jesus embodied the Realm. The apostles ate and drank with the risen Jesus. In so doing, they anticipated the eschatological banquet (Acts 10:39b-43).

Peter's audience is mainly gentile. A preacher needs to ponder the circumstances in which Peter's diplomatic "they" is a useful model for the pulpit today. Peter does not say directly that gentiles crucified Jesus. An ancient rhetor would adopt such a strategy so as not to offend the audience and to keep them listening. The preacher must ponder whether such an approach lets the congregation off the hook when they need to confront their own complicity in wrongdoing.

Connections to the Lectionary

Acts 10:34-43 occurs in Years A, B, and C as an alternate reading for Easter. This gives the preacher a natural opportunity to help the congregation see that the resurrection of Jesus is not an end it itself. It does not simply anticipate the eternal life of the individual, but empowers the reconstitution of the human community. Human beings are made to live together in the fullness of God's purposes now and forever.

Acts 10:34-43 is also found on the Baptism of Jesus, the First Sunday after the Epiphany, in Year A. This passage fits nicely with the other readings on that day as part of God's invitation to gentiles to join the movement toward the Realm. Isaiah 42:1-9 highlights Israel as "a light to the nations" (gentiles) (Isa. 42:6). Matthew's account of the baptism of Jesus echoes Isaiah 42:1 (thereby calling to mind Isaiah 42:1-9); the first gospel climaxes in the great commission to carry the gospel to gentiles (Matt. 28:16-20). A preacher might use the baptism of Jesus as the paradigm for the baptism of gentiles while explaining how Matthew, Isaiah, and Acts interpret their understandings of witness to the gentiles in different ways.

However, the assignment of Acts 10:34-43 to the Baptism of Jesus is also puzzling since that passage contains no references to baptism, whereas Acts 10:44-48, explicitly referring to the baptism of gentiles, does not occur until the Sixth Sunday of Easter, Year B. The preacher might read Acts 10:34-48 on the Baptism of Jesus, thus allowing the preacher to compare and contrast the meanings of baptism in the Gospel of Matthew and in Luke-Acts. While both the first and third gospels regard the baptism of Jesus as the model for people entering the community, Matthew prescribes baptism in the name of God, Jesus and the Holy Spirit (Matt. 28:16-28), whereas Acts only calls for baptism in the name of Jesus (Acts 10:48; cf. Acts 2:38; 8:16; 19:5). What is the congregation to make of this pluralism?

The baptism of Jesus occurs early in the calendar year—a good Sunday for the preacher to encourage the congregation to remember their own baptisms and to recommit themselves to lead a baptized life in the new year. Acts 10:34-48 reminds the church that this life includes welcoming gentiles.

Peter establishes the authority of the apostles and of the church with the statement that Jesus commissioned them to preach. The climactic message from Peter is that God has appointed Jesus as "the judge of the living and the dead" (Acts 10:42). This judgment will take place at the second coming (for example, Luke 3:17; 10:13-16; 11:29-32; Acts 17:31). God's impartiality comes into play at the final judgment: God will judge equitably all people from all nations. Those who believe God is bringing about the Realm through Jesus, and who repent, will receive forgiveness of sins.

In Luke's congregation, this emphasis on the judgment cuts two ways. To gentiles who do not believe in Jesus, it is a call to repent, be baptized, and join the movement toward the Realm. To the church, it is a reminder that the initial act of repentance and baptism are not ends but first steps on The Way. The church's mission is to witness faithfully while awaiting the second coming and the final judgment.

ACTS 10:44-48. GENTILES RECEIVE THE SPIRIT IN THE SAME WAY AS JEWISH BELIEVERS

To establish the credibility of the gentile mission, in Acts 10:1-43, Luke appeals to the events transpiring between Peter and Cornelius, to the story of Jesus, to the prophetic tradition, and to the apostles' eye witness accounts of key events in the ministry of Jesus. Acts 10:44-48 is the final piece of evidence: the experience of the gentiles receiving the Holy Spirit.

Preachers and scholars speak of this event as the "gentile Pentecost," although that phrase does not occur here, and Acts 10:44-48 does not take place on Pentecost. Nevertheless, the things that occurred among the Jewish community on Pentecost recur among gentiles. The Holy Spirit falls upon those who hear Peter's preaching. The gentiles speak in tongues (the "other languages" of Acts 2:4-1).The gentiles "extol God:" they turn away from gentile deities and acknowledge the supremacy of the God of Israel. The gentiles are baptized. By confessing God, receiving the Spirit, and being baptized, the gentiles become full participants in the community moving toward the realm.

Connection to the Lectionary

The lectionary appoints Acts 10:44-48 for the Sixth Sunday of Easter in Year B. In Connection to the Lectionary with Acts 10:34-43 (above), I propose reading Acts 10:44-48 on the Baptism of Jesus (First Sunday after the Epiphany) in Year A. If the preacher makes that change, I suggest selecting another text from Acts (not already in the lectionary) for the Sixth Sunday of Easter in Year B to increase the number of passages from Acts in the lectionary readings. Since the lectionary ignores the latter third of Acts, worship planners might draw a passage highlighting the gentile mission from there, for example, Acts 21:17-26.

Luke notes that Jewish members of the community are present as witnesses (Acts 10:45-46). Acts 11:12 indicates that six Jewish believers accompanied Peter. Peter asks pointedly, "Can anyone with hold the water for baptizing these people who have received the Holy Spirit *just as we have*." The Jewish experience at Pentecost is the norm. The gentile experience now satisfies that norm (Acts 10:48).

To the degree that Luke addresses Jewish prejudice against gentiles in the congregation, this key text points out that the gentile experience is the same as that of the Jewish believers. To the degree that Luke wants to encourage gentile respect for Jewish people in the community, this passage points out that the Jewish experience is originative. This circumstance calls gentiles to live respectfully with Jewish people since ancient people respected communities of origin.

CHIASTIC PARALLELS. LUKE 18:18-30 AND ACTS 10:44-48

The events in these chiastic elements are foils. In Luke 18:18-30 we encounter a rich Jewish ruler who wants to know what to do to inherit eternal life. The words "eternal life" are a cipher for the Realm. Because he is faithful in many ways (Luke 18:20-21) the reader expects the rich ruler will do what Jesus asks: sell all that he has, distribute it to the poor, and live out of the bounty of the community (Luke 18:28-30; Acts 2:43-47; 4:32-37). However, this ruler, though knowledgeable about Torah, has an old-age attachment to his wealth.

Acts 10:44-48 pictures gentiles who receive the Holy Spirit and baptism and who thereby receive the very thing that the rich ruler seeks: assurance they are included in the Realm and have eternal life. Whereas he "goes away very sad," the gentiles speak in tongues and extol God. These gentiles do what the rich ruler will not: they give up their attachment to the old age to gain the community described in Luke 18:30.

The sermon could help the congregation ponder the degree to which they more identify with the rich ruler or with the gentiles. Where is the congregation on the spectrum with one end being knowledgeable about the Bible and responsible in many ways, but manifesting discipleship that stops short of the Realm with other end being similar to gentiles under the power of the Spirit? Listeners have a choice: to go away from the sermon "very sad" or "extolling God."

Luke's turn to experience is the lynchpin in justifying the full standing of gentiles in the community prompts a question for today. To what degree can the church consider experience a reliable source in coming to theological interpretation of God's purposes? I return to this issue in connection with the apostolic council in Acts 15:1-35.

ACTS 11:1-18 THE JERUSALEM COMMUNITY INFORMALLY APPROVES OF THE GENTILE MISSION

Acts 11:1-3 introduces a conflict not fully resolved until the apostolic council in Acts 15:1-35. When Peter returns to Jerusalem, some Jewish members of the community criticize Peter for eating with gentiles. As in many church conflicts today, the presenting issue (eating with gentiles) is a symptom of a bigger matter (the place in the church for gentiles who have not converted fully to Judaism). A preacher could use this text to name the relationship between an immediate issue in the congregation and the larger network of issues in which it is embedded.

Peter explains "step by step" what happened to lead to the event in Acts 10:44-48. Many pastors could benefit from following Peter's model of explaining to the congregation, step by step, how they reach a theological conclusion. The congregation is typically interested not only in the preacher's opinion, but in how the preacher reached that opinion.

Thinking through an issue step by step could help many ministers clarify *their own thinking*. I know some pastors who hold opinions resulting more from theological intuition than from reasoned analysis. When confronted by congregants who want to know why preachers think as they do, such preachers are not able to give real explanations. The congregation can then dismiss the preacher's opinion. The preacher who thinks through an issue has a place to stand. Further, the sermon that works through an issue step by step helps the congregation not only with that issue but with learning how to think theologically about other issues.

CHIASTIC PARALLELS. LUKE 18:15-17 AND ACTS 11:1-18

In Luke 18:15-17, parents bring infants so that Jesus can touch them, but the disciples order the adults to stop. Overriding the disciples, Jesus invites the children to come to him. Whereas today we often make children the center of our worlds, the ancient Mediterraneans saw the child at the bottom of the social hierarchy. In this incident, the children represent all who appear to be socially insignificant. Jesus asks the disciples and all who would become a part of the Realm to identify with the children who came to him: to recognize that they do not have the power to bring about the Realm of God but can only receive it as a gift.

In Acts 11:1-18, the circumcised believers criticize Peter for eating with uncircumcised people and, by implication, criticize the gentile mission. In welcoming the children, Jesus is a model for Luke's congregation. God, through the Holy Spirit, welcomes gentile believers. The congregation should join God in doing so.

In Acts 11:4-17, Peter summarizes the events of Acts 10:1-48. To stress the reliability of this account, Peter mentions three times that he received the vision to "kill and eat" (11:10), the role of the Spirit (11:12a, 15), the presence of the six witnesses from the Jerusalem community (11:12b), and the manifestation of the same gift that the Jewish community received on Pentecost (11:17). Peter concludes not by telling the congregation what he wants them to believe but with a masterful rhetorical question that puts the listeners in the position of having to make their own decisions concerning the evidence Peter has put forward. "Who was I that I could hinder God?"

The group was silenced. Their objection lost its force. They then praised God and made a provocative statement. God long ago gave Jewish people repentance as a means to restoring life. Now "God has given *even* the gentiles the repentance that leads to life" (Acts 11:18). I know my often unconverted gentile self so well that I can only marvel that God gives *even to me* the repentance that leads to life.

Connection to the Lectionary

Acts 11:1-18 is read in public worship on the Fifth Sunday of Easter in Year C. The comments on the lectionary reading for the Third Sunday of Easter in Year C (Acts 9:1-19a) propose preaching *lectio continua* on the Third, Fourth, and Fifth Sundays of Year C. When taking that approach, Acts 11:1-18 is the point toward which Luke aims Acts 9:1-10:48: the community in Jerusalem informally approves the first expression of the gentile mission.

Another approach to the sermon might consider the different nuances in what community members are supposed to do as implied in the three main readings for the day. The Gospel of John promotes a sectarian notion of community in tension with a traditional synagogue and gives little attention to mission outside the congregation: disciples are to "love *one another.*" The Book of Revelation also promotes a sectarian congregation though one in tension with the Roman Empire. According to Revelation 21:7, the congregation is to "conquer," that is, to endure in the face of the violence of the Empire (cf. Rev. 13:9; 14:12). The Book of Revelation commissions little witness outside the congregation. By contrast, Acts 11:1-18 implicitly encourages the congregation to evangelize gentiles. After considering these different options, the preacher could help the congregation consider the question, "What are the most important things for the contemporary congregation and its members to do?"

You Will Be My Witnesses to the Ends of the Earth: Success, Providence, Tragedy, Imprisonment, Assurance, Retribution (Acts 11:19—12:25)

Acts 11:19-12:25 is a transitional section between the justification of the gentile mission in the preceding narrative and the missionary journeys beginning in Acts 13:1. In Acts 11:19-25 we go from the success among gentiles in Antioch (Acts 11:19-26) through tragedy of the execution of James (Acts 12:1-5) and the imprisonment of Peter (Acts 12:6-17) to divine retribution on Herod (Acts 12:20-25). Underneath is God's providence operating through "the hand of [God]" (Acts 11:21), through the community (Acts 11:27-30) and through an angel (Acts 12:6-17).

Each segment could become a focus for an individual sermon (as discussed below). Or a deft preacher might take the diverse stories of Acts11:19—12:25 as a kaleidoscopic lens for interpreting God's purposes in a congregation in transition as congregations in transition experience the intermixing we find in this passage of highs and lows, conflict and community. Following Luke, the preacher can help the congregation sense God's presence and providence.

Acts 11:19-27. Gentiles in Large Numbers Embrace the Realm in Antioch

In an ironic turn of events illustrating how God can make providential use of difficulty, the believers who fled Judea after the martyrdom of Stephen (Acts 6:8-8:3) established communities of the Realm in Phoenicia, Cyprus, and Antioch. The preacher could project a map so the congregation can compare this movement (northward) with the previous movements through Judea, Samaria, and southward.

The persecution intended to eliminate the church sparked the spread of the church. A preacher might muse over situations today in which leaders (ecclesial or governmental) attempt to squelch a group or a movement, only to find that the group grows stronger in response.

Since several cities in the Roman Empire were named Antioch, the preacher needs to keep track of which Antioch is in view. Here the reference is to Antioch of Syria, the third largest city in the Roman Empire. Antioch becomes an important theological symbol in Acts as a center for gentile expansion, and as a base for Paul's missionary journeys. Could the preacher's congregation have a kind of Antioch function in the neighborhood, the city, or the denomination?

The disciples speak only to Jewish people in Antioch (Acts 11:19b). However, Luke reports no response from the Jewish community. When disciples from Cyrene and Cyprus preach in Antioch, a large number respond whom the NRSV describes as "Hellenists" but whom the NIV describes as "Greeks." Some ancient manuscripts of Acts contain the word "Hellenists" (*hellēnistas*) but some use the word "Greeks" (*hellēnas*). The word "Greeks" is more likely here in view of Acts' recent discussion of the gentile mission (Acts 9:1-31; 10:1-11:8) and of Luke's contrast of the non-response of the Jewish people in 11:19b with the large welcome given by the Greeks in 11:20-21, 24.

The church at Jerusalem sends Barnabas who immediately recognizes God's hand in this gentile explosion. Barnabas brings Saul from Jerusalem. Luke makes sure readers know that Barnabas and Saul are present so readers can trust their testimony at the apostolic council (Acts 11:22-25; Acts 15:1-35).

While the gentile mission was theologically authorized through the call of Paul and the conversion of Cornelius, it springs up in Antioch without reference to those events. This mission is driven by an energy that cannot be contained. A preacher might think with the congregation about Realm-oriented grass-roots movements today that move forward under their own power. How could the congregation identify with them?

The word "Christian" first appears as a title for believers in Acts 11:26 and appears in the Gospels and Letters only here used by outsiders and in 1 Peter 4:16 where it is used by opponents. In Acts 11:26 outsiders likely used the word "Christian" derisively. A preacher might recall instances when groups have been called derisive names but have instigated reform. A matter to ponder: have Christian communities today drifted away from the values of the Realm so that we need reform? Could movements the church derides point the way to renewal?

CHIASTIC PARALLELS. LUKE 18:9-14 AND ACTS 11:19-26

Compared to other Jewish groups, Luke paints a relatively positive picture of the Pharisees in Acts (for example, Acts 5:34; 23:6-8). Nevertheless, Luke can be critical of Pharisees, especially in the Gospel as in 7:36-50, 11:37-54, and 18:9-14 as well as in Acts 15:5. In the parable of the Pharisee and the tax collector, the Pharisee violates a fundamental dictum of the Pharisees by trusting in his own righteousness, whereas the tax collector, who daily gouges Jewish people, beats his breast in repentance and goes home justified. The tax collector voices profound yearning for God.

In Antioch, the disciples initially preach exclusively to the Jewish community but Luke reports no response from that group (Acts 11:19). However, a great number of Greeks believed. The parable helps explain why the two communities responded differently. The Jewish community trusted in themselves where as the gentiles recognize their desperate situation and repent.

The preacher who ventures into these waters must help the congregation realize that Luke portrays the Pharisee and, by implication, the Jewish people, in negative light for Luke's own polemical agenda. Beyond this essential work, the preacher might encourage the tax collectors and gentiles in today's setting to recognize their need of God. A sermon can excel at that without denigrating Jewish peoples. Indeed, the preacher could help gentiles today repent of the ways in which we go along with anti-Judaism.

ACTS 11:27-30. FAMINE PROMPTS COMMUNITY SHARING

Prophets travel from Jerusalem to Antioch (Acts 11:27). The term "prophets" here refers to figures in the early church who received messages from heaven and transmitted those messages to the congregation. The early communities believed that God used such prophets to continue to speak to the church after the resurrection.

This phenomenon calls to mind the theological perspective summarized in an expression used by a contemporary denomination, "God is still speaking." According to Luke God continues to speak. For Luke the content of the prophecies must be internally consistent with the values of the Realm to be regarded as valid. The congregation today that believes God continues to speak must determine criteria by which to judge the authority of fresh interpretations. In a world of so many contradictory voices, which ones have the greatest claim to come from God?

A prophet named Agabus stands up in a community meeting and predicts a severe famine during the reign of Claudius. While a famine may not have occurred "over all the world," Josephus reports a wide-spread famine in Judea during the reign of Claudius.[3]

Upon hearing Agabus's report, the gentile disciples in Antioch act in the spirit of the ideal community (Acts 2:42-47, Acts 4:32-37, Acts 6:1-6) by sending relief to believers in Jerusalem. God uses the gentiles as an instrument through whom to provide for the church in Jerusalem. The gentile offering demonstrates the reunion of Jewish and gentile peoples. Moreover, the reader recognizes in the offering a moment in the present anticipating Isaiah's vision of the eschatological world in which gentiles place their resources in the service of the God of Israel (Isa. 64:10-12).

Many congregations and denominations collect relief offerings. My impression is that most Christians view such offerings as charity. A preacher could help today's congregation recognize these offerings as practical solidarity and eschatological anticipation similar to that in the offering from Antioch to Jerusalem.

CHIASTIC PARALLELS. LUKE 18:1-8 AND ACTS 11:27-30

The parable of the widow and the unjust judge is not an allegory but an argument from the lesser to the greater: (the lesser) if a harsh judge would finally respond to the pleas of a widow by granting her justice to get rid of her, then (the greater) how much a loving God responds to the cries of the world for justice. Justice refers to circumstances embodying God's intentions for people to live together in mutual support, peace, and provision.

In Acts 11:27-30, a situation of injustice takes hold: a severe famine denies people food. God speedily brings justice through the churches in Antioch who send food to Judea. The common life of the community is the instrument through which justice comes. Where is the world today crying for justice? How can the church become an instrument through which God acts for justice?

ACTS 12:1-5: HEROD KILLS JAMES

The central element of this text—Herod ordering James put to death—connects to the main theme of Acts 12:20-23 when God puts Herod to death as retribution. A sermon that begins from Acts 12:1-5 should include Acts 12:20-23.

Luke paints Herod in a negative light by associating Herod with the Roman Emperor and with Pontius Pilate (Luke 3:1). When John the Baptist rebuked Herod for all the evil that Herod had done, the ruler imprisoned John (Luke 3:18-20). Herod is curious about Jesus (Luke 9:7-9) but when he meets Jesus, Herod does not stand in the way of the crucifixion, and even becomes friends with Pilate (Luke 23:6-12). Luke holds Herod responsible, with Pilate, for the decision to crucify Jesus (Acts 4:27). When the angel releases Peter from prison and the guards cannot find the former prisoner, Herod follows the Roman custom of punishing guards whose prisoners have escaped (Acts 12:18-19).

Herod imprisons Peter and intends to present Peter to the Jewish crowd as Pilate presented Jesus. In the same way that Pilate yielded to the crowd in putting Jesus to death (Luke 23:13-25), Herod takes advantage of Jewish pleasure at the execution of James to imprison Peter (Acts 12:3-4).

Herod, like Pilate and the Emperor, act according to the values of the old age. Where does a minister see political authorities today—individuals, ideologies, groups—that are Herodian in their attempt to silence witnesses by putting the them to death or imprisoning them —both literally and figuratively?

Yet the preacher needs to keep the door open for the fact that God makes use of particular Roman authorities later in Acts to protect Paul. Within life-taking systems, we sometimes encounter life-giving people.

CHIASTIC PARALLELS. LUKE 17:20-37 AND ACTS 12:1-5

Luke 17:20-37 sets out present (17:20-21) and future (17:22-37) dimensions in the Realm. As the apocalypse nears, the rulers of the old age resist the representatives of the Realm (Luke 17:25). Jesus assures disciples that God is actively working to bring the Realm and that they must continue to witness or face condemnation at the apocalypse (17:26-37).

In Acts 12:1-5, Jesus's prediction that the disciples will suffer comes true when Herod has James executed. Herod is such a creature of the old age that when he sees that this action pleased the Jewish people, he imprisons Peter.

These chiastic parallels are a pastoral warning: Luke's congregation can expect threats and resistance. But, the congregation needs to endure. A preacher working with this chiasm might identify some Herods in our world. How is God is actively bringing the Realm in the present and how does God invite us to participate?

Given that some Christians in our world are threatened with martyrdom and other forms of suffering, the sermon could help the congregation identify such folk. How can the congregation be in active solidarity with such witnesses?

ACTS 12:6-19. GOD RELEASES PETER FROM PRISON

Luke tells the story of disciples being released from prison three times (Acts 5:17-21; 16:23-29). A theme is important when Luke repeats it three times. Luke wants to impress upon readers that when witness leads them into dangerous places, God cares for them. Indeed, vv. 6-9, Peter was freed while he was still in the jail building.

Luke places Peter's release from prison between Herod murdering James (Acts 12:1-2) and an angel executing Herod (Acts 12:20-23). This placement invites the preacher to contrast the behavior and fate of Herod with that of Peter; Herod commits murder and is condemned, whereas Peter is imprisoned but released. Which does the congregation choose?

The story of Peter's release is loaded with miraculous details demonstrating God's control: the angel, chains falling off Peter's wrists, passing the guards without being noticed, and the iron gate opening of its own accord. Although Peter participated in these things, he "did not realize that what was happening was real" (Acts 12:9). The preacher might help parishioners think about times when they too are in situations that seem more like vision than reality.

CHIASTIC PARALLELS. LUKE 17:11-19 AND ACTS 12:6-11

In Luke 17:11-19, Jesus heals ten people who had leprosy. The nine Jewish people who had leprosy went to the temple without acknowledging Jesus, whereas the one Samaritan returned to thank Jesus. As I say so often, Luke uses this story to cast a negative light on Jewish people. Luke seeks to prompt the community to be receptive to the Samaritan.

Similar dynamics are at work in Acts 12:6-11. Herod imprisoned Peter to please the Jewish people (Acts 12:3) and Peter expected Jewish people to move against him when the guards "brought him out" (Acts 12:5, 11). The story thus reflects negatively on Jewish people in Jerusalem in a way similar to the negative portrayal of the nine Jewish people in Luke 17:11-17. Just as God looked with favor upon the Samaritan, so God looks with favor upon Peter. Luke thus (a) warns the congregation to be wary of Jewish people who are not only ungrateful but wish to imprison the disciples, and (b) wants to hearten the congregation's confidence that their distinctive witness to the Realm is healing and liberating. Indeed, both the Samaritan and Peter were released from isolating circumstances and restored to full participation in community.

A preacher might regard anti-Judaism as similar to leprosy that discolors relationships necessary for Realm-like community, or as a prison that shuts the congregation off from relationships with the synagogue that could be liberating. The Realm calls the church to renounce anti-Jewish ideology and to work toward a world in which Jewish and Christian communities engage in mutual mission to those in prison—including prisons of prejudice—that limit so many individuals and communities today.

Luke seeks to assure the congregation that God is present and active when they face controversy, tension, and discomfort because of their witness to the

Realm. Even if they are not physically imprisoned, providence attends them. This purpose suggests a purpose for the sermon: to assure the congregation that when their witness places them in difficult circumstances, God is present in support.

In our setting, angels of the kind described by Luke seldom open prison doors miraculously. The preacher could, however, help the congregation imagine how they could act in the role of the angels in the text by supporting faithful witnesses who are behind bars and by working for their release. While the story of Peter's release has imprisoned disciples in view, the congregation could extend its vision to all who are jailed. How can the congregation become instruments of providence for the local prison population?

Chiastic Parallels. Luke 17:1-10 and Acts 12:12-19

In Luke 17:1-10, Jesus warns the disciples that occasions for stumbling are ahead. The apostles request Jesus: "Increase our faith!" (Luke 17:5). They want the confidence to live through the present and coming turmoil. Jesus responds that if they have faith the size of a mustard seed, they can cause a mulberry tree to be uprooted and planted in the sea. In this context, faith specifically means believing that Jesus is God's prophet who brings the Realm, and that the church as community continues that witness. The apostles want Jesus to increase their confidence in the presence and coming of the Realm.

The disciples do not even have faith the size of a mustard seed in Rhoda's initial report that Peter is released (Acts 12:12-17). In the context of the chiastic parallel, Luke 17:1-10, one purpose of this story is to increase the congregation's faith. If God released Peter in their season of turmoil, then they can count on God to manifest the presence of the Realm in other difficult circumstances. When the congregation prays—as they did for Peter (Acts 12:5)—they need to look for signs of the realm to follow.

Many Christians think that Luke 17:5-6 has to do with general matters of faith. A message can help the congregation move to the specific understanding of faith as confidence in the Realm. "Increase our faith!" Amid the turmoil of our time, we yearn for trust in the Realm. Yet, like the disciples in Acts 12:12-17, we often miss the signs of the Realm knocking at our door. The preacher could follow Luke's example of responding to the request to "increase our faith" by telling stories, like the release of Peter from prison, that can be interpreted as the presence of the realm around us. The homily could help us identify situations in which faith the size of a mustard seed (that is, cooperating with the purposes of the Realm) can begin to move mulberry trees.

After release, Peter goes to the home of Mary, the mother of John Mark, where the community was gathered in prayer, and knocks at the gate. When a maid, Rhoda, recognizes Peter's voice without opening the gate, she leaves him outside and runs to tell the others. Just as the apostles initially did not believe the women who came from the tomb of Jesus with the news of the resurrection (Luke 24:1-12), the crowd thinks that Rhoda is "out of her mind." When she persists, they claim, "It is an angel" (Acts 12:15). Only when the group responds to Peter's persistent knocking do they discover Rhoda's witness is true.

The preacher can help the congregation ask, "Who are the Rhodas to whom we need to listen today?" Rhoda was a maid in the lower echelons of the social pyramid of antiquity. The church today might come to a better understanding of God's liberating work by listening to people and communities in our world in social positions similar to that of Rhoda.

This text contains a sober element. Luke typically holds up women as models of faithfulness, but here Mary is at one with the other disciples in not believing Rhoda. While the church these days rightly seeks to privilege the insights and leadership of women, gender does not guarantee theological insight.

With respect to Acts 12:1-17, today's congregation may want to know, "Why did God protect Peter but not James?" Luke does not directly say. It is enough for Luke to use the fate of James as a pastoral warning, and to use the story of Peter's release from prison as an assurance of God's provision in difficulty. However, in a way that Luke never intended, the preacher could use the question just articulated as a jumping off point. To some folk a response like the following may seem adequate. "There are some things we cannot know. We can only try to accept the circumstances God gives us." For others, such a response is inadequate. A preacher in might use the latter perspective to introduce a theological meditation on the nature and extent of God's power. Does God have the power to protect Peter? If so, why does not God also protect James? If God's power is limited so that that God cannot intervene in the situations of Peter and James—and us—what can we count on from God? And what is required of us?

ACTS 12:20-25. GOD STRIKES HEROD DEAD

Meanwhile, Herod became angry with the population of Tyre and Sidon (Acts 12:20a). Those people depended on Herod for food (Acts 12:20b). The reader immediately contrasts the threat of Herod using food punitively with the largess of the Christian community in Antioch in Acts 11:27-30. Is the food-providing ministry of the congregation more like that of Herod or the church in Antioch? Are other food providers more responsive to God's purposes than the church?

Using exceptional political shrewdness, the people of Tyre and Sidon make friends with Blastus, Herod's chamberlain, hoping that Blastus would help them reconcile with Herod. Luke portrays Herod calling attention to his own self-importance by dressing grandly and acting impressively (Acts 12:21). The people declare that Herod speaks with the voice of a god and not that of a mortal (Acts 12:22). However, when Herod accepts the accolade and does not shift the glory to God, an angel strikes him down. Worms eat his body, and he dies (Acts 12:23).

O. Wesley Allen Jr. finds that such scenes were intended to communicate that deities brought just retribution on those who violated divine purposes.[4] The death of Herod demonstrates this belief. Moreover, it suggests that God will ultimately bring retribution on Pilate, Caesar, the Empire, and all who are in league with them. This idea is implied at the end of Acts (28:30-31).

While there is no evidence that the congregation to which Luke wrote was threatened with death, Herod's behavior warns Luke's people to be wary of the political authorities of their time. Moreover, the fate of Herod is intended to give that congregation the courage to endure the turbulence of their present: the power of the Empire, while brutal, is temporary.

Clergy with an apocalyptic mind-set can help the congregation take courage in the fact that God will ultimately bring down all forms of repression that function similarly to Herod. Clergy who are not apocalyptically minded but who think God acts punitively could ponder whether social forces today that seek to eat away contemporary regimes and systems could be interpreted as enacting God's judgment. Clergy who do not believe that a God actively condemns could see the downfall of contemporary empires as the consequence of those empires' misplaced values and behaviors.

CHIASTIC PARALLELS. LUKE 16:19-31 AND ACTS 12:20-26

The parable of the rich person and Lazarus in Luke 16:19-31 is a cautionary tale. The rich person ignored Lazarus lying hungry by the gate. In so doing, the rich one violated foundational Jewish teaching to care for the poor. In the next life, the rich person is in agony in the flames of hell.

Herod had a life like the rich person. As pointed out above, when Herod allows the crowd to hail him as a god, the living God strikes Herod down. The fate of Lazarus suggests that the flames of hell awaited Herod.

A preacher might see Herod and his fate in political or systemic terms. For example the death of Herod points to the downfall of capitalism or Eurocentric racial privilege or repressive political groups in the United States. However, the presence of the rich person reminds us that Herodianism is not simply "out there" in systems against which I can rail. I can align myself with Herod in the way that I personally relate to the Lazaruses of my immediate worlds. Gratefully, the purpose of the parable is to provoke a life-giving response before we reach the flames: *repent* before it is too late.

A preacher may need to help the congregation wrestle with the degree to which the congregation needs to be actively involved in dismantling Herodian systems today. Like other end-time theologians, Luke expected that God would destroy all forms of evil at the apocalypse. While Luke's congregation was not to wait passively for the apocalypse but engage in mission, that mission did not include being responsible for total systemic change.

By comparison, many preachers and congregations today think we need to be active agents of liberation. We need to participate in bringing down Herod and in bringing the Realm into expression. Even in the Christian community, we sometimes find a vengeful streak that takes pleasure in the unhappiness that comes to others as a result of their unfaithfulness. While the work of dismantling Herod may be necessary, it can be done without rejoicing over the pain that it causes others. We can celebrate God's triumph without taking personal satisfaction in the suffering it causes others. Although Jesus's act of forgiving those who crucified him may not be part of the oldest tradition of the Gospel of Luke (Luke 23:34), it points to an important work for the community of the Ream.

You Will Be My Witnesses to the Ends of the Earth: The First Missionary Journey Involves Commissioning, Confrontations, Conversions, and Mistaken Identity (Acts 13:1—14:28)

While Acts does not use the expression "missionary journey," Acts describes three trips that Paul and companions make to establish congregations: Acts 13:1-14:28, Acts 15:36-18:22, and Acts 18:23-21:17.[5] One purpose of the missionary journeys is to encourage Luke's congregation toward mission as the appropriate way to live through the delay in the apocalypse. Mission is not just an activity in which the church engages but is an expression of the church's identity. To *be* the community of the Realm *is* to reach out in the same way Paul does on the missionary journeys. This word could be renewing in congregations today who regard their mission to be maintaining the institution.

Prior to the Hellenistic age, travel and communication were limited in the Mediterranean world. Beginning with Alexander the Great, a revolution in communication possibilities took place that was important to Paul's missionary success: new roads, accessible sea travel, commonplace letter writing. We live in another communication revolution. What are theological criteria for the appropriate use of particular communication possibilities today? How can the church employ media in theologically appropriate ways? In my view, most congregations need a major infusion of creativity in these regards.

The preacher could help the congregation get a picture of Paul's travels by projecting drawings of ancient ships, maps showing Paul's movements, and photographs of the ruins of ancient roads and other artifacts associated with Paul's travels.

ACTS 13:1-3. COMMISSIONING IN ANTIOCH

Acts 13:1-3 is important for two reasons. First, it establishes that the Holy Spirit and the congregation in Antioch authorized the first mission effort by Paul and Barnabas. Luke quotes the actual words of the Spirit. Occasionally, people in the church today claim to hear such words. Others have barely any sense of what the Spirit is nor how to recognize and respond to the Spirit. This text gives the preacher an opportunity to reflect with the congregation on how to understand the Spirit and how to respond appropriately.

Second, Acts 13:1-3 indicates the leadership of the church embodied the diversity of the community of the Realm with respect to ethnicity and social relationships. The prophets and teachers include Barnabas and Saul. Simeon is called Niger (Latin for "black"), and Lucius is from Cyrene: both are Africans. Manaen is either a childhood friend or a member of Herod's court (or both), If the preacher's congregation is more homogenous than this, the message might ask what it would take for that community to move toward the Realm-like reunion of the human family taking place in Antioch.

ACTS 3:4-12. CONFRONTATION IN CYPRESS

Saul, Barnabas, and John sail to Cypress and work their way from the eastern edge of the island, stopping at synagogues, to the city of Paphos on the southwestern shore. They encounter Sergius Paulus, a proconsul (Roman governor of the province) who summons them to hear their message. A Jewish magician named Bar-Jesus (Elymas) was with the proconsul, perhaps as a religious advisor. Ancient magic attempted to manipulate force fields in the universe. Not only did the Jewish community forbid magic, but Bar-Jesus is a false prophet and a child of the devil. If the proconsul believes in the coming of the Realm, Bar-Jesus will lose the ear of the proconsul and the social standing accompanying that relationship. Bar-Jesus opposes the disciples and tries to persuade the proconsul to turn away from faith.

The proconsul faces a choice. Does he retain the familiar alliance with Bar-Jesus? Or does he believe that the God of Israel is bringing the Realm through Jesus, recognizing that such belief will bring him into conflict with some values and representatives of the old age?

Influenced by the Spirit, Paul not only names Bar-Jesus's theological and ethical inadequacy but is the channel through whom God pronounces a judgment upon Bar-Jesus in a way that also epitomizes Bar-Jesus's spiritual condition. Bar-Jesus becomes blind.

When the proconsul sees Bar-Jesus become blind, the proconsul believes. This gentile, responsible for enacting Roman rule in Paphos, shows greater theological discernment than Bar-Jesus, Jewish, but so theologically compromised that he advocates magic, and cooperates with the devil.

The preacher must mention this vignette as a part of Luke's ongoing attempt to explain why many Jewish people turned away from Realm and why Luke's church should turn its energy toward gentiles. In addition, a preacher could look for relationships in our world like that of the proconsul and Bar-Jesus in which leading people or institutions become enmeshed with false values and manipulative practices. A preacher is called to exposes the Bar-Jesuses today.

Moreover, can the preacher point to circumstances in the church and world in which proconsul-like figures exhibit more theological and ethical insight than garden-variety Christians? The proconsul is both a person of high social standing and an agent of a power (Rome) that can be repressive. Luke, of course, wants his congregation to welcome proconsul-like people.

CHIASTIC PARALLELS. LUKE 16:1-18 AND ACTS 13:1-12

Preachers and scholars put forward wildly different interpretations of the parable of the dishonest manager (Luke 16:1-9). In my view, literary context is the key (Luke 16:1-18). The parable tells of a manager, presumably Jewish, who acts unethically in the financial realm to protect his own social position. Jesus explains that if a person is not faithful with those things that belong to another, "who will give you what is your own?" (Luke 16:10-13). When Luke describes the Pharisees as "lovers of money" (Luke 16:14), we recognize that Luke regards the Pharisees as similar to the dishonest manager: they face the judgment of losing their own heritage in faithful Jewish community.

In Acts 13:4-12, the apostles encounter a proconsul drawn to their message when a Jewish magician, Bar-Jesus, a child of the devil, tries to dissuade the proconsul. When the magician behaves like the dishonest manager, the disciples temporarily blind the magician. The situation of Bar-Jesus illuminates the Pharisees: they are theologically blind; their dishonest management is no better than magic. These Jewish people make crooked God's straight paths. By contrast, the gentile proconsul—an agent of the Roman Empire—believes (Acts 13:12).

A homily should bring the anti-Jewish tone of these parallels to the attention of congregants. Beyond that, a preacher might explore tendencies toward dishonest management in the congregation and the world. How do we cross ethical boundaries—even making use of magic—in manipulating relationships and situations to maintain our own power? To do so is to invite Bar-Jesus's fate upon ourselves: Instead, we should follow the proconsul's example to repent.

Acts 13:13-52. Conversions and Controversy in Antioch of Pisidia

The witnesses travel to Antioch of Pisidia, about two hundred miles northwest of Paphos. As often in Acts, they visit a synagogue where, according to custom, the rabbi invites these learned guests to speak. Since that culture had no mass communication, such occasions could bring news, bring fresh viewpoints, and spark discussion and debate. While congregations today float in a sea of mass communication, the preacher might still take a cue from the ancient practice of the synagogue to bring into the worship space voices interpreting the realm whom the congregation might not otherwise have an opportunity to hear.

While Paul's sermon has multiple dimensions, comparison and contrast between David and Jesus is at its heart. After summarizing Israel's history from Sarah and Abraham through the Exodus, the wilderness wandering, the conquest, the judges, and the monarchy, Paul interprets David as carrying out God's wishes (Acts 13:16b-22). The story of Israel reaches its climax in Jesus, descendent of David (Acts 16:23-25),

Paul stresses that God sent the message of salvation (the coming of the Realm) through Jesus to the Jewish community. However, Jewish leaders in Jerusalem did not understand their own prophetic tradition, and asked Pilate to have Jesus killed (Acts 16:26-30). But, God raised Jesus from the dead. Through

Jesus, God is now completing the promises that God made to the ancestors as attested by Psalm 2:7, Isaiah 55:3, and Psalm 16:10 (Acts 13:31-35). Although David was God's exemplary servant, David died: his body decayed. By contrast, Jesus, though he died is now the one through whom forgiveness of sins (that is, release from the power of the old age) is proclaimed (Acts 13:36-39). The sermon closes by warning listeners not to let happen to them what happened in the days of Habakkuk (Hab. 1:5): many heard the message, but they perished when they scoffed (Acts 13:40-41).

Many Antiochenes responded favorably (Acts 13:41-43). But the Jews, jealous, begin to confute Paul. In the face of this hostility Paul declares that although God sent the message of the Realm first to the Jewish people, their animosity prompts Paul to turn to the gentiles (Acts 13:44-47; cf. Isa. 49:6 in Acts 13:47). Paul's Jewish opponents solicited people of high standing to use their social power to stir up hostility toward the witnesses, so that the Paul and Barnabas left that region (Acts 13:48-52).

An easy route to the sermon would be to ask, "Is our congregation like the Jewish people Luke pictures in Antioch of Pisidia—jealous of the ways God is at work for the Realm among those outside Christian circles? Do our reactions contradict the values of the Realm? Do we then judge ourselves unworthy of eternal life (that is, the Realm)?" (Acts 13:46). The preacher would need to follow this route without reinforcing anti-Jewish inclinations.

Connections to the Lectionary

The missionary journeys of Paul—as told in Acts—are as vivid and well known as almost any stories in early Christian tradition other than stories about Jesus. Yet, the lectionary contains only four passages from these journeys, and the readings are scattered over the three years. A preacher might depart from the lectionary to select one missionary journey, divide it into meaningful passages, and place those passages in sequence over a series of Sundays in Ordinary Time. The texts from the missionary journey could be added to the existing lectionary as an additional reading, or could replace epistle readings.

A more challenging approach would be to raise the theological question of whether the preacher and congregation believe, with Luke, that God turned away from the Jewish people when they did not come into the church. Luke's language is strong in Acts 13:46-47. A conversation beginning in the pulpit could help the congregation clarify its convictions on these matters. I do not believe a God of unconditional love would make such a move. Indeed, if God violates the promises God made to Israel by turning away from that community, what is to prevent God from turning away from Christians? The integrity of God is at stake. God is big enough to embrace gentiles without discarding the Jewish community.

A preacher could take a cue from Paul's rhetorical strategy. Paul summarizes the story of God's promises to Israel by setting out positive points with which the listeners could identify. He then invites the listeners to see the story of Jesus as the next stage in the story of Israel and to identify with the presence and coming of the Realm. A preacher might similarly tell the story of God's promises to the congregation, setting out positive points with which the congregation can identify. The preacher could indicate that Jesus is leading the congregation into the next stage of that story in which they can receive and witness to the Realm in ways appropriate for our day.

The text raises another preaching possibility, though one that is not central to the passage. When Paul and Barnabas have been driven from the city, they shake "the dust off their feet in protest." From Luke 9:5 and 10:11, we deduce the gesture of shaking the dust from their feet means, "Give up on the Antiochenes. Forget about them." Leaving people or communities alone for a time could be part of a long-term strategy for trying to communicate meaningfully. But is a congregation ever on theologically solid ground when finally and forever leaving others to stew in their own juices?

As part of justifying the growing divide between synagogue and church, Luke argues for the superiority of Jesus over David even while pointing to the positive (if limited) role of David in Israel's history. Building on a theology of continuity, a preacher could suggest a relationship of extension between David and Jesus rather than the superiority of one over the other. A preacher might identify people or movements in past or present whose values and practices complement those of Jesus and the Realm in ways reminiscent of the story of David. Instead of arguing for Jesus's superiority the preacher could seek routes to shared witness.

CHIASTIC PARALLELS. LUKE 15:1-32 AND ACTS 13:13-51

Luke 15:1-32 is comprised of four parables that come together in both invitation and warning. The parables of the lost sheep and the lost coin (Luke 15:1-10) teach that repentance is the means to be found, that is, to have a place in the community of the Realm. Luke 15:11-24 recounts a younger heir who leaves home and who effectively becomes a gentile (living with pigs), but who is welcomed home on the basis of repentance. Luke 15:25-32 tells of an older heir who refuses to participate in the homecoming. Luke's implication is clear: the older heir should repent and join the rejoicing. As the story closes, the older heir is in the field, trying to decide: do I enter the house or not?

Paul invites Jewish listeners in a synagogue in Antioch of Pisidia to become a part of the movement toward the Realm (Acts 13:16b-41). Many show interest (Acts 13:42-43). However, the Jewish people are filled with jealousy; they blaspheme, and they contradict Paul (Acts 13:44-45). Consequently, Paul turns away from the Jewish people and turns toward the Gentiles (13:46-51).

Luke used this chiastic pair to justify the growing separation between the traditional synagogue and the church in his own day: Jewish people have had their opportunities to repent but have not taken them. The preacher who simply repeats this approach will only contribute to anti-Judaism. A preacher could, however, take elements of the passage as a warning: the opportunity to repent eventually passes. I do not believe God deliberately takes away the opportunity to repent, but circumstances in which repentance would be socially meaningful do go away. God is at work restoring younger heirs, that is, people and situations to whom many conventional church members object. The church is in the field with the older heir. Will we join the reunion? Or will we, as they did in Antioch of Pisidia, lose the opportunity?

ACTS 14:1-7. OPPOSITION IN ICONIUM

An occurrence similar to the one in Antioch takes place in Iconium. Paul and Barnabas speak in a synagogue where both Jewish and Greek people (likely God-fearers) welcome the news of the Realm, but "unbelieving Jews" poison the gentiles (Acts 14:2). The witnesses persist but the city divides—some siding with the unhappy Jewish group and some with Paul and Barnabas (14:3-4). A Jewish-gentile group stones the witnesses who flee to Lystra and Derbe (Acts 14:5-7).

In Iconium the gentiles not only persecute the witnesses but join with Jewish people in doing so. While Acts endorses the gentile mission, some gentiles are antagonistic toward the representatives of the Realm. Jewish people are not the only villains. Being a gentile—as becomes even more evident in the second half of Acts—is not itself a guarantee that one has theological insight.

Gentile resistance points out why the church should continue to seek ways to witness to gentiles. A preacher might ask, "From where does such gentile resistance come? Do gentiles get bad information about the Realm—as the gentiles did in Iconium? What qualities in witness might open a gentile mind and heart to the possibility of the Realm?"

ACTS 14:8-20. CROWDS MISTAKE PAUL AND BARNABAS FOR DEITIES IN LYSTRA

Paul and Barnabas arrive in Lystra, about twenty-five miles southeast of Iconium, where they come upon a person who has never walked. That person has faith and is healed (14:8-10). The crowd makes the gentile mistake of idolatry by identifying Barnabas as Zeus and Paul as Hermes, seeing in Paul the incarnation of a god who was regarded as the sponsor of eloquence. The local priest of Zeus brings oxen and garlands to the witnesses and prepares to make sacrifice (14:11-13). In a sermon, a preacher could have a lot of fun with these latter details.

Paul and Barnabas make an impassioned, and deeply Jewish, response. The witnesses point out that they are mortals. God offers the gentiles the opportunity to turn from idolatry and to turn to the living God who made heaven and earth. While God left nations to follow their own ways in the past, God has never been without witness. Indeed, even when gentiles did not acknowledge God, God gave them rain, fruitful seasons, food, and joy (Acts 14:14-17).

This text invites listeners to turn away from idols and to turn to God. In addition to practical idols such as gender, race, nation, money, social privilege, the preacher might consider idols in the congregation or denomination, for example, the church building, particular practices, or certain ministers. Ministers sometimes make idols of careers or particular approaches to the Bible, preaching, or social justice. Scholars sometimes make idols of publications or particular appointments. John Calvin is right: Human nature, "so to speak, is a perpetual factory of idols."[6]

Instead of threatening gentiles that God will condemn them if they do not repent, Paul invites the gentiles to turn to a God already supporting them—providing rain, fruitful seasons, food, and joy. By embracing God, the gentiles increase their resonance with the power of life. The preacher could structure a sermon around such an appeal. If people follow idols with their dead-end possibilities, how much better the life of the people when they serve a God who offers the possibility of living toward the Realm.

Acts 14:16-17 is striking in another way. This passage asserts that even when peoples in the past violated God's purposes, God sustained them and did good for them. God never completely gives up but is omnipresent and is always offering life-giving possibilities. While this assertion is important in its own right, it is especially timely today when some Christian groups claim that God bestows blessing exclusively on the church.

CHIASTIC PARALLELS. LUKE 14:25-34 AND ACTS 14:1-28

In Luke 14:25-27, Jesus teaches that those who join the movement to the Realm will encounter resistance. Disciples should count the cost: they should be prepared for struggle as someone building a tower or a ruler going to war needs to count the cost of the tower or the military campaign (Luke 14:28-34).

In Iconium, some of the residents stone Paul and Barnabas (Acts 14:5). When the apostles preach in Lystra, people stone Paul and drag the body out of the city supposing him dead (Acts 14:19-20). Paul and Barnabas declare, "It is through many persecutions that we must enter the [Realm] of God" (Acts 14:22). These experiences of Paul and Barnabas are case studies of those who encounter resistance.

Similarly, the preacher can urge the congregation to count the cost, that is, to prepare to witness to the Realm and for the resistance they could encounter in response. What will it take for today's congregation to persist in the manner of Paul and Barnabas?

ACTS 14:21-28. RETURN TO ANTIOCH

The denouement of the first missionary journey is brief while adding to the narrative. The missionaries return to the churches they had established, thus calling attention to the communal character of the Realm (Acts 14:21). Paul and Barnabas remind the churches to be prepared for resistance (Acts 14:22). With prayer and fasting they appoint elders as local shepherds for the congregations (Acts 14:21, 23), a ministry detailed in Acts 20:17-38.

Paul and Barnabas return to Antioch where they report to the congregation "all that God had done with them." The most important result of their missionary work: God "opened a door of faith for the gentiles" (Acts 14:24-28). If today's preacher returns from a mission trip, what would the preacher summarize as the most important results?

A preacher could use this passage to point to the importance of members of the congregation providing the kind of pastoral support for one another that Paul and Barnabas provide for the ancient congregations as well as for congregations to support one another as congregations. What pastoral advice do we need to give one another as in Acts 14:22? What congregational structures can provide the kind of support provided by the elders in the text?

You Will Be My Witnesses to the Ends of the Earth: The Jerusalem Council Gives Theological Shape to the Gentile Mission (Acts 15:1-35)

The apostles have given informal approval to the gentile mission but have not given it their collective authorization and have not clarified the degree to which gentile converts must embrace Judaism. This issue is the most contentious internal matter faced by the church. Acts 15:1-35 recounts a pivotal meeting in Jerusalem that completes the authorization of the mission and clarifies its terms. We sometimes refer to this event as the "apostolic council," a name that does not appear in Acts. Because the council involves more people than apostles, "Jerusalem council" is a better name.

Churches today are in conflict around issues ranging from whether to fire the minister to whether believing in Jesus is the only way to salvation to whether to perform marriage ceremonies for people with same gender orientations. While churches can seldom use the apostolic council as a blueprint for dealing with conflict, Acts 15 points to key resources and to a spirit that could help congregations think theologically about issues of our day.

Acts 15:1-5. The Issue: Must Gentiles be Circumcised?

Some individuals in the churches in Judea go to Antioch to assert that gentiles must be circumcised to be saved: without circumcision they cannot be in the community of the Realm in the present and they will not be included in the Realm after the apocalypse (Acts 15:1). The underlying question is whether gentiles must be fully initiated into Judaism to in the community of the Realm?

After Paul and Barnabas debate the visitors from Judea, the church in Antioch appoints a delegation to go to Jerusalem to discuss this matter with the apostles and elders there. This is one of Luke's most dramatic indications of the centrality of the apostles as authorities for the community of the Realm.

Without intending to suggest that Luke had an attitude that is popular among many twenty-first-century pluralists, the preacher could note that the decision at Antioch to engage the council in Jerusalem underscores the value of Christian community conversing about matters of importance with a variety of voices. The future of the gentile mission was too important to be decided by Paul and Barnabas on a parking lot after the board meeting in Antioch.

The Jerusalem congregation welcomes the delegates. After Paul and Barnabas reported on the work among the gentiles, some Pharisees repeated the claim that gentiles must be circumcised and follow Torah (Acts 15:5). Some Christians today are surprised to learn that these Pharisees are Christians. By the time the council ends, they are evidently happy with the outcome voiced in Acts 15:28-29. By placing them at the council meeting, Luke may signal Pharisees of his own generation that they can think themselves faithful while endorsing the decision of Acts 15:28-29.

The church at Antioch has not denigrated the law. Indeed, there is no indication that the Jewish believers in Antioch had stopped honoring Torah. The question at Jerusalem is how to come to a faithful Jewish interpretation of the relationship of Torah and the gentiles in view of the nearness of the apocalypse.

CHIASTIC PARALLELS. LUKE 14:15-24 AND ACTS 15:1-5

In Luke 14:15-24, a host invites guests to a dinner. When the initial invitees make excuses, the host invites people who are poor and who cannot walk or see, as well as people from roads and lanes. The dinner reminds readers of the grand meal celebrating the realm, the eschatological banquet. The message is clear: those who decline the invitation are no longer welcome in the Realm, but those who accept have a place.

By the time of Acts 15:1-6, the invitation to become a part of the community of the Realm is going to both Jewish and gentile people. In Acts 15:1-6, some believers from Judea intend to deny participation in the community to gentiles who have not fully converted to Judaism. From the perspective of the parable, these Judeans received an invitation to be a part of the movement of the Realm, but by imposing circumcision on gentiles, they refuse God's invitation to the dinner. On the other hand, gentile converts are as welcome in the church as those who cannot walk or see are welcome at the great dinner.

A sermon from Luke 14:15-24, could bring the gentiles of Acts 15:1-6 into the list of those invited (14:21-24). A sermon from Acts 15:1-6 could bring the list of those invited to the great dinner (Luke 14:21-24) alongside the gentiles in Acts.

Acts 15:6-21. The Council Listens to Eye-Witness Accounts, Experience, Scripture, Reason, and the Holy Spirit

When the meeting began, the council engaged in "much debate" as was characteristic of Jewish life at that time (Acts 15:6): the believers talked directly with one another. The church today would benefit from the open interchange of views commonplace in first century life.

Luke's description of the council is masterful rhetorical strategy. The first voice that Luke presents is Peter, respected leader of the Jerusalem community with whom all would identify. Peter reminds them God made the choice "among you" that *Peter* would initiate the gentile mission. Peter provides an eye witness account of the experience of God giving the Holy Spirit to the gentiles "just as [God] did to us." Indeed, God made the gentiles clean (Acts 15:7-11). Paul and Barnabas likewise give eye witness accounts (Acts 15:12).

James, a respected member of the community, correlates the gentile experience with scripture (Acts 15:13-17). James interprets Amos 9:11-12: God long ago planned to welcome the gentiles into the community. When James says that thereby God would bring from the gentiles "a people for [God's] name," James echoes a Lukan expression for Israel (Luke 2:10, 32; 3:11; 4:10; 5:34; 10:41). Through the witness of the church, God is adding gentiles to the purposes of Israel

James reasons that these factors lead to the conclusion stated in Acts 15:19-2 (discussed below in connection with Acts 15:22-29). James reasons that the decision he proposes is faithful to Jewish tradition (Acts 15:21). The council does not turn away from Judaism, but turns gentiles toward Judaism.

Connections to the Lectionary

The lectionary never appoints Acts 15:1-35. An easy way to bring this central passage into the congregation in the context of the lectionary would be read Acts 15 alongside Paul's report of the same event in Galatians 2:1-21 on Proper 6 [11] in Year C. Reading both Acts 15 and Galatians 2 would provide the preacher with a natural platform to compare and contrast the uses Luke and Paul make of the Jerusalem council. The preacher might use the different nuances with which the two biblical authors interpret the same event as a way to help the congregation wrestle with what to do theologically when different interpreters put forward different interpretations of the same datum.

The issues at the heart of Acts 15 could become the focus of a sermon. A preacher could also develop a sermon on theological method using Acts 15:6-21 as a case study. Given the sloppy ways many congregations and individual Christians arrive at theological perspectives today, such a sermon could be hugely beneficial. The council listened to multiple people and kinds of sources—eye witness accounts, experience, and Scripture. They did not rely upon one only one person or only one source. Further, they were silent and *listened* to one another (Acts 15:12) in contrast to many church meetings today in which some participants are so full of what they want to say they talk before others have finished.

At the same time, a preacher needs to acknowledge that group process can lead to mistaken conclusions. From time to time, the individual prophet may be right, a fact that may be clear only in retrospect. In any event, a community needs criteria by which to come to such conclusions.

CHIASTIC PARALLELS. LUKE 14:7-14 AND ACTS 15:6-21

The rigid social pyramid of the Roman world is the backdrop for Luke 14:7-14. At a typical Mediterranean dinner party, people would be seated according to their social standing with the best seats going to those of highest rank. The banquet here calls to mind the eschatological banquet as a symbol for the Realm. In Luke 14:7-14, traditional social standing loses its power. The community of the Realm deliberately seeks those who would not ordinarily be invited to a banquet (represented by those who are poor and who cannot walk or see).

From Luke's standpoint, gentiles are in the same position with respect to the eschatological banquet (and participation in the Realm) as those who are poor or who cannot walk or see had to the banquet at the beginning of the parable: not welcome. To be faithful to the Realm, the council and the church must do what the host did in the parable: extend the invitation to gentiles.

ACTS 15:22-35. THE DECISION OF THE COUNCIL: A JEWISH CORE FOR GENTILES

In Acts 15:19-20 James reaches a conclusion on the basis of reason that Luke rephrases slightly in Acts 15:29. The Jerusalem congregation and the Holy Spirit endorse the decision. The council writes a letter to the church at Antioch and commissions a delegation to accompany Paul and Barnabas (Acts 15:22-23a).

The letter asks gentiles to assume four aspects of Jewish identity and practice: (1) to abstain from food offered to idols (more broadly: from things polluted by idols, Acts 15:20); (2) to abstain from blood (to drain the blood from meat before cooking); (3) to abstain from food that has been strangled; (4) to abstain from fornication (sexual immorality). From Luke's point of view, these practices are the heart of Judaism for gentiles as they prevent gentiles from idolatry and make available for gentiles the benefits of some Jewish dietary practices. These practices would facilitate Jewish and gentile people eating together in the community of the Realm.

We can see the Jewish spirit in this decision by remembering that Noah articulated God's promises to all peoples in Genesis 8:22; 9:8-17. Leviticus made it possible for gentiles to live in close proximity with Israel through similar prescriptions (Lev. 17:8-30). In the Hellenistic age, some Jewish communities foresaw a place for righteous gentiles in the world to come. The Book of Jubilees, about 200 years before Luke, formulates what are sometimes called Noahide laws, that is, principles by which gentiles may live faithfully (Jubilees 7:20-28). Later Jewish theologians articulated fuller statements in the Tosefta and Talmud. Gentiles are to avoid idolatry, murder, theft, fornication, blasphemy, eating the meat of an animal while it is still living, and are to establish legal courts to insure justice.[7] The decision of the apostolic council is thus not an independent Christian formulation but is part of a far-reaching Jewish discussion.

CHIASTIC PARALLELS. LUKE 14:1-6 AND ACTS 15:22-29

Christians today often think that Luke 14:1-6 (and similar passages in the gospels) and Acts 15:28-29 are critical of Torah itself. Instead these passages are part of a wide-ranging discussion if first century Judaism regarding how to interpret Torah. Indeed, the primary purpose of the miraculous element in the story of healing of the person with dropsy (an excess accumulation of fluid in the abdomen, legs and ankles) is to prove that Jesus has God's approval and hence is a reliable interpreter of Torah. Both Luke 14:1-6 and Acts 15:22-29 seek not to negate the law but to show that both Jesus and the apostolic council faithfully interpret the purpose of the law. The spirit of Torah is to provide for the well-being of those in the community (Luke 14:1-6). The spirit of Torah is essential for the well-being of gentiles coming into the community (Act 5:22-29). The presence (and silence) of the Pharisees in Luke 14:1-6 and at the Jerusalem council (Acts 15:5) indicates that Luke wants his congregation to see Jesus's take on Torah as more trustworthy than that of the Pharisees. Jesus's mode of interpretation in 14:1-6 authorizes the similar attitude in Acts 15:28-29.

A preacher could use these chiastic elements as the basis for a teaching sermon to help the congregation understand Torah and its interpretation in Jewish antiquity. Going farther, a preacher could use this pair of passages to help the church think about differences in interpretation of Christian tradition among Christian communities today. What is the core of the preacher's interpretation of the Christian vision, and how does it help interpret the Bible, doctrine, and stands on values and behaviors today? By what criteria does the preacher gauge a Christian interpretation to be more or less faithful?

The church often lauds the Jerusalem council and the resultant openness to gentiles. Yet few Christian grapple with the specific contents of Acts 15:28-29 and with the ongoing question of how much of Judaism the church today should actively embrace to maintain our identity. To what degree does the church today think about its life from the perspective of the categories in Acts 15:28-29? I wager that not one person in the preacher's congregation has stood in front of the meat counter and asked, "Was this food offered to an idol?" A message might ponder what qualities of life function for us in ways similar to the characteristics necessary for faithfulness in Acts 15:28-29.

On many contemporary issues, Christian communities manifest the opposite of the unified mind Luke describes in Acts 15:22. What attitude does a congregation take, and what witness does it make, when its understanding of a doctrine or an ethical situation is different from other Christian bodies?

Chiastic Parallels. Luke 13:31-35 and Acts 15:30-35

Luke 13:31-35 assumes the destruction of Jerusalem in the tradition of *vaticinium ex eventu* (prophecy after the fact). Jesus laments the destruction of the city and the temple. In contrast, Acts 15:30-35 depicts the congregation at Antioch—both Jewish and gentile members—rejoicing at the outcome of the Jerusalem council. While Jerusalem may be in ruins, God is moving ahead with the gentile mission. From Luke's point of view, lamentation is appropriate, but Luke's congregation joins God in the forward movement into the gentile mission and its faithful extension of witness to the God of the temple into new realms.

The preacher, too, can lament the destruction of the temple even while offering a theological rebuttal to Luke's claim that the collapse of the city was the result of Jewish leadership crucifying Jesus (Luke 13:33-35a; cf. Jer. 22:5-6). The preacher can argue that God did not intend for the temple to fall and Judaism to be left in disarray, yet when that event occurred, Jewish groups responded by interpreting the situation theologically and moving ahead. The

Pharisees interpreted Torah in a way that does not negate other ways forward. Without negating Judaism or the temple, then, the preacher can ask where and how God is luring the church today out of calamity and toward promising fields of witness.

You Will Be My Witnesses to the Ends of the Earth: The Second Missionary Journey Leads to Regrouping, the Macedonian Call, Lydia, Prison, and Liberation (Acts 15:36—16:40)

Paul now emerges as central human character in Acts. In the early part of the missionary journey, Paul and his companions reach Philippi in eastern Macedonia (Acts 15:36-16:4). In the next part of this journey, the witnesses go through Thessalonica and Corinth before returning to Antioch (Acts 17:1-18:22).

One effect on the reader of the long and sometimes contentious missionary journeys is to remind Luke's congregation that they have a long and difficult road to the apocalypse. However, as God sustained Paul and his fellow travelers, God will sustain the congregation. This could be an important pastoral reminder to early twenty first century Christians accustomed to things happening in nano-seconds.

Acts 15:36-16:10. The Journey Gets Underway in Fits and Starts

After the council at Jerusalem, Paul plans to take Barnabas for pastoral calls on the congregations they established on the first missionary journey When Barnabas wants to take John called Mark, Paul objects that John Mark had deserted the mission in Pamphylia (Acts 13:13). While Paul does not specify why Mark abandoned them, Luke may imply that John Mark was anxious knowing about the execution of James and the imprisonment of Paul, and having seen Satan operating through Bar-Jesus (Acts 13:4-12). Could Paul count on John Mark in the struggles ahead? While this reconstruction is speculative, it raises a question for a preacher. How long does a community continue with a leader who is struggling?

Paul adds Timothy to the mission team and has Timothy circumcised (Acts 16:1-5). The reason for the circumcision: so Timothy, who has a Jewish mother but a Greek father, will not cause offense to Jewish people. Luke might be sending a further message about Jewish customs to the church: the decision at Jerusalem (Acts 15:28-29) does not affect Jewish practices among Jewish people in the church. Luke thus signals (1) Jewish participants that they are welcome in the church as fully practicing Jews, and (2) gentiles that they are to respect circumcision and the people who practice it

This text could provide the preacher with an angle of address if the congregation is disrespectful of Jewish customs: Luke assumes the validity of Jewish practices. Such a congregation should learn to respect Jewish ways. If the congregation has a respectful attitude to Judaism, the preacher might shift the angle of address to how the church could welcome persons with cultural practices that differ from those of the congregation but are consistent with the values of the Realm.

Paul's plans to enter Bithynia do not materialize because of divine interruption. But Paul receives a vision—an indication of divine leading—of a Macedonian person calling for the missionaries to cross the northern Aegean to Macedonia (Acts 16:6-10). A preacher and congregation would do well to reflect on situations today in which individuals and communities call for similar solidarity today. One thinks immediately of churches in the developing world who literally call across the oceans for partnership. Many people in impoverished settings long for the peace, justice, and prosperity of the Realm. Macedonia can also be the congregation's silent yearnings for Realm-like qualities of life.

CHIASTIC PARALLELS. LUKE 13:22-30 AND ACTS 15:35-16:10

In Luke 13:22-30 Jesus urges listeners to remain faithful through struggle (passing through the narrow door) to be included in the final gathering of the Realm. "People will come from east and west and north and south," that is, the realm will include people from the far corners of the world and from every culture and ethnicity. Acts 15:35-16:10 pictures these realities coming to pass. Paul has such a sharp disagreement with Barnabas over whether to take John Mark on the next missionary journey that they separate(struggle) (Acts 15:35-40). Paul invites Timothy, of believing Jewish mother and unconverted Greek father—to join them and to be circumcised to facilitate his ministry with Jewish listeners (Acts 16:1-5). On their trip, Paul receives the call to Macedonia (people come from east and west, etc. Acts 16:6-10).

Going through the narrow door takes one into a world whose boundaries are as large as "east and west and north and south." But, going through the narrow door requires focus. Congregations sometimes try to do too much, even investing in things that are peripheral or antagonistic to the Realm. What does the congregation need to do to keep its focus?

Acts 16:11-15. Lydia Becomes a Part of the Community of the Realm

Acts 16:11 is the first passage in Acts in which the narrator uses the first person plural, "we." Many Christians formerly regarded the "we" passages" as autobiographical: evidence that Luke was a companion of Paul.[8] Much recent scholarship tends to think that Luke shifted to a literary convention of writing travel accounts in "we" language.

Crossing into Macedonia, the witnesses arrive in Philippi and, on the sabbath, go a place on the river bank where Jews and God-fearers pray. They meet Lydia, a gentile seller of purple, who worshipped God. The term "purple" here refers to purple cloth which only wealthy people could afford. Through baptism, she and the household she heads became part of the community of the Realm.

Lydia is noteworthy for two reasons, each of which suggests an opportunity for preaching. First, she is a woman who is head of a household making her own decisions without reference to a man. Her presence in the narrative signaled similar women in Luke's world that they are welcome in the community of the Realm. A sermon can make a similar point to women in similar situations today. A preacher may also need to make it clear to the congregation that they are to welcome such women.

Second, she is apparently a person of means. Her presence in the story signals people of wealth that they need not be afraid of the church but can enter wholeheartedly in its life and mission. Luke's message is a model for the preacher now: as wealthy people enter into the community they can discover that God can use their resources as means of providence for others; as they cooperate with God, they lose their idolatry of wealth. Sharing is a blessing to them as find security in the community. Unfortunately, many preachers are uncomfortable with people of wealth. For the preacher, learning to speak with such people may be a struggle toward more faithful discipleship.

Connections to the Lectionary

These texts are assigned to the Sixth (Acts 16:9-15) and Seventh (Acts 6:16-34) Sundays of Easter in Year C. The readings from Acts on the Sundays of Easter in Year C trace the movement of the gospel from Jerusalem through the call of Saul and the beginning of the gentile mission to the fully authorized gentile outreach (Sixth and Seventh Sundays). The church's message is moving to the "ends of the earth" (Acts 1:8).

The literary boundary of the reading for the Sixth Sunday of Easter should be Acts 16:6-15. Given the small number of texts from Acts in the lectionary, this one was likely chosen to encourage today's church to hear our own Macedonian call. The appearance of Lydia in Acts 11-15 is especially welcome in view of the scarcity of readings in the lectionary that center on women. The preacher could focus on Lydia, could develop a sermon on the theme of women in Luke-Acts, or could use the scarcity of women in the lectionary as a way to reflect critically on the gender bias in the lectionary and in the Bible itself.

The boundary of the passage assigned to the Seventh Sunday of Easter should be Acts 6:16-40. Adding vv. 35-40 includes the magistrates' reaction to the release of Paul and Silas. The latter could lead to a sermon tracing Luke's attitudes toward civil authorities in the remainder of Acts. Such an approach would give the preacher an opportunity to introduce the congregation to the latter 40% of Acts which is almost entirely omitted from the lectionary.

As was the case with Dorcas, many church women's groups in an earlier generation adopted the name Lydia. A preacher might recall the history of the group, show pictures of the meeting space, group members, and contributions to congregational life and mission. Contemporary women who share Lydia's spirit could mobilize in a way that fits the postmodern twenty-first century.

CHIASTIC PARALLELS. LUKE 13:10-21 AND ACTS 16:11-15

In Luke 13:10-17, Jesus heals a woman possessed by Satan and unable to stand upright. Jesus acknowledges that she has full standing in the community by referring to her as "a daughter of Abraham." Jesus rebuts the leader of the synagogue who object to Jesus healing on the sabbath (Luke 13:19-17). This story is followed by two parables that are parallel in structure: Jesus compares something small turning into something large to the coming of the Realm of God: a mustard seed becomes a tree in which birds nest (a symbol for gentiles; Ezek. 17:22-24) and a tiny bit of yeast leavens three measures of flour (Luke 13:18-21).

The literary relationship of the healing and the two parables suggests that the healing of the woman is like the mustard seed and the leaven: an event that may appear small but is part of the movement toward the Realm. By the time the reader gets to Acts 16:11-15, the size of movement to the Realm has expanded from one end-time prophet surrounded by a few followers to a church growing every day. The story of Lydia (a God-fearer) coming to faith reassures the reader that women are central signs of the coming of the Realm and that birds (gentiles) nest in the shade of the Realm.

As noted already, few passages in Luke-Acts have women as central characters. A sermon could cohere around the women here. How is women's experience today a sign of the Realm? What factors inhibit women's experience from partaking in the qualities of the Realm?

ACTS 16:16-24. PAUL EXORCISES A YOUNG WOMAN WHO IS A SLAVE BUT HER OWNERS RESPOND ABUSIVELY

In Acts 16:16-18, Paul and Silas meet an enslaved young woman who makes money for her owners through divination (predicting the future). She follows Paul and Silas and ironically announces they serve the Most High God and offer the way to salvation (the Realm). Annoyed by her jabber, Paul casts the demon out of her to get her to quiet down.

Although the aim of Acts 16:16-18 is to set the stage for the events that follow, a preacher might note that while Paul's motive for the exorcism is self-serving, the effect is partially liberating. Although free from the demon she is still enslaved. A message might consider how often the church finds itself in similarly muddled situations—mixed intentions leading to good but partial effects?

The owners of the young woman are incensed that their low-budget source of income is gone (Acts 16:19a). The owners drag Paul and Silas into the market place before the magistrates and make two false charges: the witnesses disturb the peace, and advocate Jewish customs that are unlawful for Romans. When the crowd attacks the witnesses, magistrates intervene to control the violence by having Paul and Silas stripped, beaten, flogged, jailed in the innermost cell and fastened in stocks.

This crowd is the epitome of unconverted gentile life. They exploit the young woman. They rely upon individual wealth (and not common life) for economic security. They lie. They are violent. The magistrates—representatives of the Roman government—go along with the crowd and lock up (silence) the very people who could help transform that gentile degradation into a community of the Realm.

A preacher can point to analogous behaviors and attitudes today. While it is easy to see exploitation, greed, lying, violence and silencing outside the church, the preacher may also want to consider how these things are manifest inside the community. The church sometimes tries to silence the very people who could help our community become more Realm-like.

Furthermore, the Realm sometimes interrupts business as usual. Liberation—even when partial—called for restructuring the lives of the young woman and the owners. The owners would have been better off had they embraced the Realm with its economic order based not on divination and exploitation but on mutual sharing.

Chiastic Parallels. Luke 13:1-9 and Acts 16:16-24

The point of Luke 13:1-5 is that those who do not repent and become a part of the Realm will perish like the Galileans or the eighteen people. The point of Luke 13:6-9 is that while Luke's listeners have time to repent, time is running out.

In Acts 16:16-18 Paul casts a demon out of a slave girl who practiced divination; she is no longer able to perform that money-making task. The crowd wants to beat the witnesses. The owners, the magistrates, and crowd must repent or face a fate like that of the Galileans and those on whom the tower fell.

According to Luke, unconverted gentiles still have time to repent, but the clock is ticking. When I worked on this part of this commentary in the winter of 2011, Hosni Mubarak was dictator of Egypt. In two and half short weeks, a popular revolution deposed him. We may have less time than we think.

Acts 16:25-34. God Releases Paul and Silas from Prison

This is the third account of witnesses to the Realm being released from prison (Acts 5:17-26; 12:6-17). Luke repeats things three times to underscore their importance. Like the two previous accounts, this one assures Luke's congregation of God's care for them when their witness brings them into difficulty. However, Acts 16:25-34 adds a new dimension: after being released from their cells, Paul and Silas make a dramatic witness to the Realm within the prison.

Paul and Silas engage in a kind of prison ministry by singing and praying in the presence of the other prisoners. A powerful earthquake opens the doors and unfastens the chains. A reader familiar with the Torah, Prophets and Writings recognizes earthquakes not only as signs of God's presence (for example, Exod. 19:16; Ps. 68:7-8) but signaling God's judgment on those who jailed the witnesses. This earthquake anticipates the earthquakes that will accompany the apocalypse (for example, Isa. 29:5-6; Joel 2:10; Zech. 14:5; 14:1-21; Luke 21:11).

The jailer sees the prison doors open and immediately starts to take his own life. According to Roman custom, such officials were responsible for their prisoners and would be punished accordingly if prisoners escaped. Through suicide, the jailer hopes to spare himself the humiliation of a public death (see Acts 12:19). However, Paul acts out the life-affirming quality of the Realm by urging the jailer not to do that since the witnesses are still in the prison, albeit free. The jailer believes in Jesus as the one bringing the Realm, takes the witnesses home and washes their wounds, after which everyone in the jailer's household is baptized. The testimony of the witnesses transformed a jailer—a representative of the Roman Empire who colluded with gentile violence—into a healer and provider, indeed, a representative of the Realm.

On the one hand, the preacher might use Acts 16:25-34 (in addition to themes that surfaced in connection with Acts 5:17-26 and 12:6-17) to help the congregation think about ways they can witness to the Realm when they find themselves imprisoned. How can I witness to the very people, institutions or systems that put me in prison?

On the other hand, when a congregation itself becomes a prison, the question is, "Who are Paul and Silas in our world? How can we listen to them to liberating effect?" We can be imprisoned by the very prisons in which we attempt to keep others. Those whom we try to imprison may have clues to *our* release.

CHIASTIC PARALLELS. LUKE 12:35-59 AND ACTS 16:25-34

In Luke 12:35-59, Luke admonishes the disciples to be steadfast in pursuing the Realm between the ascension and the second coming in the same way that a responsible slave is to keep the lamps lit when the owner is away (Luke 12:35-48). Such faithfulness may bring about social distress (Luke 12:49-53), but such distress is a sign the apocalypse nears (Luke 12:54-56). In such situations, the disciples should adopt prudent strategies enabling them to prolong their witness (Luke 12:57-59).

In Acts 16:25-34, Paul and Silas are like the faithful servant in that they have continued to witness, but they are in jail (social distress) when an earthquake releases them. They keep their lamps lit by singing. The jailer is about to commit suicide when Paul and Silas embody the concern of the Realm to affirm life: they assure the jailer—an agent of the Roman empire—of their presence. At this, the gentile jailer believes and is baptized with his household, a sign that the movement toward the Realm is underway.

A message might help encourage the congregation toward the role of faithful servant, continuing to witness by keeping lamps lit. Paul and Silas did so by singing of the presence of the Realm while in chains and through their relationship with the jailer. The sermon can help the congregation imagine situations in our setting in which the congregation can take the part of Paul and Silas.

ACTS 16:35-40. CONFRONTATION WITH MAGISTRATES

The next morning, the magistrates want to release the witnesses secretly (Acts 16:35). Perhaps they think the disciples have been taught their lesson. Perhaps the magistrates think that the disciples are innocent, or perhaps the magistrates try to cover their own mistake by having the disciples slip away. The witnesses object that they are not guilty. Paul wants public recognition of the injustice committed by the magistrates and a public escort out of town—a public exoneration (Acts 16:37-38).

Public recognition of injustice can be an important component of moving toward justice because it names victim and victimizer and allows participants to take responsibility, repent and be reconciled. Moreover, some forms of injustice are so ingrained that we are not aware of them. Public exposure can awaken us to injustice as injustice.

Luke introduces a narrative perspective that becomes more important in Acts 22:25ff. Paul is a Roman citizen.[9] According to Luke, Silas is also a Roman citizen (Acts 16:37). The title Roman citizen was a major social distinction given to only a handful of people. Citizens were entitled to certain privileges that did not extend to non-citizens. Citizens could not be punished without a trial and could not be examined by torture. Roman officials who violated these principles could be punished. Consequently Luke remarks that the magistrates "were afraid when they heard that [Paul and Silas] were Roman citizens" (Acts 16:39). The magistrates not only apologized to the witnesses but also escorted Paul and Silas out of the city. God uses Roman citizenship as one of the means of mediating providence to Paul and Silas in Philippi.

Keeping in mind that Luke's pictures of Roman officials have high and low tides across Acts, Luke's picture of the magistrates in Acts 16:19-40 is a sober caution with respect to Roman authorities. The preacher could use this profile as a way of assessing public leadership. Roman leadership can be arbitrary and violent. Romans imprison the innocent and are self-protective. They violate the best of their own principles. They try to hide their own mistakes. God sends Paul to Rome as an instrument to save Romans. But the reader knows that the Roman system itself stands under God's apocalyptic judgment. The magistrates in this text did apologize to Paul and Silas but the magistrates could have taken the next step and, like the jailer's household, joined the movement toward the Realm.

CHIASTIC PARALLELS. LUKE 12:13-34 AND ACTS 16:35-40

In Luke 12:13-34, Jesus warns the disciples against trusting the values and behaviors of the old age (represented by the barn builder who trusted in riches). If the disciples trust God to support them, they need not be anxious. As God provides for ravens, lilies, and grass, so God will care for the community on the way to the Realm. The reader recognizes this trusting attitude in Paul and Silas. When the magistrates propose to release the witnesses in secret, Paul and Silas invoke their Roman citizenship to insist upon a public release. So comprehensive is God's providence that God uses Roman citizenship as a means through which providence can work.

This parallel focuses on anxiety arising in conjunction with witness to the Realm. A preacher could help the congregation name its anxieties about things that might happen as a result of such witness. As God proved provident to Paul and Silas, How does God provide for the congregation in its seasons of anxiety? The preacher might point to something in the world of the congregation that is as surprising an instrument of providence as Roman citizenship.

YOU WILL BE MY WITNESSES TO THE ENDS OF THE EARTH: THE SECOND MISSIONARY JOURNEY LEADS FURTHER TO UPROAR, WELCOME, AN UNKNOWN GOD, A TEACHING COUPLE, AND CONFLICT (ACTS 17:1—18:22)

Like the first journey (Acts 13:1-14:28) and the initial part of the second missionary journey (Acts 15:36-16:40), this part of the journey contains highs and lows: uproar in Thessalonica (Acts 17:1-8), welcome in Beroea (Acts 17:9-15), philosophical dialogue in Athens (Acts 17:16-32), disputes over legal jurisdiction in Corinth (Acts 18:1-17) and return to Antioch (Acts 18:18-22).

ACTS 17:1-15. UPROAR IN THESSALONICA AND WELCOME IN BEROEA

When Paul and Silas arrive in Thessalonica, they follow the pattern of beginning their witness in a synagogue (Acts 17:1-3). Luke reports diverse commitments to the Realm—a few Jewish people, a "great many of the devout Greeks" and "not a few of the leading women." In their religious and social diversity, these respondents exemplify the great reunion taking place in the community of the Realm. The women evidently act on their own joining the movement.

Luke's emphasis in Thessalonica, however, is on the majority reaction in which many Jewish people become jealous and recruit ruffians who set the city into an uproar as they search for Paul and Silas. They attack the house of Jason, which may be the location of a house-church, and drag Jason to the authorities with the claim that Paul and Silas have been "turning the world (*oikoumenē*) upside down," and have claimed that Jesus should be the emperor (Acts 17:6-7). While Christians today sometimes use the expression "they turned the world upside down" in a positive way, it refers here to the serious charge of disturbing the peace of the Roman empire.

The charges function on two levels. At one level, the charges are false. The mob, not the disciples, has disturbed the peace. The Jesus movement has no plan to dethrone Caesar. On another level, the witness does disturb the old age in the sense of announcing that the old world is ending, soon to be replaced by the Realm. Jesus does simply replace Caesar in Rome but rules from the right hand of God.

A preacher today could use these two levels of interpretation. People and institutions entrenched in the old age often perceive Realm-like values and practices as threats to the old age. To those caught up in the vision of the Realm, however, the breakdown of repressive, exploitative, unjust and violent systems is not simply disturbing the peace but is part of social transformation.

Although the people and the city official were distressed by the charges, the Thessalonian city officials act according to Roman law by receiving bail money from Jason and releasing the witnesses (Acts 17:8-9). Roman legal procedure protects witnesses from possible vigilante harm.

The witnesses slip out of Thessalonica at night and travel to Beroea, located about 50 miles southwest. The response to their preaching in the synagogue is quite different from Thessalonica as many Jewish people become a part of the movement to the Realm along with Greeks (women and men) of high social rank.

Luke calls attention to the vitriol of the Jewish opposition at Thessalonica by mentioning that the Jews come all the way to Beroea to stir up unrest. The

Bereoeans send Paul to safety in Athens. Paul is safer in Athens, full of idols, than in the synagogue of Thessalonica.

CHIASTIC PARALLELS. LUKE 11:33-12:12 AND ACTS 17:1-15

Luke 11:33-12:12 puts forward two themes illustrated in Acts 17:1-15. First, in Luke 11:33-12:3, continuing Luke's attempt to discredit many Jewish leaders, Jesus warns the disciples against Pharisees and lawyers who inherited a great tradition but do not live up to it. They are guilty of persecuting and killing the prophets and apostles (Luke 11:49-52). The synagogue crowd in Thessalonica manifests such behavior. Like the Pharisees in Luke 12:1-3, the synagogue crowd is hypocritical: they claim to follow the commandments (which include "You shall not bear false witness against your neighbor," Exod. 20:16; Deut. 5:20) but lie by implying that Paul, Silas, and Jason violated the decree of the emperor (Acts 17:8). Second, in Luke 12:4-12 Jesus exhorts the disciples to witness fearlessly. While their opponents try to harm the witnesses in Acts, God has counted every hair on every witness's head and will sustain them in conflict.

In Acts 17:1-15, Paul, Silas, and Jason follow Jesus's command by witnessing fearlessly. Jesus's promise comes true: God protects them when a mob drags Jason before city authorities and is so bloodthirsty it pursues the witnesses to Beroea.

Being careful not to authorize anti-Judaism while discussing the Pharisees and the synagogue crowd from Thessalonica, the preacher could set out the principles of Luke 11:33-12:12 and then use the events in Acts 17:1-15 as examples of Jesus's teaching in action. The sermon could include examples from contemporary settings in which the church encounters conflict like that in the text and needs (1) to heed Jesus's call to fearless witness and (2) to become aware of God having counted every hair on every witnessing head.

The preacher needs to identify Luke's picture of the hostility at Thessalonica as part of Luke's invective against unsympathetic Jewish people. At the same time, Luke encourages identification with Jewish people, as at Beroea, who welcome the Realm and facilitate finding safety for Paul. With these cautions in mind, a preacher could use the responses at Thessalonica and Beroea as lenses through which to help the congregation understand responses to the witness to the Realm today. Where do opponents, like the Thessalonians coming to Beroea, continue to dog the witness? The preacher can also help the congregation look for pockets of support.

The public nature of the opposition at Thessalonica might offer an entry into reflecting on public demonstrations so common in our time. The preacher could help the congregation recognize which public actions call for values and practices consistent with the Realm, and which ones seek to maintain the powers of the old age.

Connections to the Lectionary

Acts 17:22-31 occurs on the Sixth Sunday of Easter in Year A. A preacher could look at the readings from Acts on the Sundays after Easter in Year A through the lens of different responses to the Realm. The passages on the Second, Third, and Fourth Sundays of Easter describe people who immediately embrace the news of the Realm. The Fifth Sunday of Easter focuses on Stephen and a crowd so hostile to the Realm that they stone him. Acts 17:22-31 assumes a group of Athenians who are curious about the Realm but who need further guidance. A preacher could use the Sixth Sunday as an occasion to review this spectrum and to help the congregation (1) recognize where they are located on it and (2) how the congregation might adapt its approach to people who view the Realm from these different perspectives—enthusiastic, hostile, or curious.

Acts 17:16-21. Paul and the Philosophers

Although the city of Rome displaced Athens as the center of the Mediterranean world, Athens remained a symbol of some of the best of the intellectual and cultural tradition of that time. Athens was a center of philosophy. In that time, philosophy was not an abstraction removed from real life, but was often discussed at the popular level in the marketplace, in religious meetings, and in homes. Paul thus makes use of the media of the day by talking philosophy with people in such settings (Acts 17:16-17).

While Paul is distressed because Athens was "full of idols," Paul engaged philosophers with the witness to the Realm. Luke mentions Epicureans and Stoics only in passing, but ancient readers would know that their approaches to life differed radically from Paul's end-time vision. The Epicureans believed that personal happiness is the highest goal of life and that human consciousness does not continue after death: people need to maximize happiness in the present. The Stoics did not accept the idea of personal deity but believed that universal reason (*logos*) enabled people to accept what life brought them without becoming overly happy or unduly complaining. The Stoic goal was a moderate life.

Given that Paul's gospel included resurrection from the dead, it is not surprising that the Athenian philosophers initially thought of Paul as a "babbler" proclaiming "foreign divinities" (Acts 17:18). Nevertheless, the Athenians demonstrate a key to philosophy when they say, "We would like to know what it means." They want to know how Paul interprets his own message so they can respond to what he really says, and not to their caricature of his views (Acts 17:19-20).

I see two approaches to preaching from this text. First, some people today—including some Christians—continue to operate with philosophies of life similar to those of the Epicureans and Stoics. The preacher could help the congregation compare and contrast those viewpoints with those of the Realm. These three perspectives see the purpose of life in three different ways and, consequently, lead to fundamentally different approaches to living. Why should the congregation choose The Way and not Epicureanism or Stoicism?

Second, as Paul engages best thought of his day, so the preacher could help the congregation engage the most influential thought of our day in a critical fashion. I say "most influential" and not just "best" because shoddy thought can be influential. Christians too often dismiss ideas they do not like without giving other viewpoints a fair hearing. Christians may thus overlook qualities in other perspectives that could be damaging or enriching. When taking this path, the philosophers in Athens provide a partial model for the preacher. They exhibit one of the most basic characteristics of critical thinking: knowing how others understand themselves (and not simply how we might understand them) as the basis for real interaction.

CHIASTIC PARALLEL. LUKE 11:14-32 AND ACTS 17:16-21

The ability to interpret God's presence and purposes is the lead theme in these passages from the Gospel and Acts. In Luke 11:14-26, some in the Jewish crowd think Jesus's ability to cast out demons comes from Beelzebul. When a woman cries out that the womb is blessed that bore Jesus, Jesus replies that the blessed are, instead, those recognize and follow God's purposes (Luke 11:14:27-28). However, Jesus points out that the crowd cannot read the signs of the times, thus implying they will come under judgment (Luke 11:29-32). In contrast with the Jewish people in Luke 11:14-32, some philosophers in Acts 17:16-21 want Paul to explain the "new teaching." They are more open to fresh interpretations of life than are the Jewish folk.

The pastor needs to expose Luke's ideological bias here: the passage from the Gospel is intended to underscore the reader's negative associations with

Jewish people whereas the positive response of the philosophers is designed to foster openness toward such thinkers who are open to the Realm. A preacher might take the people in Luke 11:14-26 as prototypes of Christians who fail to understand the Realm and its signs. Where does the congregation encounter the questioning, engaging spirit of the philosopher today? How can the sermon encourage the church itself to become such a community?

ACTS 17:22-34. PAUL NAMES THE UNKNOWN GOD

This passage presents the preacher with both a communication strategy and a mode of theological analysis that the preacher can employ in other settings. By way of communication strategy, Paul establishes a positive point of contact with the Athenians by affirming something right in their situation: they are interested in religion. Paul carries out a critical correlation building on Athenian interest while critiquing much of their religiosity and offering the Realm as an alternative. Preachers and congregations could consider similar strategies when reaching out to individuals and communities: begin by finding shared interests and then engage in sympathetic critical correlation.

Many people in the Mediterranean world believed that the universe was inhabited by multiple deities, each of which had responsibility for a particular geographical area or arena of life. Likely the Athenians built the altar to the unknown God as a way of covering their bases in the event that the gods with names did not protect all territories or interests.

Continuing the indirect communication, Paul does not immediately name the unknown God, but describes God in language that resonates with Greek philosophy. This God who made the world does not live in shrines. God gives life to mortals. God populated the whole earth from one couple and made it possible for human beings to be aware of some things about God so they would search for God.

In the spirit of Acts 14:17, Paul affirms that God is never far from any of us. In perhaps the boldest move of this sermon, Paul quotes two Greek sources as valid authorities: "In [God] we live and move and have our being" (perhaps a paraphrase of Epimenides) and "We, too, are [God's] offspring" (from the poet Aratus). Luke acknowledges that people outside the Jewish tradition can have theological insight. This possibility could become a sermon in its own right. What voices today outside the Christian tradition offer perspectives on life consistent with those of the Realm? Could such sources offer the church insight the church might otherwise miss?

Paul next argues from observation of life to theological claim. If human beings are God's offspring, it follows that God cannot be an idol since we are alive (Acts 17:29). A preacher could muse about what we learn about God by paying attention to life.

In Acts 17:30-31, Paul gets to the heart of the message. The unknown God is the God of Israel who has previously overlooked gentile ignorance. But time has come for Athenians to go beyond the partial knowledge represented by their idols, and to repent. Why? Because God has appointed Jesus to judge the world. While Luke is sympathetic to the presence of theological insight in other religious traditions, such insight is insufficient. Repentance is necessary.

Many people in our world have unknown gods, that is, religious impulses they do not understand; they may not even recognize such intuitions as religious. A sensitive preacher could help people name those impulses and bring them into dialogue with the God of the Bible.

Luke was not thinking about the relationship of Christianity to other religions from the perspective of the questions prominent today when churches, synagogues, mosques, and temples, sit across the corner from one another. But a pastor could certainly use this passage as an entryway into such a discussion. A key issue is how to relate Luke's conclusion in Acts 17:30-31 to other religions.

CHIASTIC PARALLELS. LUKE 11:1-13 AND ACTS 17:22-34

At the center of Acts 17:22-34 is the unknown God. Paul describes God in categories reminiscent of Greek philosophers even while chiding Athenians for worshipping idols and urging them to repent before the final judgment. In contrast, Luke 11:1-13 pictures a living God who is actively involved for good. Luke 11:2-4 names the unknown God more specifically as the one who brings the Realm. God does not simply authorize the present world order but seeks to transform it. The living God is active in ways even greater than those of the householder who gets up in the night to furnish bread (Luke 11:5-8). God will not respond with a snake (something that endangers life) when the disciples ask for a fish (something that enables life). God gives the Holy Spirit to all who ask (Luke 11:9-13).

This chiastic parallel could spark a sermon on the importance of our conceptions of God. Where does the congregation see images of deity today that are as impotent as the idols on the Areopagus? The preacher can help the congregation compare and contrast such empty deities with the living God of Luke 11:1-13, and with the differences in life that flow from those images.

ACTS 18:1-4. AQUILA AND PRISCILLA

Paul leaves Athens for Corinth, approximately fifty miles west, where he meets Priscilla and Aquila. They are Jewish refugees in Corinth: Emperor Claudius evicted the Jewish population from the city of Rome, probably in 49 CE. This detail both encourages the reader's empathy toward Judaism (the Jewish people are sometimes persecuted) and increases the reader's anxiety when Paul sails for Rome. While Paul was in Rome in the mid-sixties, long after the Jewish people were allowed to return to the city, Jewish anxiety may have lingered, associated with the eviction and with other manifestations of Roman prejudice.

Luke did not add Priscilla and Aquila to Acts to prompt the church to think about ministry with refugees and immigrants in the ways that churches must do in our setting. But a preacher could begin with their situation and move to refugee issues today.

Priscilla, Aquila, and Paul are, evidently, all tentmakers. Tents were often made of leather or of heavy cloth so tent makers were typically leatherworkers (or weavers) in a broader sense. They worked in the marketplace. People often came to the market place to discuss philosophy in the stalls operated by workers. The detail that Paul was a tentmaker helps explain how the missionary financed the mission and also how he witnessed in the marketplace.

This passage gives the church the phrase "tent maker ministry" to refer to ministers who have a job (such as tent making) outside the church to provide financial support for their ministries. Luke did not have in mind issues related to church leadership in the early twenty-first century. But as congregations get smaller with dwindling resources, increasing numbers of congregations and ministers are taking up tent maker forms of ministry. Acts 18:1-4 could give the preacher a natural platform for comparing and contrasting such situations then and now, and for helping the church think about the long-term effects.

When preaching on Acts 18:1-4, the preacher should bring Acts 18:24-28 into the sermon because this latter text reveals Luke's fuller reason for including Aquilla and Priscilla. They jointly teach Apollos, a learned and wealthy Jewish person from Alexandria. While it would be anachronistic to call them "the first clergy couple," they do share responsibility for teaching, and, hence, they model an egalitarian approach to leadership characteristic of the Realm. My spouse is a minister, and I report that sharing in leadership is indeed an experience of the Realm for me (and often for both of us). A congregation might benefit from a sermon exploring the theological rationale for shared leadership—not only among clergy but throughout the church.

Chiastic Parallels. Luke 10:38-42 and Acts 18:1-4

Luke 10:38-42 tells of Jesus's visit to the home of Mary and Martha. Christians often see this visit as a contrast between activist (Martha) and contemplative (Mary) approaches to spirituality. Another reading is more pertinent. Luke believes the Realm will restore the situation of women to that of mutual partnership with men as in Eden. That restoration is underway though incomplete. Luke 10:38-42 pictures Mary learning at the feet of Jesus as a full-fledged disciple. Jesus teaches her as he teaches the apostles (all males). In Acts 18:1-4, 24-28, then, the impulse toward restoration has taken an additional step: Priscilla is acknowledged as teacher in the community of the Realm.

A sermon could name the fact that many congregations and Christian movements today struggle with women in relationship to positions of power. Women clergy often encounter a "stained glass ceiling," a level of power beyond which they cannot rise. The preacher can help the congregation envision how we can transcend the impulse toward liberation in Luke-Acts to a much deeper sense of gender partnership, mutually supportive relationship, and shared leadership. Patriarchy may be so deeply ingrained and so resilient that the only way to purge it from the church is to privilege the leadership of women for several generations. Let males go to the kitchen and prepare the meal for Jesus, Mary, and Martha.

Acts 18:5-23. Conflict in Corinth

The witness of Paul, Silas and Timothy unfolds in Corinth much as it does in several previous cities on the second missionary journey. When Paul preaches to some Jewish people, they revile him. In protest, Paul shakes their dust of off his clothes, declares them guilty: "Your blood be on your own heads," that is, they will be judged for reviling the message of the Realm. Paul turns to gentiles (Acts 18:6). In one sense, this incident is yet another installment in Luke's attempt to get his congregation to be apprehensive of Jewish people who do not identify with the Realm. In another sense, Paul's statement that he turns to the gentiles turns out to be not quite true.

Paul's turn to the gentiles does raise a question for the church today. When, if ever, is it appropriate for the church simply to drop an individual or a group, and to go elsewhere in witness? With the apocalypse on the horizon, Luke believed the time for witness was short. Resources were limited. Opposition was intense. Paul gave the Corinthians one chance: the Realm way or the highway, Under what circumstances and to what degree is it pastorally and prophetically responsible for the preacher and the congregation to take such action?

Paul leaves the synagogue and goes next door to the house of Titius Justus, a gentile who worships God but has never converted to Judaism. Crispus—the official of the synagogue—believes and is baptized with his household. With this development, Luke gives reason to his congregation to welcome Jewish people who join the movement toward the Realm. Indeed, synagogue leadership may be among them. Many additional Corinthians come forward.

Jesus speaks to Paul in a vision directing Paul not to be afraid to speak. Not only is Jesus with Paul in a spiritual sense but Jesus has many people in Corinth. Paul demonstrated the reliability of this promise by staying in Corinth eighteen months (Acts 18:9-11). A preacher might voice the longing of today's congregation to have the same level of clarity as Paul so as to know when to remain and make a witness in a dangerous situation, and when to change locations.

Some Jewish people falsely charge Paul before Gallio, proconsul of Achaia (the area around Corinth) that Paul tries to persuade Jewish people to worship in ways not authorized by Torah. (Acts 18:12-13). Before Paul can answer the charge, a representative of the Roman legal system again comes to Paul's rescue: Gallio points out that the charge does not concern things that concern Rome. The charge concerns in-house Jewish matters that the Jewish people should settle among themselves.

A preacher might look for ways that individuals and groups outside the church contribute, like Gallio, to the witness to the Realm. Although Luke did not have early twenty-first century questions about the relationship of church and state in mind, the way in which Gallio responds to the Jewish charge does raise the question of when the state could be legitimately interested in matters within the church, and when the church can claim the attention and power of the state.

The second missionary journey concludes with Paul returning to Antioch (Acts 18:18-22). Paul cuts his hair, thus making a Nazirite vow (Num. 6:1-21). The name Nazirite derives from the Hebrew verb *nazar* meaning "to consecrate." A Jewish person would make a special consecration to God by engaging in a spiritual practice such as fasting and would indicate that vow by cutting the hair. This detail not only indicates that Paul faithfully practices Judaism and rededicates himself to the mission. The latter could be a fruitful seed for a sermon. Christians sometimes derive strength from dedicating themselves to a particular mission. What public rite could the church sponsor in which people have an opportunity to make such commitments? What symbols (comparable to cutting the hair) could the church employ that give friends and neighbors an opportunity to enter into solidarity with those making recommitments?

CHIASTIC PARALLELS. LUKE 10:1-37 AND ACTS 18:5-23

This passage from Luke sets out two motifs that recur in Acts 18:5-23. First, Jesus warns the seventy that they go as lambs into the midst of wolves (Luke 10:3). On their mission, they encounter people who are both receptive and resistant. When people receive them, they announce the Realm is present (Luke 10:5-9). But when locals do not welcome the missionaries, the missionaries are to wipe the dust from that town off their feet in protest. Indeed, judgment will fall on that town (Luke 10:10-12, 13-16). Second, readers are surprised that the Samaritan makes the Realm-like response to victim by the road. The parable prepares the reader to expect other surprising people to become agents of the Realm as the Samaritan did.

Similar themes occur in Acts 18:5-13. Many Jewish members of the synagogue at Corinth revile Paul (Acts 18:5). The unhappy synagogue members attack Paul and bring him before the tribunal on false charges (Acts 18:12). Paul effectively says, "We wipe your dust off our feet and go to the gentiles" (Acts 18:6). Other people make positive responses that surprise the reader in ways similar to the surprise of the Samaritan—Titius Justus (a worshiper of God) and Crispus (the head the synagogue that produced the reviling crowd). While Gallio (the Roman proconsul) does not rise to the height of the ministry exerted by the Samaritan, this Roman official modestly serves the Realm by refusing to elevate the charge made by the synagogue protesters to Roman legal status. A Roman idolater who does not get in the way of the Realm is less objectionable than a synagogue group who does.

The preacher can take up these themes in a sermon. The easy task is to help the congregation identify, support, and even welcome people and groups who in our day are similar to the Samaritan, Titius Justus, Crispus, and Gallio. The more difficult task is to consider when it is appropriate for today's church to shake the dust off our feet, that is, to cease witnessing and to leave an individual or a group behind, a theme taken up above.

You Will Be My Witnesses to the Ends of the Earth: The Third Missionary Journey Brings Apollos, the Holy Spirit, Imposters, and a Riot (Acts 18:23—19:41)

The first and second missionary journeys begin and end in Antioch. The third journey (Acts 18:23-21:16) begins in Antioch but ends in Jerusalem and contains a confrontation that reorients his ministry from one primarily focused on evangelism and teaching to his own defense. This first part of this third missionary journey reintroduces Priscilla and Aquila (Acts 18:24-28) and brings into view disciples who received the baptism of John but not the Holy Spirit (Acts 19:1-10), punishment of imposters (Acts 19:11-20), and a riot in Ephesus (Acts 19:21-41). Comments on the third missionary journey continue in connection with Acts 20:1-21:16.

Acts 18:23-28. Teaching Apollos

We consider key elements of the ministry of Priscilla and Aquila at Acts 18:1-4. Here it we recall that they share leadership as teachers of the Realm. Such sharing is an impulse toward restoring relationships between women and men in the Realm.

The shared teaching is impressive in view of Luke's description of Apollos as not only eloquent but well versed in scripture. Apollos is himself a teacher. However, from Luke's point of view his experience is incomplete since he received only the baptism of John. People come into the community of the Realm through repentance, baptism in the name of Jesus, and receiving the Spirit. Apollos is an incomplete disciple. The same issue recurs in our discussion of Acts 19:1-7, especially in connection with Baptism of Jesus (Year B) in the lectionary,

The preacher could take Apollo to represent a circumstance that some Christians today are reluctant to acknowledge. Apollos, though a leader, still needs to grow in discipleship. Today's preacher could use Apollos's circumstance to help members of the congregation think about points at which they could mature in discipleship.

Chiastic Parallels. Luke 9:51-62 and Acts 18:24-28

Luke 9:51 is the beginning of Jesus's journey to Jerusalem (Luke 9:51-19:27). Luke 9:51-62 describes three encounters with similar themes. In Luke 9:51-56, Jesus's messengers encounter Samaritans who do not receive Jesus. Jesus and his band go to another village. In Luke 9:57-60, someone wants to follow Jesus, but only after burying the dead. Jesus replies, "Let the dead bury their own dead, but as for you, go and proclaim the [Realm] of God." In Luke 9:61-62, someone wants to follow Jesus, but only after saying farewell to family. Jesus replies, "No one who puts a hand to the plow and looks back is fit for the [Realm] of God." The Samaritans and the two individuals in Luke 9:57-62 turn away from invitations to participate in the Realm. They prefer the known qualities of the old age rather than the risk of the journey to the Realm.

Apollos is a contrast to the characters in Luke 9:51-62. When Priscilla and Aquila advise him of the need to receive the baptism of Jesus, he immediately accedes. According to Acts 18:27-28, the community in Achaia welcomes him.

A sermon might consider the relationship between gift and response in the Realm. The Realm comes as a gift (Luke 12:32). However, becoming a part of the movement toward the Realm does call for a response. The believer must open the gift for it to become fully functional. In Luke 9:51-62, the people refuse the gift. By contrast Apollos accepts baptism as completing the gift of being in the Realm. A sermon could help the congregation recognize how God invites us to become a part of the movement to the Realm. Are we like the Samaritans and the two people who continue in the old age, or will we join Apollos?

ACTS 19:1-10. "WE HAVE NOT EVEN HEARD THAT THERE IS A HOLY SPIRIT"

After Paul leaves Corinth, he travels about 250 miles to Ephesus, a major city in Asia Minor (present day Turkey). Paul encounters people who consider themselves disciples of Jesus but who never heard of the Holy Spirit and who received only the baptism of John. Luke's conviction surfaces that full bodied discipleship includes repentance, baptism in the name of Jesus, and the Spirit. When Paul explains that John told people to believe in Jesus, the disciples are immediately baptized, receive the Spirit, and experience a version of Pentecost.

Some congregations, especially Eurocentric ones, pay little attention to the Holy Spirit. I grew up in a rationalist congregation, many of whose members could have said, "We have not even heard that there is a Holy Spirit." The preacher in a similar congregation could introduce the congregation to the Lukan understanding as well as to broader perspectives on the Spirit.

Scholars have long thought the disciples of John the Baptist and the disciples of Jesus were in conflict over which leader was more important. This text is one of many picturing John testifying to the superiority of Jesus. John may have considered himself a forerunner to Jesus, but the church may well have enhanced or created such impressions. Whatever the historical case, one preaching possibility is to identify figures, groups, movements similar to John in having religious insight that is helpful but incomplete.

Another preaching possibility—informed by the postmodern penchant for respectful pluralism—might be to criticize the way in which the Gospels and Letters portray John as inferior to Jesus. From the point of deconstruction, the church solidified its own power by downgrading that of John. Radical pluralists would simply acknowledge that John and his disciples have a different viewpoint, a perspective that raises the question of whether there are any limits to the diversity the church is willing to honor. Where—if ever—does the church draw the line on theological ideas or moral behavior that are unacceptable?

Connections to the Lectionary

Baptism of Jesus Sunday recalls the baptism of Jesus himself and baptism in the community of Jesus's followers. Acts 19:1-7, then, is a fitting text for the Baptism of Jesus. To set the stage for Mark 1:9-11 and Acts 19:1-7, a preacher could use Genesis 1:1-5 as a beginning point in explaining multiple levels of Jewish water symbolism and then tracing the history of baptism through Jewish water-rites—purification practices, immersion of proselytes into Judaism, water ceremonies at Qumran, and baptism as initiation into the eschatological communities of the John the Baptist and Jesus.

As noted in connection with the Acts 8:14-17 and 10:34-43 (the readings for the Baptism of Jesus, Years C and A respectively), Baptism of Jesus is a good day on which members of the congregation can recall their own baptisms, consider how baptism bestows identity, how it commissions for mission, brings people into common life and witness, and gives members an opportunity to renew their baptismal vows. The minister could pass through the congregation splashing people with water.

Baptism of Jesus Sunday is also good day to consider the relationship of baptism to church membership and the Realm. For people to participate fully in the church today, should the church require baptism in water in the name of Jesus (or the Trinity)? Is a particular form of baptism required—immersion, pouring, or sprinkling? John's baptism is not Christian baptism, but when the disciples in Ephesus are baptized two times, it does raise the question of whether a Christian could be baptized more than once.

Chiastic Parallels. Luke 9:43b-50 and Acts 19:1-10

In Luke 9:43b-50 the disciples not understand Jesus. They do not perceive the meaning of his teaching about his death (Luke 9:43b-45). They argue about who is the greatest (Luke 9:46-48). They try to stop an exorcist casting out demons in the name of Jesus but not following with their group (Luke 9:49-50). The disciples had yet to receive the Holy Spirit, an event not occurring until Pentecost. A similar situation pertains in Acts 19:1-10 when the disciples at Ephesus have not received the Holy Spirit. However, when they are baptized in the name of Jesus and receive the Spirit, they speak in tongues and prophesy.

Through these chiastic elements, Luke assures the congregation to accept Jesus's suffering—and their own—as part of the witness to the Realm. Through the Spirit the congregation can welcome the child and the Realm-mode of community represented therein, and the congregation can celebrate the work of exorcists outside their own community.

Acts 19:11-20. "Jesus I know. Paul I know. But who are you?"

People in Ephesus touched Paul with handkerchiefs and aprons and took them to the sick with the result that healings and exorcisms took place in those who were touched by the handkerchiefs (Acts 19:11-12). This motif is similar to Acts 5:15-16 when God heals through Peter's shadow when it falls across the sick. Many people in the ancient world believed that healing power could be transferred from one person to another via physical means such as pieces of cloth. Acts makes use of popular folk thinking.

Some Christians have taken this passage quite literally A few years ago a radio healer sold handkerchiefs that he had blessed. At a key moment in the radio broadcast, he would ask people to hold their handkerchiefs to the radio and expect healing as he prayed. I do not know whether healings actually resulted. I do know that ministers in circles in which I move made fun of this practice.

Luke's deeper point might help the preacher toward a sermon that does more than critique radio preachers: the healing power at work in the Realm is at work not only through the word and touch but through multiple media. Moreover, the healing power is not confined to the immediate presence of the person through whom God heals. The healing power can travel. Yes, a preacher needs to caution a congregation against superstition with respect to handkerchiefs. At the same time, physical objects can become powerful symbols that evoke life-giving responses. Churches who anoint those who have an illness with oil seldom believe that the oil itself heals. Rather, the oil is a physical reminder of God's presence. When I was in high school, our congregation gave everyone a pocket-sized aluminum cross which I carried until I lost it. That cross was not magic, but it reminded me of God's presence.

Acts 19:13-16 casts another negative light on some Jewish people by portraying seven itinerant exorcists, children of the high priest Sceva, who attempt to exorcise in the name of Jesus. Exorcists and other charismatic miracle workers were often itinerant. Many people believed that knowing the name of a spirit gave the possessor access to the power of that spirit. However, Jewish records remember no high priest named Sceva.

In Acts, the name of Jesus belongs to the community of the Realm. The Jewish exorcists are not members of the community and are, thus, imposters when they use it. They are not inhabited by demons, but they behave as creatures of the old age. When they attempt to exorcise an evil spirit, the spirit makes a reply that may be humorous. "Jesus I know and Paul I know; but who are you?" At that point, the person with the evil spirit physically overpowers the seven exorcists and they flee.

Two things occur in this incident that could become the start of a sermon. First, while the imposters attempt to exorcise in the name of Jesus, they are exposed as having no real power. They promise qualities of the Realm (freedom from demons) but they cannot deliver. The sermon could help the congregation name this phenomenon today in ideas, behaviors, and groups today. Second, the exorcists are punished by the very thing they attempt to manipulate: the demon, which is so powerful it gives the one person it inhabited the power to wreak violence on the exorcists. The sermon could alert the congregation to the fact that such an outcome awaits those—including the congregation—who are imposters. God does not destroy the exorcists. Their false behavior creates its own destruction. A preacher can move from this threat to the positive question: What can the congregation do to become genuinely representative of the Realm?

Acts 19:17-20 contrasts the fate of the seven exorcists with those who believe. The former are overpowered and naked. The latter are filled with awe and give up magic. They collect the books that held the magic spells and formulas needed to practice magic, and burn them publicly. When we remember one silver coin was worth one day's wages, the value of these books is staggering: fifty thousand silver coins. The believers did not simply sell these books, but destroyed them presumably to get rid of the temptation to return to the behavior of the old age represented by magic.

A bold preacher can ask: is the congregation ready to give up its ties to magic—its reliance on old age values and practices? The preacher could explore whether the congregation is ready to burn its books—its stocks and bonds and other investments that prolong the old-age qualities of the present world.

Chiastic Parallels. Luke 9:37-43a and Acts 19:11-20

These texts center on demons that wreak havoc on human life. The sermon could point to contemporary equivalents of demonic possession. The texts point to different ways of approaching possessions the preacher could use as analogues for different responses today.

In Luke 9:37-43a, the disciples are impotent in the face of a demon inhabiting the young person, but Jesus, representative of the Realm, rebukes the demon. The person in Acts 19:16 is possessed. These aspects assume the congregation to whom Luke wrote struggles with demons (as the disciples do in Luke 9:37-41). Yet this passage assures the community that the power of the Realm is now resident through the Spirit. The congregation is called to act in the manner of Jesus and Paul.

In Acts 19:13-17, the Jewish exorcists try to use the name of Jesus to exorcise demons. By treating the name of Jesus (the hope for the Realm) in an old-age way, they invite condemnation on themselves represented in the demonic leaping on them. They are destroyed by the very means by which they sought to manipulate the demons.

When the congregation faces demonic possession, they have a choice. They can struggle for a Realm-like world in Realm-like ways, knowing that even as they struggle the Spirit is with them. Or they can try to control the demons in demonic ways, and thus become the victims of their own methods.

Acts 19:21-22. "I Must Also See Rome."

In Acts 19:21-22, Paul makes a statement that shapes the reader's perception of the rest of Acts. When Paul says, "I must also see Rome," he employs a Greek expression that implies divine necessity (*dei*). Rome is the pre-eminent symbol of the "end of the earth" (Acts 1:8). Paul's statement shows that his journey to Rome is the result of God's initiative and is not simply a happenstance resulting from his arrest in the temple and legal entanglements. This detail highlights a theme pervading Acts: the movement of the witness to the Realm takes place under divine guidance. By reintroducing it here, Luke wants the reader to remember that God's providential hand leads Paul to Jerusalem and thence to witness in Rome.

When Paul says, "I must also see Rome," he gives the preacher an image with which to discuss the mission of the congregation. Rome represents empty splendor and falsehood, abusive power and corruption, privilege of the few and violence toward the many. Yet Rome is the ultimate place where Paul witnesses to the Realm. Where is Rome for the congregation? In the Pauline sense, what must the congregation see?

The deeper point of Luke's notion of divine necessity is not that God guides each event in the life of a person or congregation but that God's purposes are deep and unrelenting. Making the hermeneutical move from point of view of the process theology to which I subscribe, divine necessity means that God never gives up on a person or situation but continually tries to offer the possibilities of the Realm, even to the Romes of the world.

Acts 19:23-41 assumes that readers are aware that the popular goddess Artemis (Diana in Roman mythology, daughter of Zeus) was recognized in first-century Asia minor as a fertility goddess. Indeed, archaeological remains picture Artemis with a chest covered either with breasts or with bull's testes. A preacher could project such a picture as part of the sermon.

Paul's powerful witness in Ephesus (Acts 19:17-20) prompts many people to stop buying shrines of Artemis. Demetrius points out not only that Paul costs the silversmiths income but that some people are beginning to scorn the temple of Artemis which will deprive her of adoration. We might assume that Demetrius fears that a neglected Artemis will then neglect the Ephesians (Acts 19:23-27). Demetrius is engaged in intertwined idolatries—worship of money and Artemis. The latter reinforces the former.

Enraged, the silversmiths confess faith in Artemis (Acts 19:28). However, subsequent developments reveal the fallacy of this faith. Her devotees drag two of Paul's companions, Gaius and Aristarchus, to the theater. Paul wants to join Gaius and Aristarchus in the theater but both the disciples and some friendly local officials try to prevent him from taking such a stand. (Acts 19:29-32). This detail should give today's preacher pause. Members of a congregation sometimes warn a preacher that a particular fray is too dangerous. How can a minister or congregation gauge when hesitation is a practical strategy for the moment or the result of fear?

Alexander tries to address the crowd but the crowd dismisses him because he is Jewish. The crowd erupts into two hours of uproarious confession of Artemis (Acts 19:33-34). The behavior of the crowd demonstrates one of the primary consequences of idolatry: social chaos.

A town clerk—a civic official approved by the Roman Empire—serves the purposes of the Realm by quieting the crowd (Acts 19:35-41). The clerk points out that the witnesses have not acted illegally: they have not robbed the temple nor have they blasphemed Artemis. Demetrius and his companions should take truly legal complaints against the witnesses to the courts that are open even now. Further charges should be settled in the regular assembly. Demetrius and the artisans must follow Roman legal protocol. As for now, the group should break up to avoid being charged with rioting—a very serious matter in an Empire that valued *Pax Romana*.

Where might the preacher point the congregation toward idolatry in our culture that results in chaos like that in Ephesus? What functions as our Artemis, spawning dependencies and threatening behavior such as that of Demetrius and the silversmiths?

This text is appropriate for churches in capitalist cultures in which making money is important. How much money is the congregation willing to give up to be part of the movement toward the Realm? The preacher can portray the economy of the Realm—which relies on mutuality, sharing, and acting for the common good—as more inviting than an economy based on Artemis.

The preacher should attend to gender dynamics. Although Acts presents an impulse toward the liberation of women, none of the pictures of faithful women in Acts take up as much narrative space as this negative story of Artemis. The positive qualities associated with women on the way to restoration in Acts are seldom as emotionally powerful as the negative feelings associated with the riot around Artemis. The preacher needs to warn the congregation against unconsciously transferring negative associations with the goddess and the riot to women today.

Chiastic Parallels. Luke 9:18-36 and Acts 19:21-41

The structure of these two chiastic elements is similar, thus setting in motion a pattern in the reader's mind that goes from the Gospel to Acts to the congregation to whom Luke wrote to today. In Luke 9:18-26 the pattern is: confession that Jesus is God's agent bringing the Realm (Luke 9:18-20), Jesus teaching that the disciples will suffer (Luke 9:21-27), and divine assurance through a momentary realization of the Realm in the present (the transfiguration) that Jesus's words are true.

This pattern recurs in Acts 19:21-42. The text assumes that Paul witnessed to the coming of the Realm (Acts 19:17-20). The artisans drag Paul and his companions to the theater and engage in threatening behavior (Acts 19:23-34). Providence comes through the town clerk who calms the crowd by explaining that Paul and his companions are not lawbreakers (Acts 19:35-41).

The preacher might explain how Luke intended for the congregation to which he wrote to apply this pattern to its own life: engaging in witness that leads to resistance within which to be aware of divine support. Thinking about today, a preacher might help the congregation remember events in its own history when this pattern has proven true, and then invite listeners to imagine a situation in the present or future that is challenging: it calls for witness but presents the potential of threat. The congregation can proceed in the confidence that God's providential care will be present.

You Will Be My Witnesses to the Ends of the Earth: The Third Missionary Journey Brings Macedonia, Greece, Raising the Dead, Teaching the Elders, Prophetic Women, and Anticipating Paul's Death (Acts 20:1—21:16)

Acts 20:1-21:16 is the last part of the third missionary journey. Paul departs for Macedonia, visits Greece before returning to Macedonia (Acts 20:1-6), from whence he passes through Troas where God raises Eutychus (Acts 20:7-12), thence to Miletus (Acts 20:8-16) where he teaches the elders from Ephesus (Acts 20:17-38). After being in Caesarea on the Sea, encountering prophetic women, hearing Agabus prophesy Paul's death, Paul leaves for Jerusalem (Acts 21:7-16). The feeling is much the same as when Luke says that Jesus's "face was set toward Jerusalem" (Luke 9:53). This part of the narrative, especially Acts 20:22-24 and Acts 21:10-14, prepares readers for the climactic events of Paul's life ahead by assuring readers of God's aegis and Paul's courage.

Acts 20:1-16. Macedonia, Greece, and Raising the Dead in Troas

Acts 20:1-6 is a transitional section describing how Paul made his way from Ephesus to Troas and Miletus. However, the narrative is more than a travelogue: it emphasizes the importance of community. Paul's visits were a source of encouragement to the believers. When a plot was made against Paul, the believers provided safe passage. Indeed, some believers preceded Paul to Troas (located on the ocean of the northwestern corner of modern day Turkey) to prepare for his arrival.

A minister could develop a sermon on the importance of members of the community of the Realm supporting one another, a theme highlighted in connection with the chiastic parallels Luke 9:1-17 and Acts 20:1-6 (below). Luke's mention of so many specific places and the names of so many of Paul's companions reminds the preacher that the witness to the Realm takes place in specific contexts among specific people. The preacher might interview members of the congregation: "Would you tell us when this community was a real support for you?"

Luke sees the life of Jesus as a model for the church in Acts. This motif comes to the fore in connection with the last phase of Paul's life when Luke draws parallels between the arrest, trial, and death of Jesus and of Paul. Acts 20:6 contains such a parallel when Luke mentions that Paul sailed from Philippi toward Troas and Jerusalem "after the days of Unleavened Bread." The events leading to Jesus's death take place in the shadow of "the festival of Unleavened Bread" (Luke 22:1). One reason that Luke emphasizes the suffering of Jesus and that of the church is to encourage the congregation to which he wrote in their own suffering through the examples of Jesus and Paul.

Chiastic Parallels. Luke 9:1-17 and Acts 20:1-6

Luke 9:1-17 is made up of three parts whose themes appear also in Acts 20:1-6. In Luke 9:1-6, Jesus gives the twelve authority over demons and diseases, and sends them on a journey to proclaim the Realm. In Luke 9:7-9, Herod, having beheaded John, wants to know who Jesus is. In Luke 9:10-17, the twelve return to Jesus but find themselves in a wilderness with 5,000 hungry people. Jesus feeds the 5,000, assuring readers that God indeed will support them in difficulties.

In Acts 20:1-6, Paul is on a journey on which he proclaims the Realm and exercises authority over demons and diseases. He is threatened by a plot against him (Acts 20:3b). Yet God provides companions and a safe journey to Troas. Indeed, he sails after the days of Unleavened Bread. His travelling companions are the means whereby God provides for Paul in his wilderness moment (the plot against him).

The preacher might find a clue for the sermon by suggesting that Luke wants readers to find parallel situations in their own settings. The church is to witness on its journey (exemplified in Luke's distinctive title for the church: the Way). When encountering difficulty, they can count on God for support. In the wilderness this support came in the form of bread and fish. In Acts, the support came through the community in the form of Paul's traveling companions. The preacher can offer encourage the congregation to become such a means of grace.

In Acts 20:7 the church meets to break bread on the first day of the week. Paul converses with the congregation until midnight. A young person named

Eutychus, sitting on the window ledge, went to sleep, fell three stories to the ground, and died (Acts 20:8-10). The power of the Realm moves through the preacher to raise Eutychus from the dead.

The preacher could make much of a central point of this narrative. God restores Eutychus to full participation in the community. How is God at work to restore people who are dead to community today?

As Paul turns to Jerusalem and his eventual martyrdom, he becomes a channel for the power that raises the dead. Being God's representative in raising Eutychus assures Paul (and the reader) that although Paul will die, his ultimate destiny is in the hands of a God whose power has flowed through the missionary's own hands. Paul's ministry is a means whereby God's grace comes to Paul as part of his preparation for what lies ahead. A homily could help the congregation recognize how their own ministry becomes a means whereby ministry itself becomes an experience of the Realm. Preachers might take the lead by sharing such stories from their own ministries.

Among contemporary clergy, this story is sometimes a source of humor. Paul must have been daydreaming in preaching class when they talked about the length of a sermon. He preached six hours, took a break to raise the dead, and then preached six more hours! And Paul must also have been daydreaming when the preaching professor discussed how to help sermons connect with the congregation: Paul's sermon first put Eutychus to sleep then killed the young person. While Luke did not include this incident as a lesson in homiletics, a preacher might encourage the congregation to make their witnesses in ways that do not put people to sleep.

Paul sails to Miletus, on the seacoast almost 200 mile south of Troas, to get a good start on the trip to Jerusalem, which he hoped to reach by Pentecost. Paul does not stop in Ephesus, evidently to avoid a prolonged visit. Paul was not the first preacher to see a talkative parishioner in the aisle of the supermarket and to take evasive action.

CHIASTIC PARALLELS. LUKE 8:22-54 AND ACTS 20:7-16

In Luke 8:22-25, Jesus calms a storm. In Luke 8:26-39, Jesus exorcises a demon from a person in the country of the Gerasenes. In Luke 8: 40-56, Jesus heals a woman who had suffered from a hemorrhage for twelve years and raises a young woman from the dead. These miracle stories demonstrate that in the Realm, natural disaster, illness and death lose their destructive power. These stories invite the community into mission as Jesus tells the twelve in Luke 9:1 that they have such authority, as do the seventy in Luke 10:8-9.

The stories in Luke3 8:22-54 climax with power over death, the archenemy of the Realm. Healings and exorcisms have occurred in Acts (for example, Acts 2:43; 3:1-10; 5:12-16; 9:32-43; 14:8-18; 19:11-12), but thus far only Peter has been God's agent in resurrecting the dead (Acts 9:36-43). Now Luke assures the reader that life-giving power did not end with Jesus or Peter but continues through Paul, and the church. The preacher might identify individuals and situations that are figuratively dead and suggest how they could come to life in the Realm. The preacher might also explore how the congregation could become, like Paul, an instrument of life.

Acts 20:17-38. In Miletus Paul Teaches the Elders from Ephesus

Paul wants to talk with the elders from Ephesus. Elders are local leaders of the congregation who are concerned with preaching and teaching, while deacons focus on the physical care of the congregation (Acts 6:1-6). The eldership was likely modeled on similar figures in the synagogue. The elders make the 25-mile trip from Ephesus to Miletus to talk with Paul.

Acts 20:18-35 is Paul's farewell address to the elders. Typical of farewell addresses in antiquity, this one summarizes the core of what Paul hopes his legacy will be. In the process, he imparts his most sustained reflection on a key purpose of the elders.

Paul recalls his own attempt to endure amid the trials that came from Jewish people (Acts 20:18b-19). Paul did not shrink from pain but continued to offer the opportunity to repent to both Greek and Jewish people (Acts 20:20-21). Paul is on the way to Jerusalem where, the Spirit has revealed, he will face imprisonment and persecution. Yet, Paul hopes that he can finish his course (Acts 20:22-24).

Paul's faithfulness in difficulty adds to the credibility of the guidance he gives to the elders. Paul wants them to know he is not responsible for tensions that will soon come among them; he has prepared the community for the savage wolves who come from the outside, and from some members within the community who distort the truth (Acts 20:27-32).

Paul draws on historic Jewish language to speak of the congregation as a flock, which implies that the elders are shepherds and overseers. The word "overseer" renders the Greek *episkopos,* "bishop." The bishop is a local leader who oversees the congregation as a shepherd cares for the flock by keeping the flock together for safety, providing food, keeping predators at bay, tending to wounded sheep, and disciplining wandering members.

Luke makes use of a modest form of *vaticinium ex eventu* (prophecy after the fact) in which he speaks in the future tense as if predicting events that have already come to pass in Luke's congregation. Luke borrows Ezekiel's description of unfaithful Jewish leaders as "wolves" to evaluate some Jewish leaders of Luke's own day (Ezek. 22:27; Acts 20:29).

The role that Paul implies for the elders is valid in almost any time and place: to impart a message to build up the church so participants will receive their inheritance, that is, a place in the eschatological Realm (Acts 20:31-32). The elders are to teach the Realm so as to maintain the congregation in the face of attacks from the outside and distortion from within.

The preacher could reflect on these dynamics and on how awareness of the Realm can help the congregation. The wolves are no longer Jewish leaders, but people and groups from outside who seek to undermine the vision of the Realm as the goal of world community. People within the church continue to attempt to distort the church's vision of God's purposes through the Realm.

More generally, a preacher could use this text to help the congregation understand the big picture of the ministry of elders. In my tradition, the Christian Church (Disciples of Christ), the service of elders (lay leaders elected by the congregation) is often limited to praying over the loaf and the cup. Luke envisions elders teaching the congregation the ways of the Realm. The preacher could underscore the fact that teaching can be more than giving lectures to students; it can take place in any settings and any mode.

The preacher can call the attention of the congregation to a painful irony. Luke perceived the Jewish leaders of his day as savage wolves. At most, such leaders might have attempted to discipline the Jewish members of Luke's congregation. However, in only a few years, the roles would reverse: the church becomes the savage wolf at the door of the synagogue. The savagery of the church would lead through segregation, pogroms, and the inquisition to the Holocaust and the murder of six million Jewish people. This is what can happen when the church does not teach adequately.

Paul concludes by returning to his own example. The Ephesians can believe him because he earned his own keep (Acts 20:33-34). Indeed, Paul is a fully functioning member of the community of the Realm by providing materially for those who resources are marginal (Acts 20:35).

Paul quotes a line from Jesus with which worship leaders continue to introduce the offering. "It is more blessed to give than to receive" (Acts 20:36). This saying is not found elsewhere. Luke may have heard it from an early Christian prophet, may recall it imprecisely, or may have created it. To be blessed means to be aware of being part of the Realm. Those caught up in the movement toward the Realm experience the presence of the Realm ever more fully as they make their resources available to the community. The more they invest themselves, the more their own sense of well being increases.

CHIASTIC PARALLELS. LUKE 8:4-21 AND ACTS 20:17-38

Luke 8:4-21 is intended to encourage the congregation when it becomes discouraged as members drift away. This passage assures the congregation that faithful witness will bear fruit now and at the apocalypse. According to the allegorical explanation of the parable in Luke 8:11-15, people are similar to four kinds of soil (path, rock, thorns, and good). People who are like the first three kinds of soil struggle, and some fall away. But, the good soil—people who are patient and who endure with a good heart—bear fruit.

The teaching of Paul to the elders of Ephesus in Acts 20:17-38 illustrates the allegorical explanation. Paul had scattered the seed among the Ephesians (Acts 20:17-27). However, savage wolves disrupted the flock, while some of the community's own members distort the truth (Acts 20:28-32). Those who endure will bear fruit in ways such as supporting those who are weak (Acts 28:33-35).

The preacher might sketch the feelings of discouragement in Luke's congregation to which Luke 8:4-21 is addressed. The preacher might then identify similar feelings in the congregation today. After discussing the discouraging circumstances in Luke's community as revealed in Acts 20:28-31, the preacher could identify similarly circumstances in the contemporary church. To address such circumstances, Luke 8:4-21 urges the congregation to remember that the harvest is coming. Those who endure can live in hope. In Acts 20:17-35 Paul urges the elders—like the sower in the parable—to continue teaching and exercising pastoral care. Such sowing will bear fruit at the apocalypse.

ACTS 21:1-16. FINAL JOURNEY TO JERUSALEM, PROPHETESSES IN PTOLEMAIS, AND PREDICTION OF PAUL'S DEATH

Acts 21:1-6 is similar in function to Acts 20:1-6 discussed above. However, while Paul has his sights set on Jerusalem, the Spirit intervenes with the message that he should not go there yet (Acts 21:4). Luke implies that the Spirit then gives Paul the go-ahead (Acts 21:5).

The reference to the Spirit reminds readers that God presides over Paul's witness. The deep point is that God is always with Paul. Some Christians believe not only that God is omnipresent but that God orchestrates all of life's events. This text could launch a sermon considering the relationship of God's initiatives to human life. How much does God do? By which criteria can we gauge God's presence and activity? What is our responsibility?

Chiastic Parallels. Luke 8:1-3 and Acts 21:1-6

In the days of Luke, itinerant charismatic preachers and healers often lived on the hospitality of those among whom they traveled. That is the case in Luke 8:1-3. Luke emphasizes that women support Jesus and his band. Since these women evidently act without reference to men, and seemingly have their own funds, their appearance here points toward the restoration of women in the Realm. Their generosity is the practical means through which God provides for the traveling witnesses.

A similar situation pertains in Acts 21:1-6. Paul and his companions are traveling. The disciples in Tyre provide for them. The community is the instrument through which God provides practical support to witnesses with Luke highlighting the presence of women at the send-off.

The preacher could urge both (1) the members of the congregation to rely upon God's providence mediated through the community and (2) the congregation to become such a supportive community. Since the central characters in Luke 8:1-3 are women, a message could help the congregation recognize the providential ministries of women and could urge women to become such agents.

Acts 21:7-16 plays an important role in foreshadowing what will happen to Paul in Jerusalem and beyond. At Caesarea on the Sea Paul stays with Philip the evangelist (the same Philip of Acts 8:26-40). Recalling Acts 2:17-18 and its vision of young women prophesying, we now encounter the four daughters of Philip who have the gift of prophecy. While this reference is brief, it reminds the reader of both the impulse toward the restoration of women and of the ongoing office of prophet.

Luke mentions these details with a casualness that might be worth a preacher's consideration. Often we are attracted to dramatic signs of the Realm. Here Luke matter-of-factly reports that young women are prophesying in Caesarea. While the full restoration is yet to come, signs of the restoration are taking place without fanfare at Philip's house. Where can the congregation see similar signs occurring today?

Agabus follows the prophetic tradition of Israel by making use of a prophetic gesture in which the prophet acts out the message. Agabus takes Paul's belt and binds the missionary's hands and feet thereby representing Paul's upcoming captivity. The prophet interprets the gesture: it predicts some Jewish people binding Paul and handing Paul to gentiles (Acts 21:10-11). These events parallel what happened to Jesus: arrested by Jewish leaders and then crucified by Rome.

When Agabus's prophecy comes true, the reader's confidence is reinforced in the story that Luke tells in Acts and in its implications for Luke's own time. That Agabus's prophecy comes true encourages Luke's congregation to trust the prophets speaking in their own time. The preacher wants to encourage the congregation to attend to prophets today. Yet, the prophetic message can be verified only when it comes true, namely, in retrospect. The preacher might suggest that when prophets today speak in ways consistent with the values and practices of the Realm, the congregation can respond positively. When a prophecy goes against the grain of the Realm the community should consider it false.

Although some locals try to persuade Paul not to go to Jerusalem, Paul asserts that he is ready to be imprisoned and to die (Acts 21:12-13). Paul joins Jesus as a model witness to the Realm. If Paul could maintain this courage for witness when confronting death, surely congregations can do so when facing their lesser struggles.

The preacher might help the congregation imagine situations today in which the congregation could enact a prophetic gesture, that is, situations in which the congregation could act out a Realm message. Preachers might also consider acting out such gestures within their congregations.

CHIASTIC PARALLELS. LUKE 7:36-50 AND ACTS 21:7-16

The story of Jesus and the woman who anointed him in Luke 7:36-50 underlines the identity of Jesus as a prophet and the openness of the community of the Realm to people who are in situations like that of the woman. While Christians sometimes assume the woman was a prostitute, the text says only that she was a sinner and does not specify her sin. Jesus demonstrates he is a prophet by reading Simon's mind and by interpreting the woman's situation (Luke 7:39-47). A technical theological point is important. In Luke 7:38, Jesus does not say, "I forgive you." When Jesus says, "Your sins are forgiven," he uses a grammatical construction called the divine passive to imply that God is the one who forgives sin.

In Ptolemais, the prophet Agabus foresees Paul's death. Reading the main theme of Luke 7:36-50 into Acts 20:7-14, Luke's implication is that Paul is in the prophetic tradition of Jesus. Luke elsewhere reminds the reader that the prophets suffer (for example, Luke 11:47-50; 13:31-35 Acts 7:51-8:1). Paul's death, then, is not simply legalized murder but is proof that Paul continues the tradition of the prophets. Correlating Paul's suffering with prophetic witness is important to members of Luke's community who might regard Paul's death (like that of Jesus) as shameful. As we soon see, Paul is initially arrested on grounds related to the fact that he welcomes gentiles (sinners) into the community of the Realm (Acts 21:27-34).

This chiastic pair gives the preacher an opportunity to talk with the congregation about the Lukan meaning of the notion of prophet of the Realm. The preacher shares Luke's hope that the congregation will become a prophetic community, yet with prophetic ministry sometimes comes suffering. Such ministry includes creating space in the community for women such as the one who sinned in the Gospel passage and gentiles who were a focus in Paul's ministry.

You Will Be My Witnesses to the End of the Earth: Paul Is Falsely Arrested in Jerusalem (Acts 21:17—22:21)

Acts 21:17-36 describes the fulcrum event on which turns the rest of Paul's story in Acts : Paul's false arrest in the temple. This arrest and its consequences become the means by which Paul gets to see Rome (per Acts 19:21). James warns Paul of tensions awaiting him (Acts 21:17-26). The arrest itself incites a mob action (Acts 21:27-36) and brings Paul before a tribune who allows the missionary to make a defense (Acts 21:37-21).

Acts 21:17-26. James Prepares Paul for Arrest

After rejoicing at Paul's report of his ministry among the gentiles, James indicates that thousands of believers among the Jewish people are "zealous for the law:" they continue to practice Judaism while believing that Jesus is God's representative in bringing the Realm (Acts 21:17-20). However, they mistakenly believe the claim that Paul teaches Jewish people living among gentiles to abandon Jewish customs (Acts 21:21). The reader knows these charges are not true.

To avoid a confrontation, James recommends that Paul demonstrate his faithfulness to Judaism by joining a group people performing a Nazirite vow (see Num. 6:1-21). A Nazirite vow was an act in which Jewish people consecrated themselves to God, demonstrating their commitment through public acts such as cutting their hair. By so doing, Paul would symbolize his faithfulness to Torah (a point already established: Acts 16:3; 18:18; 20:16). As a special act of devotion, people who supported those taking the Nazirite vow often paid for the sacrifices of Nazirites. Luke interprets Paul paying for the shaving of the heads as declaring Paul's innocence (Acts 21:23-24). Paul purifies himself and only then enters the temple (Acts 21:26). Paul, following Torah, would never suggest that other Jewish people abandon Torah.

James reminds Paul (and the reader) of the letter from the Jerusalem council sent to Antioch (Acts 15:27-29). This letter asks gentiles to manifest core Jewish values and practices.

A message might struggle around the question of how to respond to false accusations. James proposes that Paul make an indirect response by demonstrating faithful behavior rather than confronting the charges directly. That strategy does not work for Paul (Acts 21:27-36). When might a more direct approach be useful?

This text brings to mind an issue not on Luke's mind but one with which many people struggle. When we know something that someone else does not know, when is it faithful to tell them, if at all?

CHIASTIC PARALLELS. LUKE 7:18-35 AND ACTS 21:17-26

Luke 7:18-35 climaxes with poetic images that compare Jesus (and other witness to the Realm) to children playing a flute to which no one danced, and to wailers to whom no one responded with mourning (Luke 7:32). The reference to the flute is from ancient celebrations (such as weddings) in which the playing calls forth dancing, while the reference to wailing is from professional mourners whose wailing announces a death and, hence, the time for mourning. Witnesses announce the Realm, but many people do not respond.

In Acts 21:17-26, Paul—the great flutist of the Realm, so to speak—has played. The community of Jewish and gentile believers is a sign of the Realm. But Paul's Jewish opponents have spread the lie that Paul teaches Jewish people to forsake Torah and Jewish identity. James proposes that Paul adhere to a public vow to demonstrate that he lives according to Torah. But instead of dancing when they hear this tune, Paul's opponents take mob action against him.

The preacher might ask, "Where is the flute playing today, that is, where is our congregation being invited to join Jesus and Paul in the movement to the Realm? Are we dancing?" If not, the preacher can help the congregation imagine why they would want to dance. The preacher might also ask, "Is our congregation playing the flute? Is our ministry inviting people into the Realm in the tradition of Paul?"

ACTS 22:27-36. PAUL IS ARRESTED ON FALSE CHARGES IN THE TEMPLE

When Paul's vow is almost complete, some Jewish people from Asia (western Turkey today) stir up a crowd to seize Paul with a dramatic charge: they claim that Paul teaches "everyone everywhere" against Torah, and has brought Greeks into the temple. Gentiles were welcome as far as the court of gentiles—the outermost court. The Asians had seen Paul with Trophimus (a gentile) and presumed that Paul had taken his companion deeper into the temple (Acts 21:27-29).

The crowd becomes a vigilante mob trying to kill Paul. (Acts 21:30). The preacher needs to critique the false charges and the mob actions as Luke's negative stereotype of many Jewish people.

When word of the crowd's violence reaches the tribune of the cohort, the Roman officer and some of his cohort (a unit of about six hundred soldiers) save Paul by arraigning Paul for questioning. The tribune wants Paul's version (Acts 21:32-36). Even after Paul is in custody, the soldiers must protect Paul as the crowd cries "Away with him!" The Roman soldiers and the Roman legal system behave in more Realm-like ways than the bloodthirsty Jewish mob who would violate their own ethics by putting an innocent person to death without a trial. Roman arrest is the means to salvation from the Jewish mob. Luke's polemic is on overtime here.

The preacher could ask the congregation to enter the story from the perspective of the crowd. The actions of the mob reveal their guilt since they violate foundational Jewish tenants. The mob's actions are especially reprehensible since they take place in the temple. If appropriate the preacher could point to ways that the congregation is like the mob: accusing others of being unfaithful when the congregation itself behaves in rogue fashion.

The preacher could ask the congregation to enter the story from the perspective of Paul. The preacher could name some false charges from outside against the community of the Realm in our time. In addition James indicates that concerns about Paul also come from Jewish folk who are within the community. The preacher could explore similar ways that Christians disagree—sometimes with hostility—over God's purposes today.

The preacher could reflect on contemporary analogies to the Roman presence providing safety and seeking justice for Paul. Can the preacher name individuals, groups, or forces who are as hostile to the Realm today as the Roman Empire was in antiquity, but who mind-bogglingly serve the purposes of the Realm?

CHIASTIC PARALLELS. LUKE 7:1-17 AND ACTS 21:27-36

Luke 7:1-10 is the healing of the slave of a centurion, a Roman officer in charge of 100 soldiers. Luke 7:11-17 is Jesus raising from the dead the male heir of a widow from Nain, a town near Nazareth. These stories demonstrate that Jesus is the prophet of the Realm restoring the brokenness of the old age a healing and a raising that benefit a gentile male and a Jewish woman.

In Acts Paul continues the work of Jesus in representing the Realm by performing miracles and by welcoming gentile people as well as women and men. Whereas the centurion, the widow and the crowd welcome the Realm in Luke 7:1-17, the Jewish leaders and the crowd in Acts 21:27-36 falsely arrest Paul in an attempt to end his witness. Whereas Jesus heals and raises the dead, the crowd beats Paul and tries to kill him. Whereas Jesus helped a centurion, a tribune helps Paul, even saving the missionary from death.

The preacher might ask when and where we experience signs of the Realm in our midst on the order of the ministries of Jesus and Paul? Do we respond as they do in Luke or in Acts? What motivates each response? How can the preacher encourage the congregation to be more like the crowd in the Gospel?

ACTS 22:37-22:21. PAUL MAKES A DEFENSE BEFORE THE MOB IN JERUSALEM

The Roman Empire was a highly stratified social system with people in the upper echelons accorded more respect and power than those in lower ranks. Paul plays on this structure by speaking to the tribune: Paul is a citizen of the impressive city of Tarsus, which had a reputation for being a place of culture and education. Paul appeals to his privileged social standing to win the tribune's favor. While the tribune is Paul's immediate savior, the tribune reveals his own theological and ethical parochialism by surmising that Paul was an Egyptian who organized four thousand assassins When told that Paul is Jewish the tribune gives Paul permission to address the crowd (Acts 27:37-40a).

Paul motions as a skilled orator and speaks in Hebrew, silencing the crowd as they hear their own language (Acts 21:40b; 22:2). We like to hear one of our own. Paul explains that he is making a defense (*apologia*), a rhetorical category that people in antiquity recognize in much the same way that an audience today knows something of what to expect when they read an editorial. Paul uses a narrative mode of defense telling the story of his life, call, and mission.

Paul's defense is the second of three narratives of Paul's call in Acts. Luke presents a motif three times to emphasize its importance. This was a defining story at the outset of the gentile mission (Acts 9:1-19). It recurs at Paul's arrest, and yet again when Paul is leaving on the final journey to Rome (Acts 26:12-23).

Paul invites identification by stressing his Jewish roots and his persecution of the Way (Acts 22:3-5). Paul explains the transformation from persecutor to preacher, emphasizing that the "God our ancestors" orchestrated this event to call Paul as a witness "to all of the world." (Acts 22:6-16). Since the Jewish people saw Paul's sincerity as a persecutor, they should recognize his sincerity as a preacher (Acts 22:17-20).

The point Luke wants to make: God called Paul as a missionary to gentiles (Acts 20:21). The reader recognizes two things. First: Paul echoes the call of Isaiah, thus placing Paul in the prophetic tradition. The other: Paul's mission to the gentiles takes place under the aegis of the Jerusalem council (Acts 15:27-29; cf. 21:25).

The church today must sometimes defend the values of the Realm. The preacher could use Paul's narrative mode of defense as a model for doing so, or for helping the congregation understand how the preacher has come to a particular position. Instead of presenting logical arguments, the preacher might sketch the background of the issue, trace how the congregation or preacher interacted with issue, name resources that help us think about the issue, unfold the resolution and its effects. This approach could be especially useful in connection with controversial subjects. Instead of confronting the issue directly (and risking immediate polarization in the congregation), the preacher invites identification and exploration.

When helping the congregation think about sensitive issues, the preacher might also invite people from the congregation to share their own experiences around the issue in the way Paul does. The sermon might include testimonies (either live or on DVD). If such a presentation would not be at home in the congregation the preacher might consider what kinds of communication events could function in our setting similarly to the apology in the world of Luke.

Paul is clear about his mission. If the congregation is unclear about its mission, the preacher could use this text to help the congregation think about that matter.

Chiastic Parallels. Luke 6:37-49 and Acts 21:37-22:21

Luke 6:37-49 is part of the call the Sermon on the Level Place (Luke 6:17). Jesus urges disciples not to condemn (Luke 6:37-38) but to take the logs out of their eyes (Luke 6:39-42). A good tree will bear good fruit, whereas a bad tree does not (Luke 6:43-45). The house built on a foundation of rock will stand, as do people who hear Jesus's words and act on them (that is, who embrace the witness to the Realm). The house built without a foundation will fall, as will people who hear Jesus's words and do not act on them.

Acts 21:37-22:21 depicts a scene in which Jewish leaders from Asia had judged Paul falsely and condemned him. The crowd illustrates those who have logs in their eyes, who are bad fruit, and who build houses without foundations. By the time of Luke, the Romans had destroyed the temple, illustrating the truth of Jesus's teaching. Paul's defense is Luke's way of encouraging readers to remove the logs from their eyes, to be good fruit, and to lay a foundation on rock by embracing the Realm, especially the gentile mission.

Paul's witness to the Realm—represented by his defense—gives specific content to what it means to judge, to have a log in one's eye, to be bad fruit, and to lay the foundation of the house on rock. When are we tempted to condemn manifestations of the Realm? When do have a log in our eye such that we fail to see the Realm? When are we bad fruit rejecting the Realm? When are we inclined to build our houses without foundations by avoiding the repentance and other hard choices required by the Realm?

You Will Be My Witnesses to the Ends of the Earth: Paul Invokes Roman Citizenship and Makes a Defense in Jerusalem (Acts 22:22—23:35)

The tribune orders Paul to be flogged to persuade the missionary to reveal the reason for the outcry against him when Paul reveals he is a Roman citizen (Acts 22:22-29). This revelation prompts a hearing before the council in which dissension breaks out, and the Pharisees find nothing wrong (Acts 22:30-23:11). When some Jewish people plot to kill Paul (Acts 23:12-22), the tribune again saves Paul's life sending Paul to Felix in Caesarea (Acts 23:23-35).

In Acts 21:17-22:20 and 22:22-23:35, we are reminded of the importance of respecting the complexity of individuals and groups in the dynamics of Paul's situation. We cannot speak simply of "the Jews" (even if Luke occasionally does) or "the Romans" but must recognize that some Jewish people opposed

Paul while others supported. While the Empire eventually murders Paul, some Romans, and the Roman legal system, provide safe passage. Many gentiles welcome the Realm but some do not. In a season in the United States in which individuals and groups increasingly caricature one another, this complexity in Acts reminds the preacher always to honor particularity.

ACTS 22:22-29. PAUL REVEALS TO THE TRIBUNE THAT HE IS A ROMAN CITIZEN

A crowd in antiquity was expected to listen to the whole of a defense before rendering judgment. The crowd in Acts 22:3-21 is rude when they listen only to a certain point when they renew their cries to kill him (Acts 22:23). The tribune again seeks to take Paul into the barracks to flog the missionary to get Paul to give his version of what happened (Acts 22:24). This brutal practice was legal: officials had the authority to torture non-citizens to get information from them.

Paul is tied with thongs. The flogging is about to begin when Paul makes a statement to the centurion (an officer over one hundred soldiers) that changes the rest of his life: "Is it legal for you to flog a Roman citizen who is uncondemned?"

Paul's Roman citizenship, introduced in Acts 16:37-38, plays a more formative role in the next chapters of Paul's life. The term "citizen" was much more restricted than today (when almost everyone living in a nation, state, or municipality is a citizen). In antiquity, citizen was a distinct class, usually from the upper social echelons, with rights not available to ordinary residents. While cities granted citizenship (Paul was a citizen of Tarsus, Acts 21:39), Roman citizenship was the most valued and was conferred by Rome on people who served the Empire. Once granted, citizenship passed from generation to generation, through it could also be purchased. Inherited citizenship was often more respected than purchased citizenship, much like old money often has more social cache than new money in North America. Citizens had distinct legal rights pertinent to Paul. A citizen could not be punished without a formal trial. A citizen had the right to appeal to Caesar, that is, to be heard by the imperial court (Acts 25:10-12). Citizenship was so serious that Rome punished officials (and even whole populations) when the rights of citizens were abused. The emperor Claudius (10 BCE-54 CE) deprived Rhoads of independence when Roman citizens were unjustly executed there.

When Paul reveals he is a Roman citizen, the centurion immediately recognizes both he and the tribune could be punished for flogging a citizen, and goes to the tribune (Acts 22:27). In a reversal of roles, Paul's inherited citizenship has a higher social standing than the tribune's purchased citizenship. Paul, as bound citizen about to be flogged, controls the destiny of the tribune.

The preacher could use Paul's citizenship to start a conversation about social status in Christian community. When I was a child in Bible school, our teachers often spoke about Paul's Roman citizenship with a measure of wonder. To our middle class congregation, Paul's Roman citizenship represented the presence and approval of an upper class. By contrast, Luke envisions the community of the Realm as socially and economically diverse; social distinctions give way to the common purpose of witnessing to a new world which does not have such social segregation. Yet churches today often look upon the upper social standing of members in ways that reinforce the social segregation of the old age.

Luke presents Paul's citizenship as the means whereby the sovereign God uses Rome to protect Paul from the mob and to facilitate Paul reaching Rome. However, the Realm assumes that all people should have access to such justice.

Citizenship was awarded for serving the interests of the Empire. While Paul's citizenship was inherited, that citizenship meant that he benefitted from the idolatry, injustice, exploitation, and violence of the Empire. Is it legitimate for a witness to the Realm to benefit from oppression, even when the ultimate purpose of the witness is to stand for the Realm? Should Paul have directly protested the Roman Empire? Should Paul have attempted to resign his citizenship?

Torture as a means of investigation is not at the heart of this text. Nevertheless, the presence of binding and flogging here means brings to mind facts the preacher cannot ignore. (1) Torture is practiced today, including by the United States. (2) Torture is contrary to the Realm of God.

Chiastic Parallels. Luke 6:20-36 and Acts 22:22-29

Luke 6:20-36 begins the Sermon on the Level Place (Luke 6:17) with blessings on the poor, hungry, weeping, and those persecuted because of their witness to the Realm (Luke 6:20-23) as is Paul in Acts 22:22-29. Jesus pronounces woe (eschatological condemnation) over the rich, the full, the laughing, and those of whom others speak well from the perspective of old age values. The disciples are to love their enemies (Luke 6:27-31). Why? Because if you love those who love you, that is no credit to you. Even sinners do that. Jesus's disciples are to be merciful even as God is merciful (Luke 6:32-36).

The reader aware of this chiastic parallel sees Paul in the position of Luke 6:22: persecuted, hated, excluded, and reviled. The mob is in a position similar to that of those over whom Jesus spoke the woes in Luke 6:24-26. The tribune initially thinks Paul may be an enemy: the Egyptian who led four thousand assassins (Acts 21:38). By halting the flogging, the tribune does not come off as a full-fledged representative of the Realm, but, the tribune does good to Paul even if to save himself from being punished for flogging a citizen. Roman law is merciful toward the citizen by sparing flogging even if such mercy does not flow to non-citizens.

A preacher might examine the degree to which the church that hears the Sermon on the Level Place is like the mob: acting in ways that violate the Realm. The preacher could look outside the church to determine whether individuals, groups, and forces in our world are like the tribune: implicated in idolatry and empire but enacting (even if grudgingly) values and practices resonant with the Realm. Indeed, can the preacher point to modern day tribunes who are more faithful than some Christians? What motivates them?

ACTS 22:30-23:11. PAUL AND DISSENSION WITHIN THE COUNCIL

The tribune, wanting to know the charges against Paul, ordered the Jewish council to convene like a grand jury. Instead, Luke paints the council as inept, divided, and in violation of its own principles. In Acts 23:12-15, the chief priests and elders cooperate with the forty people who want to murder Paul.

Paul states that he has lived with a clear conscience, that is, whether as persecutor or preacher he was faithful to God's purpose as he understood that purpose at the time. He did not violate his own integrity (Acts 23:1). The high priest immediately orders those standing nearby to strike Paul, evidently rejecting Paul's claim. Paul responds by drawing on Ezekiel 13:10-16 in which people build a weak wall then cover it with whitewash to conceal the faulty construction. A deluge causes the wall to fall, exposing the poor construction. So it is with false prophets, says Ezekiel, and so it is with the council, implies Paul who accuses the high priest of violating the law by assuming that Paul is guilty before hearing any witnesses (Acts 23:2-3).

Bystanders accuse Paul of insulting the high priest only to have Paul respond that he did not realize he was speaking to the high priest (Acts 23:4-5). While the council has gone against its Jewish principles by accusing Paul without witnesses, Paul proves himself more Jewish than the crowd by quoting Exodus 22:28: he would not knowingly violate Jewish precedent.

In a clever rhetorical move, Paul notices both Pharisees and Sadducees in the council and identifies himself as a Pharisee on trial because of the resurrection. Dissension breaks out between the Pharisees and the Sadducees over the issue of the resurrection since Sadducees did not accept end-time theology and the resurrection of the dead (Acts 23:6-9).

The Pharisees declare that they find nothing wrong with Paul; indeed, Paul may have received a message from an angel or a spirit. This is the last direct reference to the Pharisees in Acts, and it leaves a positive impression of Pharisees, thus supporting the idea articulated earlier that Luke's relatively favorable picture of the Pharisees in Acts suggests that Luke seeks a level of rapprochement with the Pharisees of his own day (Acts 23:9).

The dissension becomes so violent that the tribune fears the Jewish crowd will tear Paul to pieces. The tribune again saves Paul by sequestering the missionary. This scene concludes with Luke's editorial comment that the risen Jesus stood near Paul that night, encouraging Paul to be courageous, and indicating that Paul would bear witness in Rome (Acts 23:10-11).

A sermon on this passage must bring Luke's polemical intent to the awareness of the congregation so the congregation will not walk away from the passage thinking that it represented an accurate picture of the council. As I have said repeatedly, to let such a picture stand without comment is passively to reinforce anti-Judaism and even anti-Semitism.

Paul's indictment of the council as a whitewashed wall flaunting its own principles could become a lens though which to look at the church. To what degree is the church nicely painted on the outside but poorly constructed on the inside? To what degree is the church a false prophet? Can the preacher point to groups outside the congregation who better exemplify the values and practices of the Realm than do many Christians and the church as community?

The figure of the high priest, assuming that Paul is guilty without hearing witnesses, may suggest a sermon. Christians sometimes assume the worst about individuals and groups without taking the time to investigate. Indeed, one of the most serious problems facing the United States today is the breakdown of critical thinking. Many people have opinions but cannot articulate respectable reasons for their opinions. Public discourse often consists of slapping the face of our opponent but with no real interaction of ideas. The preacher could use this text as a warning against such behavior and as a call to more critical thinking, and to genuine conversation.

The behavior of the Pharisees defending Paul suggests an intriguing approach to a sermon. Judaism today is descended from the Pharisees. The preacher could help the congregation remember occasions when Jewish leaders and communities, despite the millennia of anti-Judaism and anti-Semitism perpetrated by the church, have stood with the church, or have even spoken a good word in behalf of the church. Such an approach could help the church develop attitudes of solidarity with Judaism.

CHIASTIC PARALLELS. LUKE 6:12-19 AND ACTS 22:30-23:11

In Luke 6:12-19, Jesus chooses the twelve apostles, and teaches and heals as he prepares to begin the sermon on the level place. For Luke, the apostles are to help Jesus's followers maintain their identity as a community and their witness to the Realm. Paul is a leader under the aegis of this body. The council in Acts 22:30-23:11 is supposed to perform a function in Judaism similar to that of the apostles in the community of the Realm. However, the council becomes a hubbub of dissension wanting to tear Paul apart, all in violation of Jewish legal procedure. The forty would-be murders of Paul are under the aegis of this body.

This chiastic parallel focuses on institutions of leadership. Luke's purpose is for the reader to contrast the leadership of the council with that of the apostles (the body authorizing Paul's mission). Luke wants to discourage trust in the council and its heirs, and to encourage trust in leadership in the tradition that Paul represents. This suggests a twofold purpose for the sermon. One is to help the congregation identity institutions of leadership in the church that share the qualities of the council and of the apostles. The other purpose is to help listeners ponder the degree to which the congregation as an institution of leadership in the wider world is more like the council or more like the apostolic tradition with its witness to the Realm.

ACTS 23:12-15. THE PLOT TO KILL PAUL

The next day, more than forty Jewish people join in a conspiracy to kill Paul. They are so determined that they bind themselves with an oath, and they fast (neither eating nor drinking) until they kill Paul. Israel took such oaths when it vowed to destroy God's enemies (for example, Num. 21:2-3). The conspirators believe that Paul is God's enemy. Even worse, chief priests and elders join with them in a deception. The leaders and the council ask the tribune to "bring [Paul] down to you on the pretext that you want to make a more thorough examination." The conspirators will kill Paul on the way.

Luke thus completely erodes the credibility of the high priests, the elders, and the council by portraying them as conspirators, liars, and murderers. As commented above, such qualities dishonor the spirit of Judaism. However,

Luke seems not to notice that shaping the story in this distorted way is itself a violation of Judaism. By misrepresenting Jewish people Luke bears false witness.

Many Christians today are disturbed by the plot against Paul. The preacher can help the congregation recognize that this behavior is not a thing of the past. In some parts of the world, Christian and Jewish communities are targeted for harassment and death. Within the church, plans for actual murder are rare, but Christians sometimes plot against one another (and against others) in ways that violate the values and practices of the Realm.

Beyond the church, many governments today, including the United States, engage in similar behavior by targeting individuals or groups for death. Baptized Christians sometimes lead such plots. The preacher could lead the congregation in reflecting on the appropriateness of such actions even in the name of national security.

CHIASTIC PARALLELS. LUKE 6:1-11 AND ACTS 23:12-15

Luke 6:1-11 consists of two controversy stories reinforcing Luke's negative caricature of Jewish leadership—the question of whether Jesus and his disciples were working on the sabbath (Luke 6:1-5) and the question of whether it is lawful to heal on the sabbath (Luke 6:6-11). From Luke's perspective, the Jewish leaders in these stories do not understand their own tradition.

The same thing is true in Acts 23:12-15. Forty Jewish vigilantes conspire with the chief priests and elders to murder Paul. They do not understand that their own tradition insists on formal legal procedure and prohibits wanton murder.

The pervasive negative attitude toward Jewish people in this chiastic set give the preacher another opportunity to devote a entire sermon to deconstructing Luke's negative evaluation of many Jewish leaders and, people. Luke may have intended to warn the church against such folk, but the preacher needs to warn the church against Luke's unfair characterizations and the damage they continue to cause.

ACTS 23:16-23. THE TRIBUNE PARTNERS WITH PAUL TO PLAN THE RESCUE

Paul has a sister whose heir learns about the conspiracy to kill Paul and reports the plot to Paul who asks a centurion to take the younger person to the tribune with this news (Acts 23:16-18). In the nephew and the centurion, we see the value of go-betweens, people who are not primary decision makers but whose ministry brings people together in ways that lead to major decisions. How can the sermon support such go-betweeners in the congregation? Can the congregation itself become such a messenger in the larger world?

The tribune interviews the nephew privately. The nephew divulges the plot. The tribune orders the nephew to silence (Acts 23:19-23). This detail raises questions about an issue that nags some ministers and congregations: confidentiality. In today's church, some types of confidentiality are given. But where does the congregation (and other bodies in public life) draw the line with information that should be known by all.

Groups today often speak of "partnering" with one another to do more than one group could by itself. The agreement between Paul and the tribune, is not a pure example of partnering but it does point in that direction. The homily might consider partnerships today in which the church could engage to magnify the witness to the Realm. Particularly noteworthy: the partnership between the tribune and Paul brings together people from two different spheres of life. Indeed, the values of their sponsoring bodies—the Roman Empire and the community of the Realm—contradict one another at points. But Paul cooperates with the tribune and the larger Roman system in the rescue that allows Paul's testimony to continue.

The preacher could build on the help for Paul that comes from a source who has not previously appeared in Acts—Paul's nephew. While Luke did not have such an application in mind, the minister might encourage the congregation to look within itself for persons, groups, or connections that it has not previously recognized as providing leadership.

Chiastic Parallels. Luke 5:27-39 and Acts 23:16-22

Luke 5:27-39 is the call of Levi the tax collector (an agent of the Empire) to follow Jesus, subsequent complaining by the Pharisees and scribes that Jesus associates with people who are such threats, and Jesus's response that leads to the affirmation that new wine should go into fresh wineskins. The Realm creates a new community in which tax collectors who repent are included in the new wine, that is, in the community of the Realm. The Realm is not a patch on the old world but a new world.

Acts 23:16-22 include an analogue to Levi, as well as new and old wine. The tribune (like Levi, an agent of the Roman Empire) does not repent, but, like Levi, he serves the Realm. Those conspiring to murder Paul are old wineskins. Putting the fresh wine of the witness to the Realm into the context of the old wineskin has most caused the wineskin to burst: Jewish people are now conspiring to commit murder.

While recognizing contentious shadow in which Luke paints the Pharisees, scribes, and conspirators, the preacher needs to help the congregation recognize the presence of the Realm, and to assess whether they are an old wineskin or a new one. Is the church ready to expand as the members receive the fresh wine of the Realm, such as Levi and Paul's witness to the reunion of people of different ethnic backgrounds? Or is the congregation already at the limits of its present ability to receive? If receiving further new wine is a threat, perhaps the preacher could help the congregation imagine how to become a new wineskin.

ACTS 23:23-35. ROMAN LEGAL CUSTOM FACILITATES PAUL'S SURVIVAL

The tribune facilitates Paul's survival by sending the missionary to Caesarea where Felix, the governor, can question Paul in a safe environment. There are forty murders. The tribune assembles a travel party for Paul of four hundred seventy foot soldiers, riders, and soldiers equipped with spears (Acts 23:23-25). By assembling such an entourage, the tribune insures that the Roman citizen will be safe. The reader, of course, contrasts the hostile behavior of the Jewish assassins with the protection afforded by Rome.

We now learn the tribune's name: Claudias Lysias, who follows the form of the typical Greek letter in his communication to Felix in Acts 23:26-30. The letter summarizes the circumstances that brought Paul to his attention, his attempt to ascertain the charges against Paul, and his determination that the charges pertained to Torah and not to Roman law. The tribune sends Paul to Felix, and also orders the accusers to appear there, so the governor can sort out the charges.

Claudias Lysias revises his telling of the story of what did to cast himself in a positive light (and to avoid punishment for mistreating a citizen). Revising events to promote our own interests was no stranger then or now, even in the church.

The soldiers transport Paul to Caesarea. Ironically, Felix lodges Paul in Herod's quarters. The house that sheltered the killer of John the Baptist and James now shelters a representative of the Realm. Herod was killed by his own unfaithfulness. Paul is saved from being killed so he can witness to Rome, the death-dealing power that Herod served. What can the church do to help buildings, neighborhoods, and communities that have sheltered death become shelters for life?

The tribune and Felix want to make sure Paul is in a safe place. The preacher might help the church ask what we can do to help people who are in threatening situations find safe places. The preacher needs to consider the degree to which the church is a safe place.

The tribune has confidence that official channels—represented by the legal system–will protect Paul and will be fair. The sermon could instigate a dialogue on what to do when we no longer have confidence in official channels, including the legal system. Official channels sometimes quash the values and practices of the Realm. Indeed, imprisonment puts inmates in danger.

CHIASTIC PARALLELS. LUKE 5:12-26 AND ACTS 23:23-35

Luke 5:12-26 tells the stories of the cleansing of a person with leprosy (Luke 5:12-16) and of the healing of a person who was paralyzed, setting off a conflict over whether Jesus forgives sin (Luke 5:27-26). In each case God acts providentially to manifest the Realm. God heals the leprosy. God ends the paralysis, and forgives sin.

In Acts 23:23-35, Paul is in the presence of threat (the plot to murder him) but God acts providentially to continue Paul's witness to the Realm when the tribune sends Paul to Felix in Caesarea. To protect Paul from the murderers, the tribune secures Paul within a traveling group of two hundred soldiers, seventy riders, and two hundred warriors with spears.

A homily might consider how we are threatened, and how God's providence works for us. The range of threats in the texts opens several windows through which the congregation could enter the sermon—leprosy, paralysis, and threat from other people. In Luke 5:12-26, God acts through Jesus and in Acts 23:23-35 God acts through the tribune and soldiers. Through what agencies is God working today? How can we cooperate? The preacher might also help the congregation think about how they can become an instrument of providence.

YOU WILL BE MY WITNESSES TO THE ENDS OF THE EARTH: PAUL MAKES A DEFENSE BEFORE FELIX IN CAESAREA (ACTS 24:1-27)

Paul is now in Caesarea awaiting a hearing before Felix who ruled during social unrest, including frequent political intrigue and the emergence of the *sicarii*, people who used short swords (Latin: *sicae*) to assassinate victims in crowds. Felix employed violence trying to keep the peace. For Paul to be associated with mob violence when coming to Felix is a serious matter. While Felix seeks to conduct a fair hearing, the unhappy history associated with Felix is on the edge of the reader's consciousness. This behavior, while not violent, is consistent with the popular picture of Felix as a leader associated with social tension (Acts 25:22-27). Tertullus brings charges against Paul (Acts 24:2b-9). Paul makes a defense (Acts 24:10-21). Felix holds Paul in custody for two years before Felix is replaced as governor (Acts 24:22-27).

ACTS 24:1-10. AN ATTORNEY BRINGS CHARGES AGAINST PAUL

Felix adheres to the principle of waiting until all parties in the dispute arrive before beginning the hearing (Acts 24:1-2a). In Acts 24:2b-8, Tertullus articulates charges against Paul. The attorney begins as orators often did by praising the audience in the hope of disposing Felix favorably (Acts 24:2b-4). Even allowing for the hyperbole to which rhetoricians sometimes rose in Luke's time, Tertullus's description of Felix stretches credibility in view of the reputation of Felix set out above: peace, reforms, foresight, a leader welcomed in every way. Young people today would call Tertullus a "suck up." A preacher could delve into ways people in our settings—including the church—inflate our representations of other people to serve our own purposes.

Describing Paul's behavior as "pestilent" from the time of Paul's entry into the temple (twelve days ago) to the present, the attorney claims hyperbolically that Paul was "an agitator among all the Jews throughout the world," and that Paul was a "ringleader" in the "sect of the Nazarenes." Moreover, Tertullus states that Paul profaned the temple, which was why Jewish leadership seized him (Acts 24:5-8). Tertullus's use of "Nazarenes," the only one in the Gospels and Letters, may be a slur.

While "the Jews" asserted that Tertullus told the truth, the reader recognizes immediately they lie (Acts 24:9). In a formal court of law, Jewish authorities have again betrayed their own legal tradition. Furthermore Tertullus intimates that Paul may be a source of the social chaos that disturbs the reign of Felix when, in fact, Paul preaches a Realm that will bring about absence of violence and the presence of supportive community.

This speech is yet another instance when the preacher must blow the whistle on the foul on the truth committed by Luke's propensity to demonize Jewish people. At the same time, the preacher can use Tertullus's speech as a pattern to lay over leaders and situations today to look for points at which our patterns of behavior follow that of Tertullus's: making public and private statements that misrepresent other people to suit our own convenience.

Chiastic Parallels. Luke 5:1-11 and Acts 24:1-9

In Luke 5:1-11, Jesus calls the first disciples to follow him to learn to witness to the Realm. A key part of the call is Jesus's instructions to "Put out into the deep water." The reference to the deep (*bathos*) recalls the primeval chaos of Genesis 1:1-2. Jesus tells the disciples to put down their nets into the chaos, from which comes an abundant catch.

In Acts 24:1-9, the behavior of the Jewish leaders creates chaos for Paul. Often, when Paul puts down his net into social chaos (that is, when he makes his witness), God brings forth a haul for the Realm. When the Jewish leaders put down their net (that is, when they give testimony about Paul), they intensify chaos.

The preacher could take Luke 5:1-11 as a call to regard the chaos of the world as the lake into which do drop our nets. The preacher can help the congregation recognize forms that chaos takes today. The materials in chaos are not evil in and of themselves. In Genesis 1:1-2, the primeval sea was a body of incredible energy, but the energy was unfocused and destructive. God in creation focuses the energy into energy that creates community. Jewish writers in antiquity sometimes describe gentile existence as chaos. The church offers the gentile world the re-creative power of the Realm. The alternative is to become like Tertullus and his companions: people who increase chaos in the world.

Acts 24:10-21. Paul Makes a Defense

Paul's defense is his own version of the events that took place in Jerusalem (Acts 22:22-23:35). Paul begins by acknowledging that Felix has been judge over the nation for many years (Acts 24:10-11). Paul is emphatic that he (Paul) did not dispute with anyone in the temple, nor did Paul stir up the crowd in the synagogue or the city (Acts 24:12-13). The missionary confirms he is a member of the Way. Paul makes a confession of faith: Paul worships "the God of our ancestors" (thereby playing on the respect that people in antiquity showed for historic things) and believes everything in the law and the prophets (the Jewish scriptures at that time) (Acts 24:14). Paul is the picture of the practicing Jewish person.

In Acts 24:15, Paul brings to the fore a something he shares with the Jewish prosecutors: belief in the resurrection of both the righteous and the unrighteous. This language is from end-time theology and presumes an apocalypse at which time all people—past and present—will be judged. Those deemed righteous join God in the Realm while those judged unrighteous are punished. The distinctive belief of the church—in comparison to other Jewish communities of the period—is that this age has begun through the ministry of Jesus and will climax with his second coming. Paul assumes that the other Jewish people present are still awaiting the end-time. Paul implies that Felix, the high priest, elders, Tertullus, and "the Jews" must give an account to God at the judgment.

Paul portrays himself as practicing key elements of Judaism—living in covenant with God and other people (Acts 25:16) and bringing the offering he collected in the Diaspora to the church in Jerusalem (Acts 25:17). Furthermore, Jewish people in the temple witnessed Paul completing the rite of purification in peace (Acts 25:18). As his defense climaxes, Paul reiterates that he is innocent. The only thing of which Paul is guilty is calling out, in a previous hearing, that he was on trial because he believes in the resurrection of the dead (Acts 24:19-21). Believing in the resurrection of the dead—and end-time theology—is not a crime. If it were, Tertullus and his companions would be guilty.

Unlike Tertullus, Paul tells the truth. Nevertheless, telling the truth does not solve Paul's problems. A preacher might look at the question of where we get the strength, especially when we are under pressure, to tell the truth. And what do we do when the truth has even less effect than it did when Paul spoke before Felix?

When evaluating the charges of Tertullus and the defense of Paul, the reader has the advantage of knowing the entire story from the perspective of the narrator. The reader recognizes falsehood in Tertullus and truth in Paul. But, the preacher might want to wrestle with the congregation over what to do in situations today when the congregation does not have the advantage of a narrator's point of view, when the congregation is in the middle of a conflicted situation, and the congregation has no independent way of adjudicating truth.

CHIASTIC PARALLELS. LUKE 4:38-44 AND ACTS 24:10-21

In Luke 4:14-31, Jesus begins ministry in the synagogue at Nazareth by announcing that the final manifestation of Realm is beginning in his preaching and healing, and in the mission to the gentiles. The exorcism of the person with the unclean spirit verifies the truth of Jesus's claims (Luke 4:31-37). In Luke 4:38-41, Jesus heals Simon's mother-in-law and other people. Several demons recognize power in Jesus (v. 41). In Luke 4:42, the crowds who have been with Jesus in the area around Nazareth and Capernaum want Jesus to stay, but God has made it clear to Jesus ("I *must* proclaim . . .") that the time has come for the witness to the Realm to expand to other cities. *God* leads the witness to the Realm.

In Acts 24:10-21, the tone of the group is different from the crowd in Luke 4:38-44 but one aspect of their purposes is the same: the group in Acts wants Paul to stay. However, the crowd wants Felix to *prevent* Paul from witnessing. Paul explains that he is not guilty of the crime with which Tertullus charges him. Against the background of Luke 4:42-44, we realize again that Paul, like Jesus, will go forward to witness because God guides.

The preacher might lead the congregation to recollect how, like the crowd with Jesus, we want to remain where we are in size, in program, in outreach, in organization, in liturgy, in theological and ethical vision. Indeed, the preacher might help the congregation recollect how, they, like Tertullus and his companions, resist the witness to the Realm. Yet, the preacher could remind the congregation that God is with us as God was with Jesus and Paul, enlarging our vision of the realm and empowering us to press ahead even when confronted by hostility.

ACTS 24:22-27. PAUL IN CUSTODY FOR TWO YEARS

Luke presents Felix as knowledgeable about the Way but not sufficiently informed. To Felix's credit, he evidently wants evidence from Claudias Lysias independently from both Tertullus and Paul. To Felix's credit while he follows the customary Roman procedure of confining the witness (Paul), the governor gives Paul a lot of freedom of movement (Acts 24:22-23).

After a few days, Felix and his spouse, Drusilla, who is Jewish, listen to Paul speak "concerning faith in Jesus Christ." In view of Luke's end-time theology, "faith in Jesus Christ" refers not simply to believing certain things about Jesus but also to believing that Jesus is God's representative in the apocalyptic transformation of the ages. This larger way of thinking is implied in Acts 24:25 when Felix is frightened when Paul speaks about justice and self-control as preparation for the coming apocalyptic judgment. Felix knows about the Realm, but not enough. While Luke does not specify why Felix became frightened, we could imagine that Felix was enervated at the prospect of the Roman Empire (and his social world) disappearing and of Felix himself being judged at the apocalyptic tribunal.

While Felix may have been frightened at the prospect of judgment, the anxiety was not enough to repress his old age inclination. In Acts 25:26, Felix hopes Paul will bribe him. Felix's old age character is revealed further when he keeps Paul in custody for two years as a favor to the Jewish leaders (Acts 25:27).

While Luke's judgment on Felix is not as harsh as his judgment on the Jewish leaders, Felix is hardly a model of virtue. The legal system of the Roman

Empire saves Paul's life, but the Roman in charge, Felix, is trapped in old age perspectives.

The preacher could use the figure of Felix as template for interpreting leaders today—leaders aware of possibilities in the direction of the Realm, but finally afraid to act on those possibilities. The prospects of justice, self-control, and the resurrection of the dead prompt Felix to say to Paul, "Go away for the present." The preacher can point to modern day Felixes—leaders of nations, states, municipalities, institutions, corporations, and other groups who fear the risk of the Realm. Felix is more comfortable in the world that he knows, even with its conniving and violence, to the unknown of the Realm.

Preachers may lay this template over the congregation. When are we in the church more like Felix than Paul? Felix keeps the threat of the Realm represented by Paul at bay by keeping Paul in custody. How do we avoid the unsettling possibilities of the Realm by keeping them at bay?

Chiastic Parallels. Luke 4:31-41 and Acts 24:22-27

In Luke 4:31-37, Jesus confronts a person with an unclean spirit. The demon recognizes something of who Jesus is and is afraid that Jesus has come to destroy them. Jesus casts the demon out, the crowd responds with awe, wanting to know the source of Jesus's power. The report about Jesus begins to spread.

Like the demon knowing something about Jesus in Luke 4:31-37, Felix knows something about the Way, (Acts 24:24). However, when Felix hears Paul discuss the coming of the Realm (and its call for self-control and justice, as well as the coming judgment), Felix becomes frightened, as the demon did in Luke 4:31-36. The text of Acts 24:22-27 does not say that Felix has a demon, yet the chiastic pair prompts the reader to recognize similarities of behavior between the demon and Felix.

The preacher could compare Luke and Acts in this chiastic set. In Luke, Jesus sends the demon away. In Acts, Felix sends Jesus away (to custody). Jesus releases people from captivity. Felix puts Paul into captivity. In so doing, Felix demonstrates he himself is captive to his fear of the Realm.

You Will Be My Witnesses to the Ends of the Earth: Paul Makes a Defense before Festus, Bernice, and Agrippa (Acts 25:1—26:32)

The story takes a dramatic turn in Acts 25:1-12 when Paul as Roman citizen presses his right to have his case heard by the emperor. Before Festus can send

Paul to Rome, Agrippa II and his sister Bernice (great grandson and great granddaughter of Herod the Great) come from Jerusalem to welcome Festus. Agrippa wants to hear Paul (Acts 26:13-27). While Agrippa had sympathies for the Jewish population, his final loyalty was to Rome. After hearing Paul's defense (Acts 26:1-23), Agrippa—like Pilate at the trial of Jesus—concludes that Paul is innocent. However, according to Luke, Paul's appeal to the emperor could not be reversed (Acts 26:24-32).

ACTS 25:1-12. PAUL APPEALS TO THE EMPEROR

Festus has taken office and Paul is imprisoned in Caesarea. Festus goes from his headquarters in Caesarea to Jerusalem where the chief priests and other Jewish leaders report their negative perception of Paul, and request that Festus transfer Paul to Jerusalem for trial. They want to go through with the plot to murder Paul (see Acts 23:12-22). However, in a move that continues Roman protection for Paul, Festus announces that Paul is housed in Caesarea and invites pertinent Jewish witnesses to the hearing there (Acts 25:1-5).

In Caesarea, the Jewish leaders bring false charges against Paul who replies that he has not committed offense against Torah, the temple, or the emperor (Acts 25:6-8). Festus, however, seeks to do a favor for the Jewish leaders, and asks Paul if the witness would like to be tried in Jerusalem (Acts 25:9).

Paul appeals to the tribunal of the emperor to hear his case (Acts 25:10-12). As a Roman citizen, Paul had a right for his case to be heard by the emperor. Scholars generally agree that Luke's picture of the right to appeal to Caesar in Acts is within the range of Roman practices, though scholars debate whether Paul's case is more properly *appellatio* or *provocatio*. In Roman law, *appellatio* took place after a lower court had reached a verdict and the defendant sought to appeal the verdict. *Provocatio* came into play before a verdict had been rendered but when a defendant sought a change of venue. It appears that Paul exercises *provocatio* to request a change in venue from Caesarea to Rome. Officials such as Festus may have had more authority than is presumed in Acts 26 to consider whether to forward to Rome cases in which appeal had been made.

When interpreting Acts for preaching, the question of the legal umbrella Luke presumes is secondary to the function of the appeal in the narrative of Acts. Preachers sometimes say that Paul appealed to the emperor because he feared that he could not get a fair trial because of the favoritism that Felix and Festus show to Jewish leadership. Yet, Paul is not afraid to die (Acts 21:13l 25:11). The primary concern is not Paul's fear but the fact that witness to the Realm has not reached Rome: Paul's goal (for example, Acts 19:21; 23:11).

The appeal ensures that the Jewish plot against Paul will not succeed, thus demonstrating to Luke's congregation that God has the power to work through adverse circumstances.

Paul's appeal climaxes a theme winding through Acts: God uses some Romans and aspects of the Roman system to accomplish God's purposes. The preacher might explore how God might be at work through empires today in ways similar to appeal to the emperor.

The preacher might take a clue from a rabbinic theological method Luke employs elsewhere: an argument from lesser to greater (Luke 11:5-8; 18:1-8). If God can use the idolatrous, unjust, exploitative, violent Roman Empire to serve God's purposes, how much more can God use communities that intentionally seek to serve God's aims? The preacher could lead the congregation to reflect on how it could become less like Rome and more available to God.

Luke pictures the legal practices in both Judaism and the Empire as old age, though the Roman Empire does protect Paul as he achieves the goal of Acts 1:8. The preacher might point to instances when the church has not been as helpful to God as the Roman Empire; for example, the church was instrumental in putting Jewish people to death in the inquisition. The preacher should also remind the church that Roman justice is flawed. The standard for the church is the Realm.

Paul's appeal was not successful: Rome executed Paul. Paul himself has such a premonition. A minister might wrestle with the question of when it is important to press ahead with a witness when the congregation knows that immediate circumstances will not change. Where is the line between a futile gesture and a symbolic statement?

CHIASTIC PARALLELS. LUKE 4:14-30 AND ACTS 25:1-12

Luke 4:14-30 and Acts 25:1-12 contrast two realms: those of God and the old age, especially that of Caesar. Luke 4:14-20 is a lens through which to understand the rest of Luke-Acts. Jesus is the prophet of the Realm that will restore the world (Luke 4:18-19, cf. Isa. 58:6; 61:1-2l; Luke 4:24-27, cf. 1 Kgs 17:1-16; 2 Kings 5:1-14). The movement toward this Realm is underway through the ministry of Jesus (Luke 4:21). However, many people resist it (Luke 4:28-29). Nevertheless, God guides those who, like Jesus, witness to it (Luke 4:30).

Beginning with Acts 9:1-19, Paul witnesses faithfully to the Realm (per Luke 4:16-27). However, Paul encounters opposition (Acts 22:27-36; 23:12-22; cf. Luke 4:28-29) that leads to appearing before Festus in Acts 25:1-12. Not finding justice, Paul appeals to Caesar. At one level, as we frequently note, the Empire gets Paul to Rome to bear witness at the end of the earth. At another level, the reader recognizes the injustice of Paul's situation: innocent, yet kept in captivity, and finally killed, perhaps as a favor to the Jewish leadership (per Acts 24:27; 25:9).

A preacher might contrast the visions of the world represented by Jesus in Luke 4:14-30 and by Caesar in Acts 25:1-12. Which vision does the congregation prefer—one that provides sustenance for all, releases captives, enables people to perceive, frees people from demons, renews the cosmos, and reunites the human family? Or one based on scarcity, enforcing its will by threat of captivity, misleading people regarding ultimate reality, cooperating with demons, exploiting the cosmos, profiting from social division, and operating its legal system to preserve its own power? Do we trust the God behind the overflowing vision of Luke 4:14-30 or the emperor behind the limited vision of Acts 25:1-12?

ACTS 25:13-22. FESTUS INTRODUCES PAUL'S CASE TO AGRIPPA

Agrippa and his sister Bernice travel from Jerusalem to Festus in Caesarea, not only making a social call but currying favor with the Roman governor (and thus exhibit the political savvy that kept Agrippa in Roman favor). The ambiguity of Rome in relationship to the community of the Realm surfaces here.

Festus summarizes his version of the events of Acts 25:1-12 for Bernice and Agrippa. The chief priests and elders came from Jerusalem and asked Festus for a verdict against Paul. Festus, however, follows Roman precedent by not rendering a verdict until accusers and accused meet face to face. However, the charges against Paul pertain not to Roman legal matters but to differences in the Jewish house (Acts 25:13-20).

Festus was "at a loss as to how to investigate these questions," so asked if Paul wanted to go to Jerusalem. If heard by itself, this offer may sound like an attempt on Festus's part to gain a more fair hearing for Paul by having Paul tried in a court familiar with the charges, but Acts 25:9 indicates that Festus takes this action as a favor to the Jewish hierarchy. When Paul appealed to the emperor Festus kept Paul in protective custody until Paul could go Rome (Acts 25:21-23).

By bringing Agrippa into the picture, Luke shows that all levels of leadership related to Palestine have an old-age character. The Jewish leadership is vitriolic toward Paul. Agrippa and the Roman governors are more passive, but unjust in the end. Agrippa perceives Paul's innocence, but does not have the courage to defend Paul before Rome (Acts 26:32). The Roman government through Felix and Festus has two opportunities to adjudicate Paul's case justly but fails. The reader inevitably compares and contrasts the rulers of the old age with the rule of God.

CHIASTIC PARALLELS. LUKE 4:1-13 AND ACTS 25:13-22

In Luke 4:1-13, Satan tempts Jesus in the wilderness. Luke, like many end-time theologians, believed that Satan would confront the faithful as the final manifestation of the Realm nears. In Luke 4:1-13, the Spirit initiates such a confrontation. The major temptation in its three forms (to turn stones to bread, to rule the present world, to leap from the temple) is to settle for the rule of Satan amid the brokenness of the old age rather than to follow the journey to the Realm. The temptation of Jesus is a paradigm for the temptation that church and world repeatedly face.

By reading Acts 25:13-22 (and the narrative through Acts 26:32) through the lens of the chiastic pair, we see that Festus and Agrippa face temptation prompted by Satan. Whereas Jesus resists temptation, Festus and Herod yield by accommodating to the injustice of the old age.

The manner in which Festus and Agrippa encounter temptation and yield is instructive for today. Temptation does not always come in dramatic encounters with Satan but through everyday life circumstances. Unfortunately Luke portrays the Jewish leaders as instruments of temptation who offer Festus an old-age understanding of Paul. Festus relies on Agrippa, an old-age figure, for guidance. Agrippa recognizes Paul's innocence (Acts 26:30-32) but refuses to do anything about it. When do we take our places with Festus and Agrippa, yielding to temptation, even when we know better? Nevertheless, just as the Spirit empowered Jesus to resist temptation and Paul to remain faithful, so the Spirit is at work among us.

ACTS 25:23-27. FESTUS PRESENTS PAUL TO AGRIPPA

Festus presents Paul to Agrippa and Bernice. The brother and sister arrive "in great pomp" surrounded by prominent people. Luke thus subtly suggests that Agrippa and Bernice are self-important creatures of the old age who revel in the present social structures privileging them. They are free but represent the false values of the old world whereas Paul, the representative of the new age, is in custody. Agrippa shows real interest in the Realm, but is unable to turn away from his entanglement with the old world. A homilist could consider ways in which many people today are counterparts to Bernice and Agrippa in their shallow values.

Festus introduces Paul by explaining that Festus has decided to send Paul to Rome, but Festus does not have a legal reason for doing so. So, Festus presents this interview with Paul as a time for others to help formulate charges. There is no suggestion that Festus seeks to help the emperor determine Paul's innocence. The reader might wonder whether Festus is trying to make sure that the Emperor does not think ill of Festus for sending Paul to Rome for no good reason. By bringing Bernice and Agrippa into the picture, it appears that Festus seeks to enlarge the circle of responsibility for the injustice being done to Paul.

A preacher could use this situation as a case study in which people today act similarly. We are sometimes afraid to take responsibility for our actions and attempt to protect ourselves by getting others to take some of the heat.

This passage and its larger context indicts the Roman legal system. Luke presents the system as inflexible and insensitive to truth. Festus knows there are no Roman legal grounds on which to send Paul to Rome, yet Festus is obligated to send Paul to the emperor. Consequently, Festus seeks Agrippa's help in manufacturing such grounds. While the system may have been intended to provide more possibilities for justice than a system that depended only on local magistrates, the Roman system does not provide sufficient justice to exonerate Paul.

This situation prompts me to think about the fairness of judicial systems in the United States. The preacher might help the congregation discover how the system is prejudiced in favor of people of Eurocentric origin. Occasional candidates for judge run on platforms that seek to deny rights to certain parts of the population. The preacher could help the congregation identify opportunities to become advocates for people who are disadvantaged by our system of justice and to become agents for a system that provides Realm-like justice for all.

CHIASTIC PARALLELS. LUKE 3:23-28 AND ACTS 25:23-27

In the ancient world, genealogies were important because identity was communal: one's ancestry indicated identity, character, and purpose. The genealogy of Jesus in Luke 3:23-28 begins with Jesus as the son of Joseph and moves backward until it places Jesus as heir of Adam, who with Eve was the first human couple created by God. By tracing Jesus to Eve and Adam and to God, Luke shows that the mission of Jesus ultimately points beyond Judaism to gentiles. Scholars sometimes say that the end-time is like the beginning-time, that is, the eschatological world is similar to the world at creation before the fall.

In Acts 25:23-27, Paul, representing the Realm with its outreach to gentiles prefigured in the genealogy of Jesus, stands before the gentile Festus and before Agrippa. Paul offers Festus and Agrippa the opportunity to become part of the community of the Realm (Acts 26:24-32). However, Festus, Bernice and Agrippa are not willing to act in a bold way on what they know is true—namely that Jesus is innocent. By acting in Paul's behalf, Festus, Agrippa and Bernice could have been grafted into the genealogy of Jesus, Eve and Adam.

A preacher can have fun with the genealogy of Jesus while getting to the serious point that we are often like Festus. The possibility of the Realm is before us even as Paul was before Festus, Bernice, and Agrippa, offering us the opportunity to join the movement toward ultimate blessing that began with Eve and Adam. We may be attracted even as we are unwilling to commit. By his indecisiveness, Festus chooses to continue to live in the lineage of the emperor, and, therefore, will ultimately share the fate of the Empire: condemnation.

ACTS 26:1-23. PAUL MAKES HIS DEFENSE BEFORE AGRIPPA

This is Acts' third account of Paul's experience on the Damascus Road (Acts 9:1-19; 22:3-21). Luke repeats material in order to emphasize it. In Acts 22:3-21 and now Acts 26:1-23, Luke shapes the presentations in view of the differences in audience pictured in Acts. The speech in Acts 26 contains material not found elsewhere that raises potential preaching points.

Luke again paints Paul as an accomplished orator by describing Paul as raising his hand (Acts 26:1). Following the custom of orators in antiquity (and suggesting a way whereby preachers can many begin sermons) Paul begins by complimenting the audience and thereby establishing identification (Acts 26:2-3).

Paul next enhances the credibility of his witness saying that "all the Jews" are aware of Paul's exemplary life in Judaism. Paul wants them to believe he is on trial not for an idiosyncrasy but for Paul's "hope in a promise that God made to our ancestors," and one toward which the twelve tribes are oriented. That hope is the coming of the Realm, here represented by the resurrection from the dead (Acts 26:4-8). Paul: this hope is the core of Judaism.

By recounting his life as a persecutor, Paul invites identification from the Jewish members of the audience (Acts 26:9-11). Paul implies, "I was once like many of you are now."

Paul adds the voice of the risen Jesus to this account of the Damascus Road: "It hurts you to kick against the goads" (Acts 26:14b). A goad was a pointed stick used to prod an animal pulling a plough or a wagon. This saying was a conventional expression by the time of Luke. As in Acts 17:28, Luke quotes a source from outside of Judaism as a theological authority, thus prompting ministers to consider where we might find theological wisdom in popular culture.

The risen Jesus calls Paul to testify to the Realm. Paul cites Jesus saying that Jesus will rescue Paul from both Jewish and gentile forces. This rescue motif does not appear in previous narrations. Jesus sends Paul to open the eyes of others so they will turn (repent) from darkness and from "the power of Satan" to God, and to a place in the Realm (Acts 26:12-18). Paul suggests that those who live according to old age principles are allied with Satan, another theme that does not appear in the previous accounts

Paul's address emphasizes that he was obedient (a classic Jewish motif) by witnessing to the Realm in Damascus, Jerusalem, Judea and to the gentiles. The message: people should repent and live in ways consistent with the Realm ("do deeds consistent with repentance"). This message is the real reason a Jewish conspiracy developed against him (not, as Jewish leaders said, his disobedience in the temple). The Jewish leaders are so entrenched in the old age they lie (Acts 26:19-21)

At the climax, Paul uses language to touch the deepest chords of the Jewish heart: *God* supports the witness; Paul has preached only Moses and the prophets, which point to Jesus as God's representative who brings light to both Jewish and gentile peoples (Acts 26:22-23).

The pastor might consider individuals, groups, and forces that have force-fields in today's world in the same way that Agrippa and the people in the hall emanated force-fields at the time of Paul—upper class people, including Agrippa, ruler of much of Palestine—who have power to shape local life. How can the congregation bring the values of the Realm to their attention? Some of those people may be in the congregation, in which case the preacher needs to explore how the sermon can help them take Realm values into account as they lead community life.

The themes of Paul's defense pose possibilities for preaching sermons on other texts today. Without directly confronting them, Paul wants Agrippa and other Jewish members of the audience to believe that by opposing Paul, they oppose their own tradition. Paul wants them to think, "Since we believe in the same God as Paul, we should believe what Paul says." Paul invites a change of mind through positive identification and through indirectly inviting listeners to reconsider the logic of their own position. Of course, preachers sometimes need to call a spade a spade.

This defense also opens the door for a discussion of theological method today. Paul changes the words of the risen Jesus from Acts 9:14-17 by adding the proverb about the goad and by adapting other words to appeal to the audience in the hall. Paul changes what the tradition said to suit his immediate purpose. Christians today sometimes do similar things. When we come upon something in the Bible or church doctrine that does not suit our purposes, we sometimes try to change the tradition itself. Some such efforts are genuine reappraisals. But Christians sometimes try to resolve theological problems at the level of exegesis by getting the text or the doctrine to say something other than what it patently says, so that today's congregation is not theologically offended. Paul does not go that far. But his revision of the tradition could prompt a preacher to reflect on the degree to which it is appropriate for a congregation to honor the integrity of a text by letting it say what it says, conversing with the text, perhaps disagreeing with it, and formulating what the congregation truly can believe.

CHIASTIC PARALLELS. LUKE 3:21-22 AND ACTS 26:1-23

In Luke 3:21-22, Jesus is baptized. God through the Holy Spirit empowers Jesus to serve as eschatological prophet who announces and initiates the final movement toward the Realm. Luke 3:21-22 draws on Psalm 2:7 and Isaiah 42:1. Israel used the Psalm when a royal youth was elevated to monarchy. The power of the Realm becomes operative through Jesus in the way the power of the monarch becomes operative at enthronement. Isaiah 42:1 begins the first servant song in which the prophetic vocation of the servant community points to the manifestation of God's rule liberating exiles and giving light to gentiles (Isa. 42:6). As Israel (servant community) witnessed to God's purpose at the time of the exile, so Jesus continues that witness in the last days.

In Acts 26:1-23, Luke reminds the reader of Paul's vocation as representative of the Realm to carry the witness to the Realm to gentiles. Acts 26:23 refers directly to Isaiah 42:6.

These texts invite a sermon on baptism, identity and mission. For Jesus, baptism confirmed identity and mission. Baptism similarly represented the transformation in Paul's life from old-age persecutor to new-age witness. For the congregation baptism confirms identity and bestows mission: we are beloved of God, commissioned to witness to the Realm. The preacher might compare and contrast this theology and ecclesiology of baptism with understandings of baptism operative in the congregation. Baptism gives us visceral assurance of God's presence and leading through the Spirit, so that when we find ourselves in situations like that of Paul in Acts 25:1-26:32, we know who we are and what we are to do.

ACTS 26:24-32. PAUL APPEALS TO AGRIPPA TO JOIN THE MOVEMENT TO THE REALM

Festus declares that Paul is out of his mind. The idea of a Realm that transcends Rome is too much for Festus (Acts 16:24). Paul, however, asserts that as a person familiar with Jewish tradition, Agrippa "knows about these things." Moreover, the witness to the Realm has been a matter of public record (Acts 26:24-26).

Paul boldly asks Agrippa, "Do you believe the prophets?" Does Agrippa believe in the coming of the Realm and is he ready to join its movement? Today's preacher could put Paul's question to the congregation. "Do *you*, congregation, believe?" Such simple, direct questions often create space in the listener for serious reflection.

Paul surmises, "I know that you [Agrippa] believe" (Acts 26:27). Paul thinks that in his heart of hearts, Agrippa wants to join the movement to the Realm.

The preacher could use Agrippa's response as a lens. "Are you so quickly persuading me to become a Christian?" Without hearing the tone Luke intended for Agrippa's voice, we do not know whether this statement indicates sympathy with Paul or is an ironic criticism. That Paul is a prophet, and that Agrippa looks favorably upon Paul in Acts 26:32, incline me toward the former. If so, Agrippa's situation is poignant—so close to joining the movement to the Realm but unwilling to take the final step. He may be afraid to imagine a world that does not revolve around him. Perhaps he fears loss of power. Whatever his case, the congregation may contain people who are in similar near-belief—wanting to be part of the movement toward the Realm but unable to commit.

Bernice, Agrippa and their companions agree Paul has done nothing wrong. Agrippa says that Paul would be set free had he not appealed to Caesar (Acts 26:31-32). Agrippa may be right about Roman practice. But as noted above some scholars of Roman law think that local officials had authority to deal with such cases before they were dispatched to Rome. Either way, Luke's critique of the Roman system is evident. If Agrippa did not have such authority, then the system itself is arbitrary and depends upon an idolater (Caesar) to render final judgments. If Agrippa did have such authority, he and Festus are spineless for not freeing Paul. The figures of Festus, Agrippa, and Bernice warn the congregation (again) that while God may use the empire to transport Paul safely to Rome, the empire itself—its systems and those who operate them—is a creature of the old age. The preacher could use this observation as basis for naming and criticizing similar phenomena in our own world.

When Luke pictures Paul appealing directly to Agrippa to believe, Luke signals the congregation to which he was writing that officials of the Roman Empire are welcome in the community of the Realm. Even though Luke assumed that joining the movement involved repentance, baptism, and living toward the Realm empowered by the Spirit, Luke also seems to assume that Agrippa, Bernice, and Festus could continue as functionaries of the Empire. Some contemporary Christians are troubled by the idea that a repentant Christian would draw a paycheck from an oppressive power. The preacher could help the congregation identify the various viewpoints in this discussion and wrestle with them. Should we withdraw from evil systems? Should we continue to work in them while attempting to transform them? Should we ignore the systems themselves and attempt only to be moral in our personal lives?

The church today might be as direct as Paul to Agrippa in inviting the unconverted to become a part of the movement to the Realm. To be sure context and audience always plays roles in determining moment and approach. But many congregations today are reluctant to extend this invitation directly. But the Spirit can bring courage forward.

CHIASTIC PARALLELS. LUKE 3:1-20 AND ACTS 26:24-32

John the Baptist alerts people that the final movement toward the Realm is about to begin and prepares them through repentance and baptism. Repentance means turning away from the old age and embracing the Realm. Baptism means becoming a part of a community awaiting the Realm (Luke 3:1-20).

In Acts 26:17-20, Paul highlights God's call to represent the Realm. Paul thus invites Agrippa, and Bernice to repent (Acts 26:24-32). Agrippa, while Jewish in family tree, was an ally of Rome. Paul extends the possibility to become a part of the movement toward the Realm even to those who enchain him. Festus refuses to repent declaring instead that Paul is out of his mind (Acts 26:24). Agrippa and Bernice join Festus in recognizing Paul's innocence, but are too entangled with the old age to repent (Acts 24:30-32). They all face the final judgment as creatures of the old world.

The preacher might identify individuals, communities, values and behaviors that the congregation would find analogous to Festus, Agrippa, Bernice, and their companions, that is, people and forces entangled in the old age and distasteful to the congregation. Yet, the invitation to repent is to be offered to all, including representatives of the Empire and people such as Agrippa and Bernice who exploit their own people.

You Will Be My Witnesses to the Ends of the Earth: God Preserves Paul amid Shipwreck on the Way to Rome (Acts 27:1—28:10)

Paul is placed in the custody of a centurion, Julius. The first days of sailing are uneventful, though Paul prophesies difficult waters ahead (Acts 27:1-12). The ship is pounded (Acts 17:13-26) when Paul prophesies they must lighten the load to be saved (Acts 17:26-38). When the ship breaks apart, some soldiers want to execute the prisoners but Julius intervenes to save Paul and others (Acts 27:39-44). They wash ashore on Malta where a poisonous snake bites Paul only to have Paul emerge without being hurt. God, through Paul, healed the father of Publius (Acts 28:1-10).

Luke-Acts is set up as a journey: from Galilee to Jerusalem to Judea, Samaria, and the ends of the earth, from Elizabeth in Judaism to Paul and Rome and the gentile mission, from the old world through tribulation to the apocalypse and the Realm. Indeed, as I have noted previously, the church is called the Way in Acts in part because that name exemplifies the nature of the church: a people on a journey.

The Way is marked by interplay of conflict and confidence, suffering and support. Paul's journey from Caesarea to Rome is an intense experience of the way in which Luke uses the powerful image of the sea as a symbol of chaos to assure readers of God's ability to bring them to a successful landing. The preacher can build on these themes in preaching.

The congregation might benefit from seeing a map of Paul's journey as well as drawings of ancient ships and photographs of pertinent archaeological artifacts.

Acts 27:1-12. Paul Sails for Rome

Paul is transported under guard from Caesarea to Rome. Julius a centurion (officer in charge of 100 soldiers) from the Augustan Cohort, a prominent unit of the Roman army named after Caesar Augustus (Acts 27:1). The word

Augustus is less a name and more a title meaning "revered," and reminds the reader of the pretention of the emperor. However, Julius comes to Paul's rescue, another Roman who serves God unknowingly by preserving Paul for witness in the imperial city.

They have easy sailing from Adramyttium to Myra where they change ships. Luke encourages the reader's sympathy for Julius by saying the centurion treats Paul kindly (Acts 27:2-5). From Myra the sailing is difficult to Fair Havens as they are against the wind (Acts 27:6-8).

The delay puts them in peril because they are now into the fall when bad weather increases. The Fast (the Jewish Day of Atonement occurring in September or October) had passed (Acts 27:9). Paul's role as prophet emerges as he offers the first of several prophecies on this voyage: the trip will be difficult, leading to loss of cargo and threat to their lives (Acts 27:10). This prophecy comes true, thereby continuing the pattern of prophecy-fulfillment fortifying the reader's confidence in the story and in the second coming. However, leaders of the voyage disregarded Paul. When the harbor was not suitable for winter, they put to sea hoping to reach Phoenix.

A minister might compare the situation on the boat with situations of leadership in the church and in the world. Paul, the prisoner, had the acumen to interpret the situation. The centurion, the pilot and the owner talked only among themselves, and soon put the ship in danger. How are we tempted to overlook Paul-like figures today and to turn instead to conventional sources of perspective? The postmodern world is marked by the breakdown of traditional lines of authority; the church contemplates sailing into a future era of history that is different from our recent past; the church might seek out today's Pauls. If we listen only to credentialed experts, our ship may continue to break up in the storm.

While Paul's prophecy may have been inspired by the Spirit, he also evidently paid attention to what was happening around him. This, too, is something congregations need to do: look at the world as it is and not as we wish it were.

CHIASTIC PARALLELS. LUKE 2:41-52 AND ACTS 20:1-12

In Luke 2:39-52, Mary and Joseph lose track of the youthful Jesus visiting the temple. They find him with the teachers, listening and asking questions. Because of his young age, he is a surprising contributor. The structure of this incident—trustworthy insight coming from an unexpected source—is also the structure of the chiastic pair.

In Acts 20:1-12, Paul is a prisoner, an unlikely source of insight. When Paul prophesies the voyage will be dangerous, the centurion pays little attention. Had the pilot taken advantage of Paul's insight, they might not have shipwrecked.

The preacher could help the congregation pay attention to sources of theological guidance that are as unlikely today as a twelve-year old and a prisoner. While the youthful Jesus and the imprisoned Paul can represent a wide range of theological resources, the sermon could highlight the insights that children and prisoners contribute to our understanding of the Realm.

ACTS 27:13-26: POUNDED BY A STORM AT SEA

The structure of Acts 27:13-26 suggests a possible structure for a sermon. Acts 27:13-20 describes the desperate situation of the ship. Acts 27:21-26 offers hope in the midst of chaos.

Almost immediately after leaving port, the voyage is a struggle. A violent wind made the boat unmanageable. The measures they took failed to control the vessel so they lowered the sea anchor to prevent running onto Syrtis. The wind was so violent the next day they casting much of the cargo overboard. When that was insufficient, they threw the ship's tackle over. The sun and stars disappeared amidst the tempest making it impossible to navigate. "All hope of our being saved was abandoned" (Acts 27:13-20).

While this situation is not an allegory of the situation of the congregation to whom Luke wrote, that congregation could identify with the floundering ship and the tensions in it. Today's congregation may also identify with Paul's situation.

To save the ship, they lightened the load. Without attributing this idea to Luke, we might do the same in situations of difficulty. We often deal with too many things at once. We carry things in our hearts and in our congregations that are too heavy. We need to lighten the load.

In Acts 27:21, Paul points out to the shipmates that they should have listened to him earlier (see Acts 27:10). Since Paul was right previously, Paul must be right now. While his rhetorical move is well-intentioned, it could easily backfire in today's culture if spoken in an arrogant tone. I can imagine someone dismissing Paul by saying, "A know-it-all is in the room."

Nevertheless, Paul encourages the shipmates to keep up their courage. Furthermore, in the midst of the storm, an angel assured Paul that Paul would stand before the emperor and that everyone on board would arrive safely. The means to safety: running aground on an island, which occurs in Acts 27:39-44.

In the storm, God gives Paul a tangible sign of assurance. The preacher might lead the congregation to recognize such signs of assurance in the storms assailing the witness to the Realm. Often signs come through people. They come through scripture and events in history. In the next section, Luke points to the breaking of the bread as such a sign (Acts 27:35).

The sign gave Paul the confidence he would carry out his mission of taking the gospel to the end of the earth. However, today storms sometimes overwhelm particular goals and missions. The most important assurance may be not that we will reach Rome but that God is with us.

CHIASTIC PARALLELS: LUKE 2:21-40 AND ACTS 27:13-26

Luke 2:21-40 tells the stories of Jesus being presented (dedicated) in the temple by Mary and Joseph who are poor enough that they buy turtledoves or pigeons for sacrifice rather than a sheep. Simeon and Anna prophesy that the Realm of God will include gentiles, and that Jesus, the representative of the Realm, would be endangered by opposition.

In Acts 27:13-26, Paul, a prisoner, is endangered by the storm. Yet, Paul, inspired by an angel assures the people in the boat that all—presumably all gentiles except Paul—will reach safety. The angel reassures Paul that he will reach the goal of the gentile witness by standing before the emperor.

These elements, coming near the beginning of the gospel and near the end of Acts, function like parentheses within which much of Luke-Acts takes place. On the one hand, each element soberly assumes that the witness to the Realm is accompanied by difficulty. On the other hand, the tone of each element is assurance: in the midst of chaos, Jesus, Paul, and the congregation can be certain that God is always with them. As a congregation today follows Anna, Simeon, and Paul in looking to the future, the preacher can help the community recognize that its journey continues to take place within these great parentheses.

ACTS 27:27-38: PAUL PROPHESIES WHAT THEY MUST DO TO SAVE THE SHIP

About midnight, the sailors believe the ship is dangerously near land, so they take soundings, fearing the ship will run on rocks. They let down four anchors and pray for day to come so they can better assess their situation (Acts 27:27-29).

A group of sailors board the ship's small boat as if to put out the anchors. However, they try to escape. Paul, the captive, now says to his captors that the sailors must stay with the ship, or the crew and passengers cannot be saved. The soldiers call the sailors back, and set the small boat adrift (Acts 27:30-31).

Are there occasions when we, like the sailors, flee ships that are in trouble? The sailors flee the ship and their commitment to care for ship and passengers. Yet God through Paul invites them to return and find safety through their service on the ship.

At the risk of going in directions Luke never intended, a preacher may be struck by the fact they are saved as a community. Maintaining community—reclaiming the sailors—makes it possible for them to survive. A sermon could explore how community can function in this way now.

Paul urges them to eat. When Paul says, "None of you will lose a hair of your heads," he invokes Jesus's affirmation that "even the hairs of your head are numbered" (Luke 12:7; cf. 21:18). Since God has numbered their hair, they can count on being saved, so they need food for strengthen (Acts 27:33-34).

Paul eats, but he does more than munch bread. The confluence of the verbs took, gave, broke in Acts 27:35 indicates that Paul partook of the sacred meal (cf. Luke 9:16; 22:19; 24:30). For Luke, the presence of the risen Jesus becomes known in the breaking of bread (Luke 24:31). For Luke-Acts, the Lord's Supper is a bread-only meal: in the storm, the presence of the risen Jesus becomes known to Paul. The other people on the boat also eat bread and gain energy.

The preacher can help the congregation recognize that as Paul encounters the strengthening presence of the Risen One through the bread. Luke's congregation encounters that same presence in their own storms. Today's congregation is strengthened by the breaking of the bread in the midst of struggles.

The others eat and then lighten the ship further by throwing over the cargo of wheat. For survival, they are now left to the providence of God. On the one hand, the preacher can commend this as a bold move. What can we throw off—things on which we have relied but that are no longer necessary or appropriate? On the other hand, the preacher needs to be careful not to encourage irresponsibility.

Chiastic Parallels. Luke 2:8-20 and Acts 27:27-38

In Luke 2:8-20, the angels announce the birth of Jesus to shepherds. Shepherds' lives were difficult as they spent long periods of time in isolation, dealt with wild animals and other dangers, struggled with food and water as well as the value of sheep in shifting economic times. Shepherds were sometimes dirty and looked upon as anti-social. They represent for Luke people who need to have confidence that the Realm is coming. The angels' visitation assures them.

In Acts 27:27-38, the ship is in danger. Paul urges the hungry passengers and crew to eat so they will be strong enough to survive. At the climactic moment, Paul takes bread, gives thanks, breaks it, and begins to eat. As noted above, Paul partakes of the Lord's Supper.

The chiastic pair suggests that in the breaking of the bread, the angel choir again announces the presence of the Realm. Whether on a dark night in Palestine among shepherds or in the midst of a storm, Realm-possibilities are present.

Acts 27:39-44. In the Midst of Shipwreck, Paul Is Saved

In the morning, they awake to find themselves off land they do not recognize. They take Paul's advice and try to run the boat aground, but the ship strikes a reef—an invisible obstacle—and the ship becomes stuck with the stern breaking up (Acts 27:39-41). How often this is the case in the church and in other groups, witnessing to Realm-like values. We are moving toward a significant witness when something happens to derail the movement. What are the reefs the congregation strikes? This story affirms that even when things break down, God continues to work to bring the witness to life.

They are within sight of safety, but a new threat appears for the prisoners. They are close enough to land that most of the soldiers want to kill the prisoners to prevent the prisoners from escaping. If the prisoners escape, then Rome will hold the soldiers accountable and will severely punish them. Julius persuades the other soldiers to abandon their plan. The centurion gives the order to abandon ship: everyone is saved by swimming or by hanging onto pieces of the ship (Acts 27:42-44).

This was not the smooth landing that Paul anticipated in Acts 27:26, but his words come true again. A pastor might help the congregation embrace circumstances in which things do not end in the upbeat way planners anticipated, but nevertheless end in a Realm way.

A Roman again saves Paul, this time from a Roman threat. A preacher may again invite the congregation to turn to unexpected sources that can facilitate the witness.

CHIASTIC PARALLELS. LUKE 2:1-7 AND ACTS 27:39-44

Luke 2:1-7 describes the birth of Jesus under difficult circumstances. Luke 2:1-2 reminds the reader of the omnipresence of the Roman Empire. The registration was for the purposes of establishing the tax base and accumulating names for conscription. Mary gave birth not in her home in Nazareth but in quarters used temporarily by travelers. Since the space was crowded, the parents laid Jesus in a manger (a box for feeding animals). Such a birth is a sign that God can be trusted to supply witnesses to the Realm even in difficult circumstances.

Paul is in a similar situation: circumstances are grim as the ship breaks up. Not only is the ship in peril from the storm, but soldiers (representatives of the Empire) want to kill the prisoners to prevent them from escaping. But the birth of Jesus in difficult circumstances is the paradigm for Paul: in a perilous situation, God can be trusted to support the witness to the Realm.

The preacher might lead the congregation to identify circumstances in our setting that are similar to the old-age circumstances at the birth of Jesus (Empire, taxation, conscription, shortage of resources) and around Paul on the ship (danger from nature and from the social world). How does God offer the congregation possibilities of the Realm, represented by Jesus's birth and by Paul swimming safely to shore?

ACTS 28:1-10. PAUL ON THE ISLAND OF MALTA

The travelers discover they are on Malta, an island south of Sicily. The locals welcome the survivors (Acts 28:1-2a) reminding Luke's readers indirectly of God's covenant with the whole human family through Noah: God creates structures of hospitality so that people who do not even know God can cooperate with God's purposes.

Since it was cold, they build a fire. As Paul gathers brushwood, a poisonous snake fastens on his hand. The natives make a logical conclusion from the perspective of the ancient assumption that punishment ultimately happens to wrongdoers. The word justice in Acts 27:4b may refer to Dike, the goddess of justice (The Greek word *dikē* means justice). The Maltans think Paul is a murderer, who having escaped death on the sea is now receiving just condemnation (Acts 27:2b-6).

The preacher might ask, "Who is similar to the residents of Malta today—welcoming, hospitable, but inadequately informed theologically?" The preacher might ask, "Are members in the congregation analogous to Maltans?" Their presuppositions do not prepare them to recognize the Realm.

Unfortunately, even when the residents of Malta realize that something unusual is happening with Paul, their lenses lead them to conclude that Paul is a god.

Can the preacher point to material from the media, or conversations with church members or church meetings when Christians miss the Realm because they do not have adequate theological frames of reference? The preacher can help the congregation see that this reaction underscores the importance of witnesses to the Realm offering explicit interpretations that help people name their worlds in the terms of the Realm. Paul does not even attempt to do that in this passage. A Christian today might do better than the ancient archetypal witness.

This part of the story has contributed (with Mark 20:17-18) to handling venomous snakes as a religious exercise. The preacher might alert the congregation to this phenomenon, explain the ritual, its significance, and the degree to which the preacher thinks such practices are consistent with the purposes of the Realm.

Publius is the leading resident of the island, but his father is sick in bed with fever and dysentery. In those days, dysentery—a severe inflammation of the colon resulting in diarrhea, dehydration, fever, and pain in the abdomen—could easily lead to death. However, Paul visits the father, lays on hands, and prays. Not only is Publius healed, but "the rest of the people on the island also came and were cured" (Acts 27:7-9). These healings prove the presence of the Realm, while embodying the character of the Realm: restoring the human being to the way God intended.

The people of Malta—unlike Paul's most recent encounters with Jewish leaders and provincial leaders of the Roman Empire—bestow honors on Paul and provide all the provisions Paul needs for the final sail to Rome (Acts 27:7-10). This summary statement reaffirms the power of witness among gentiles. Paul thus heads for Rome on a high note.

CHIASTIC PARALLELS. LUKE 1:57-80 AND ACTS 28:1-10

Luke 1:57-80 contains the birth of John the Baptist and Zechariah's prophecy after the birth. The birth of John prompts people to ponder what John signifies (Luke 1:57-66). Zechariah, John's father, affirms that the God of Israel promises to preserve Israel and to bring forth a representative who can lead gentiles into the Realm (Luke 1:66-80, esp. 78-79).

On Malta, these promises come true. God preserves Paul from the threats of the storm and of being murdered (Acts 27:39-44). Now God preserves Paul from death from the viper attack. Paul manifests the Realm in behalf of gentiles by healing the parent of Publius and others.

On the one hand the preacher can point to God's promises in Luke coming true through Paul in Acts. Furthermore, while the congregation might think of Malta as a side stop, it becomes a place where the Realm is revealed. Where is Malta for the congregation—within the community? Beyond?

On the other hand, sometimes snakes come out of the fire and attach themselves so that people cannot shake them off. People die. Fever and dysentery sometimes get the best of Publius 's father. The preacher needs to help the congregation recognize the presence of the Realm in such circumstances.

You Will Be My Witnesses to the Ends of the Earth: Paul Witnesses to the Realm under House Arrest in Rome (Acts 28:11-31)

We now arrive at the point toward which the Gospel and Acts have been reaching—Paul witnesses in Rome. They sail from Malta to Rome where Paul encounters believers (Acts 28:11-16). In house arrest, Paul reports to local Jewish leaders the false charges that sent him to Rome: they listen (Acts 28:17-22). When a dispute breaks out in the Jewish community regarding whether to accept Paul's witness, Paul draws on Isaiah to say that the news of the Realm will now go the gentiles (Acts 28:23-29). The book ends with the report that Paul lived in Rome for two years proclaiming the Realm (Acts 28:30-31).

Acts 28:11-16. Paul and the Witness to the Realm Reach Rome

Paul spends the rest of the winter in Malta before sailing for Rome, boarding a ship that had the twin brothers Castor and Pollux as its figurehead. Many people believed that these siblings, children of Zeus, protected seafarers. The reader knows, of course, that safe travel comes from God and not from Zeus, but God can make use of the children of Zeus (so to speak). The idea of God using people who do not believe in God is a theme in Acts around which the preacher could develop a sermon. Who are the children of Zeus through whom God works today?.

A map on a screen or in the bulletin would help the congregation imagine Puteloli, Paul's last stop before Rome. The news of the Realm had already reached this community that extended its hospitality to Paul (Acts 28:11-14a).

In a phrase with deep evocative power, Luke says, "And so we came to Rome" (Acts 28:14b). This phrase pulls together the narrative of Acts from 1:8 to now.

Believers immediately come—from as far as the Forum of Appius and from Twin Taverns, almost forty-five and thirty-five miles away, respectively (Acts 28:15). Paul lives under house arrest with only a soldier guarding him (Acts 28:16). In addition to watching over Paul, the guard protects Paul.

The emphasis on community is striking here. In both Puetioli and Rome, people come together with Paul and they all strengthen one another. The preacher might meditate on the strength for the Realm that encouraged within the congregation and when the congregation connects with Christians far away.

CHIASTIC PARALLELS. LUKE 1:39-56 AND ACTS 28:11-16

In Luke 1:39-56, Mary arrives in a town in the Judean hill country and visits Elizabeth who declares that Mary is blessed for believing that she (Mary) would be a vessel through whom God would birth the one who would announce the final manifestation of the Realm. Elizabeth encourages Mary (Luke 1:39-45). Mary affirms God is now moving to complete the promises that God made to Israel by manifesting the Realm (Luke 1:46-56).

Paul visits with believers in Puteoli before arriving in Rome and visiting with believers there. Acts has established that the Realm of God is the subject of such interchanges. Paul, like Mary, gives thanks to God and takes courage.

Women are the first characters in the Gospel to embrace the Realm. Both Elizabeth and Mary welcome the news whereas Zechariah is slow to believe and Joseph is secondary to the process. The women are paradigmatic for Paul in Rome. He visits with people about the Realm. He extends the witness initiated by the women in an obscure hill town into the capital of the gentile world. How do women today welcome the Realm and witness in ways that help males recognize the Realm and respond appropriately?

ACTS 28:17-22. PAUL BRINGS THE NEWS OF THE REALM TO JEWISH LEADERS IN ROME

After being in Rome only three days, Paul meets first with the local Jewish community, explaining the false charges. Paul explains that the Romans recognize that he had done nothing to deserve death and wanted to release him.

Paul was held only because Jewish leaders objected, which necessitated Paul's appeal to the emperor (Acts 28:17-19).

Paul, however, does not assume that the Jewish people in Rome are guilty by association with the Jewish leaders in Jerusalem. The witness explains that his message and imprisonment "are for the sake of the hope of Israel." The gentile mission is the goal of Israel's life. Paul hopes that the Jewish people in Rome will embrace the Realm. Paul is reaching out to the Jewish community in Rome to help them avoid the mistake made by the Jewish leaders in Jerusalem (Acts 28:20).

The leaders respond they have received no negative letters or other reports about Paul. They have heard negative reports about the community of the Realm ("this sect") but they want to hear what Paul has to say (Acts 28:21-22).

The early twenty-first century is a contentious time. The preacher could use the encounter in Acts 28:17-23 as a model for interactions around contentious matters. Paul and the Jewish leaders come together in a spirit of good will. Paul speaks in a pastoral way directly about his situation. He does not pussyfoot around the fact that a Jewish misstep is responsible for his situation. He is forthright about favorable Roman attitudes. Yet he emphasizes he has the best interest of the Jewish community at heart, even encouraging them to recognize that his work is an expression of their deepest hope. For their part, the Jewish leaders want to give Paul a fair hearing. They do not prejudge Paul on the basis of the negative reputation of "the sect." The conversation between Paul and the Jewish leaders leads to disagreements within the Jewish community (Acts 28:23-25a), but the interaction begins in respectful critical thinking together.

The homily could identify issues in the congregation and in the larger world around which the congregation needs to have conversations in a similar spirit. Indeed, the interaction within the church should serve as a model for the larger culture (a light to the gentiles). The church might initiate such conversations in the broader world.

CHIASTIC PARALLELS. LUKE 1:26-38 AND ACTS 28:17-21

In Luke 1:26-38, Gabriel announces to Mary that she, surprisingly because of her social status, will give birth to the one through whom God will manifest the Realm. Scholars describe Mary as the model believer: when she receives the news of the Realm, she says yes. Her faithful response makes possible the movement to the Realm even though a sword will pierce her (Luke 2:35)

Paul with his history of persecution, is as surprising a vessel as Mary to carry the witness to the Realm. Yet he followed Mary's example: when the risen Jesus called, Paul said yes. A sword is about to pierce Paul. Yet he is obedient to the call, and now meets with Jewish leaders in Rome (Acts 28:17-22).

Mary, the peasant woman, is the model witness. She is even the model for Paul who, by virtue of gender, education, and place in Jewish society, is much higher on the social pyramid. Their opposite points on the social spectrum make a point: the Realm is for all. For both Mary and Paul, the structure of the experience is the same: the news of the Realm comes as an act of unmerited favor; they welcome it; God empowers them; they do what they are called to do.

ACTS 28:23-31. PAUL INTERPRETS THE REALM AND ITS FUTURE DIRECTION

We are now at the climactic moment of Acts. In ancient literature, the last words and impressions of a character are important.

Paul explains the Realm of God by telling the story of Jesus and by drawing from the Torah and the prophets. Some in the Jewish audience are convinced while others do not believe. "So they disagreed with each other" (Acts 28:23-25a).

As they were leaving, Paul says that the Holy Spirit was right in Isaiah 6:9-10 quoted in Acts 28:26-27.[10] In Isaiah 6:1-8 God calls Isaiah in the temple: Isaiah sees God high and lifted up. After being touched by hot coal, Isaiah declares, "Here am I; send me." In the Septuagint version of Isaiah 6:9-10, God immediately says to the people: you will hear the prophet's words, but you will not understand them (Isaiah 6:9). God explains that Isaiah's preaching will not lead to repentance but to its opposite: the unrepentant people will soon be ready for judgment. Their minds are dull; their eyes and ears do not perceive what they need to perceive. Hence, they will not turn and be healed (Isaiah 6:10).

According to Acts, many Jewish people in Paul's day respond to the news of the Realm in the same way as the contemporaries of Isaiah: by failing to repent. Judgment came to Israel through national collapse and exile (Isa. 6:11-12). Paul implies that Jewish people of his day who do not repent face a similar judgment, though ratcheted from national disaster to apocalyptic condemnation.

Paul concludes, "Let it be known to you then that this salvation has been sent to the gentiles; they will listen" (Acts 28:28). While this statement sounds like a flat rejection of the Jewish community, the very next line reports that Paul "welcomed all who came to him." While we cannot be sure that Jewish people were included in the "all," Luke could have easily made Jewish absence explicit. Twice previously Paul has said the gospel is going only to gentiles, but each time he soon engaged Jewish people (Acts 13:46-48 but 14;1-7; 18:5-6 but 18:18-21). Acts 28:28 seems to mean that Paul will no longer take the initiative with Jewish people, but he still works with those who come to him.

Acts 28:25b-28 presents the preacher with a complicated theological challenge. I do not believe it is appropriate for the church to attempt to convert Jewish people from Judaism to Christianity. God's promises to the Jewish community are irrevocable. In a twisted way, then, the text sanctions a behavior that I consider appropriate: not seeking to testify to Jewish people. Yet, a preacher might be able to use Paul's diminution of the mission to the Jewish people as the starting point of a conversation regarding whether the church should permanently ignore communities with which it disagrees. The church might adopt short-term disengagement in contexts in which some open space might create a better opportunity for people to consider the Realm. But if the church believes in a God of unconditional love, then denying the opportunity to become aware of that love is inappropriate. The preacher might help the congregation identify people, groups, or situations we are tempted to write off, and propose appropriate forms of pastoral engagement.

Acts 28:30-31 puzzles some contemporary readers because it appears to be a non-ending. However, Luke has prepared the reader for two things. (1) Paul was executed by Rome (Acts 19:21; 20:22-25; 21:11-14; 23:11; 26:32; 27:23-25). (2) Caesar and Rome are soon to fall. In connection with the death of Herod in Acts 12:1-4 and 20-24, we noted an ancient assumption in which a leader who offends the gods is struck down in a demonstration of retributive justice. According to O. Wesley Allen, Jr., this motif is in the back of the reader's mind at the end of Acts: we fill in the next stage in the drama in which Paul is executed by Caesar and in which God punishes Caesar, and, I would add, the Roman Empire, in the apocalyptic judgment.

If Caesar, the ruler of the empire, cannot destroy what God intended, then neither can opposition to the church in the time of the reader. Luke encourages readers to complete the story by recognizing continuity between the story of Acts and their own experience of God's providence.[11]

To be sure, the idea of divine retribution is theologically problematic. But the deeper purpose for that phenomenon, as O. Wesley Allen points out, is to assure the church that God can carry the church into the future. It is hard to imagine a more timely entry into a sermon. Given the struggles faced by individual Christians, congregations, and the larger church, Luke reaches across the centuries with a word that is pastoral and empowering. In the midst of our struggles to witness, God who was faithful to Israel, Jesus, and Paul is also faithful to us.

Chiastic Parallels. Luke 1:5-25 and Acts 28:23-31

Luke 1:5-25 takes place in a Jewish atmosphere. Zechariah and Elizabeth are an exemplary Jewish couple. Zechariah is a priest. Gabriel announces they will give birth to John, who will prepare people for the final manifestation of the Realm. Zechariah resists this news, but Elizabeth—in the first sign in Luke-Acts of the impulse toward the restoration of women—embraces it.

In Rome, Paul meets with Jewish people day and night to persuade them the final manifestation of the Realm is at hand. While some embrace the news, others turn away. Paul is so distressed by their disagreement that he quotes Isaiah as the basis for declaring that God is sending salvation to the gentiles (Acts 28:23).

As the beginning element in the chiasmus, Luke 1:5-25 helps the reader understand that the story of the Realm is a Jewish story. As the Gospel and Acts unfold, we learn that a goal of this story is to welcome gentiles into the Realm. As the ending element in the chiasmus, Acts 28:23-31 is the capstone in the explanation of how a movement that began in Judaism turned to gentiles.

The preacher could use these first and last elements of the chiasmus as an opportunity to tell the story of Luke-Acts as a whole. The preacher would need to be selective and concise in telling the story. The sermon could help the congregation take its place in the story.

Since Christian congregations are almost exclusively gentile, a preacher could encourage the congregation to thank God for Judaism as our parent. The preacher could encourage the congregation to repent for the ways the church has abused our relationship with Judaism, and to imagine ways whereby the church can take steps to restore communion so that our relationship might itself be a sign of the Realm.

Notes

1. Kathy Black, *A Healing Homiletic: Preaching and Disability* (Nashville: Abingdon, 1996).
2. The historical Paul makes a similar statement in Romans 2:11.
3. Josephus, *Jewish Antiquities,* trans. Louis H. Feldman. Loeb Classical Library (Cambridge: Harvard University Press, 1965), 27–31.
4. O. Wesley Allen, Jr. *The Death of Herod: The Narrative and Theological Function of Retribution in Luke-Acts.* SBL Dissertation Series 158 (Atlanta: Society of Biblical Literature, 1997), pp. 204–5.

5. Scholars have differing views on the specific identification (by chapter and verse) of these journeys, especially the third. Some scholars think that the notion of "missionary journeys" is itself mistaken.

6. John Calvin, *Institutes of the Christian Religion*, trans. Ford L. Battles, ed. John T. McNeill (Philadelphia: Westminster, 1950), 1:108.

7. For example: Abodah Zarah 8:4-8 in *The Tosefta: Translated from the Hebrew with a New Introduction*, trans. Jacob Neusner (Peabody: Hendrickson, 2002), 2:1291–92; Sanhedrin 56a in *The Babylonian Talmud: A Translation and Commentary*, trans. Jacob Neusner (Peabody: Hendrickson, 2005), 16:296.

8. The "we" passages are Acts 16:11-17; 20:5-15; 21:1-18; 27:1—28:16.

9. Scholars debate whether the historical Paul was likely a Roman citizen. But such citizenship is important in the narrative of Acts.

10. Isaiah 6:9-10 was an important text to the writers of the gospels with excerpts appearing in the mouth of Jesus is Mark 4:10-12; Matt. 13:10-17; Luke 8:9-10; and by the gospel writer in John 12:40. Each context uses Isaiah 6:9-10 in a slightly different way.

11. O. W. Allen, *The Death of Herod*, 205.

Appendix 1: The Chiastic Structure of Luke-Acts

Chiasm was a commonplace literary structure in antiquity in which an author arranged the elements of a text in inverted parallelism. The name chiasm derives from the Greek letter *chi* (which is made like the English letter "x") because chiastic structure follows the pattern of the letter x: In antiquity, a chiasm could be as short as two lines or as long as an entire document. Within a chiasm, the parallel elements could be as short as lines or as long as paragraph.

For convenience, scholars label the corresponding elements of the chiasmus by the letters A and A' (pronounced "A" and "A-prime"), B and B', C and C', etc. and arrange them as follows:

   A
      B
         C
         C'
      B'
   A'

Scholars print the text in this visual pattern on the page so that readers today can easily identify the chiastic element. Ancient texts were not laid out this way. They were written or spoken from start to finish. Chiasmus was such an ingrained phenomenon in antiquity that listeners or readers could identify the presence of a chiasmus without special visual or auditory prompting.

The central element of the chiasmus (C and C' above) reveals the most important concern of the chiasm. The elements that precede the central element lead to the central concern. The elements that follow the central element draw out the implications of that concern.

I believe the Gospel of Luke and the Book of Acts is a giant chiasmus in which the Gospel provides the elements A through GGGG and Acts provides elements GGGG' through A'. The elements of Luke-Acts are in a relationship of synthetic parallelism: the elements in the Gospel tell the story of the manifestation of the Realm through the ministry of Jesus while the comparable elements in Acts show how these themes play out in the life of the church.

The main theme of Luke-Acts is that God has begun the final and full manifestation of that Realm through the ministry of Jesus. The Realm will come finally and fully only when Jesus returns. Before that event, God must complete the promises God made to Sarai and Abram to bless gentiles. According to Luke, God's way of doing so is to welcome them into the Realm. Acts tells the story of God using the church as means of reaching out to gentiles and incorporating them into the movement toward the Realm.

However, the community to whom Luke wrote was beset by conflicts both within the church and between the church and outside groups. Luke wrote the Gospel and Acts to empower the community to witness by assuring it that God through Christ was in control of the movement of history.

The chiastic structure of Luke-Acts embodies this purpose in literary expression. The central element of the chiasmus is the ascension of Jesus (see GGGG and GGGG' below). The Gospel shows that God was controlled the birth of Jesus in Judaism, and guided the ministry of Jesus in announcing the Realm through the conflicts that led to his crucifixion, resurrection, and ascension. The ascension confirms that God was working through the ministry of Jesus to manifest the Realm and to create a community to witness for we see Jesus at the right hand of God. Acts draws out the implications of the fact that God is at work through the Jesus movement to extend the community of the Realm into the gentile world. Just as God guided the ministry of Jesus and brought him safely to resurrection and ascension, so God guides the church as it witnesses to the Realm in its seasons of conflict.

The parallel elements in the chiasm of Luke-Acts enrich one another. The elements in the Gospel point to themes and developments in the elements in Acts. The elements in Acts presuppose the parallel elements in the Gospel. The commentary proper explains in more detail how awareness of the parallel elements illumines our understanding of them.

Ordinarily the elements of a chiasmus would be presented on the page as they are above. Because of the length of biblical material examined here, and because of page space constraints, I set out the elements of the chiasmus in two parallel columns.

A. Luke 1:5-25. The story of the final manifestation of the Realm begins in a Jewish atmosphere.	A'. Acts 28:23-31. The story of the final manifestation of the Realm ends by looking toward the gentile mission.
B. Luke 1:26-38. When an angel confirms to Mary that the child to whom she will give birth is God's representative to bring the Realm in the end-time, she immediately agrees, and becomes the model of obedience.	B'. Acts 28:17-21. When Paul confirms to Jewish leaders in Rome that Jesus is God's representative in bringing about the final manifestation of the Realm, disagreement results

Appendix 1: The Chiastic Structure of Luke-Acts

C. Luke 1:39-56. Mary visits Elizabeth and praises God for the final manifestation of the Realm taking place through the birth and ministry of Jesus.	C.' Acts 28:11-16. Paul visits with Jewish leaders in Rome and explains that the manifestation of Realm through Jesus is the hope toward which Israel has been living.
D. Luke 1:57-80. After the birth of John, Zechariah prophesies that God through Jesus will give light to those who sit in darkness, i.e. will manifest the Realm to gentiles.	D'. Acts 28:1-10. On Malta, two remarkable incidents show that God is working through Paul to manifest the Realm to gentiles.
E. Luke 2:1-7. The birth of Jesus takes place under difficult circumstances, a sign that the promise of the Realm can be trusted, even in difficult circumstances.	E'. Acts 27:39-44. Paul is saved in the difficult circumstances of shipwreck, a sign that the promise of the Realm can be trusted, even in difficult circumstances.
F. Luke 2:8-20. Angels announce the birth of Jesus as assurance that God is bringing the Realm.	F'. Acts 27:27-38. The breaking of bread assures Paul that the risen Jesus is present to sustain Paul and the sailors.
G. Luke 2:21-40. Simeon and Anna prophesy that the Realm will include gentiles.	G'. Acts 27:13-26. Paul prophesies the circumstances that can lead to the safety of the gentiles in the boat.
H. Luke 2:41-52. The young Jesus instructs the leaders in the temple.	H'. Acts 27:1-12. Paul instructs the leaders of the boat on his trip to Rome.
I. Luke 3:1-20. John the Baptist calls people to repent, and is imprisoned.	I'. Acts 26:24-32. Paul calls Agrippa to repent, and is sent to Rome as a prisoner.
J. Luke 3:21-22. The baptism of Jesus confirms that Jesus is God's prophetic agent in manifesting the Realm.	J'. Acts 26:1-23. Paul recounts his call to become a prophetic representative of the Realm.
K. Luke 3:23-38. The genealogy of Jesus, representative of the Realm, locates him as descendent of the God who created the whole human family and whose Realm is therefore trustworthy.	K'. Acts 25:23-27. Festus, representative of Rome, cannot locate Jesus in relationship to Roman justice and seeks help in writing a charge that justifies sending Jesus to Rome, thereby exposing the old-world character and untrustworthiness of the Roman system.
L. Luke 4:1-13. Jesus resists the temptation to turn away from his mission of witnessing to the Realm.	L'. Acts 25:13-22. Festus is tempted to accede to the false charges against Paul, but does not.

M. Luke 4:14-30. Jesus's inaugural sermon announces the coming of the Realm, the great restoration in which all things will manifest God's purposes.	M'. Acts 25:1-12. Paul appeals to Caesar, yet the reader recognizes that Caesar's rule belongs to the old world and will give way to the Realm of God.
N. Luke 4:31-41 Jesus models what disciples should do when faced with temptation.	N'. Acts 24:22-27. Felix yields to temptation by seeking money from Paul.
O. Luke 4:42-44. Jesus explains his mission: to manifest the Realm	O'. Acts 24:10-21. Paul explains his mission: to manifest the Realm among gentiles.
P. Luke 5:1-11. Jesus calls the first disciples to serve the Realm by putting their nets into chaos (the deep) to bring forth a catch.	P'. Acts 24:1-9. The high priest and other Jewish leaders resist the Realm and create chaos.
Q. Luke 5:12-26. In the presence of threat, God acts providentially through miracles to manifest the Realm.	Q'. Acts 23:23-35. In the presence of threat, God acts providentially to preserve Paul, agent of the Realm.
R. Luke 5:27-39. Putting fresh wine (the witness to the Realm) into old wineskins destroys the skin; fresh wine requires fresh wineskins.	R'. Acts 23:16-22. The fresh wine of the witness to the Realm has burst the old wineskins (the Jewish plot to murder Paul) while the fresh wineskin (the Tribune) preserves the fresh wine.
S. Luke 6:1-11. Jesus's witness to the Realm provokes controversy.	S'. Acts 23:12-15. Paul's witness to the realm provokes a plot to kill Paul.
T. Luke 6:12-19. Jesus calls twelve apostles, and teaches and heals—all in demonstration of the Realm.	T'. Acts 22:30-23:11 The leaders of the council and their actions (striking Paul on the mouth) undermine the Realm. Their behavior contrasts with that of the Twelve.
U. Luke 6:20-36. The members of the community of the Realm are to love their enemies and thereby embody the Realm.	U. Acts 22:22-29. A Roman tribune shows Paul justice whereas the Jewish people abuse Paul.
V. Luke 6:37-49. In the Realm, people are not to judge. A good tree bears good fruit but a bad tree bears bad fruit.	V'. Acts 21:37-22: 21. The Jewish crowd judges Paul. Paul's testimony shows that the Realm is the good fruit but those who have arrested him are the bad.

Appendix 1: The Chiastic Structure of Luke-Acts

W. Luke 7:1-17. The Realm reaches out to gentiles.	W'. Acts 21:27-36. Some people object to the Realm reaching out to gentiles through the invitation of Paul.
X. Luke 7:18-35: John and Jesus played the flute and wailed (i.e. announced the Realm) but many people did not dance or mourn (i.e. turned away from the Realm)	X'. Acts 21:17-26. Some people turn away from the Realm by claiming that Paul teaches Jewish people living among gentiles to forsake Moses.
Y. Luke 7:36-50. A woman who is a sinner confirms that Jesus is the prophet of the Realm. The community of the Realm should welcome her.	Y'. Acts 21:7-16. Paul is in the prophetic tradition. The community of the Realm should welcome gentiles.
Z. Luke 8:1-3. Some women are companions of Jesus and the disciples on the way to the Realm.	Z'. Acts 21:1-6. Households encourage Paul and his companions on their journey to witness to the Realm.
AA. Acts 8:4-21. The parable of the sower depicts the Realm as a seed growing quietly that will one day bring things to light and constitute a family or community.	AA'. Acts 20:17-38. Paul described his ministry Ephesus in ways that are reminiscent of a growing seed.
BB. Luke 8:22-54. The Realm is manifest through four miracle stories climaxing with a raising from the dead.	BB'. Acts 20:7-17. God through Paul manifests the realm by raising the dead.
CC. Luke 9:1-17. Jesus commissions the twelve to witness to the Realm and provides for them in the midst of difficulty.	CC'. Acts 20:1-6. God provides for Paul, who had been commissioned to witness to the Realm, in the midst of difficulty.
DD. Luke 9:18-36. Confession of faith followed by teaching that disciples will take up their crosses daily, and the transfiguration—a momentary realization that the Realm in the present.	DD' Acts 19:21-41 Confession of faith leads to suffering during the riot in Ephesus climaxing in a reprieve—a realm-like moment
EE. Luke 9:37-43a. The disciples cannot cast out a demon when they have an inadequate grasp of the Realm.	EE'. Acts 19:11-20. God demonstrates the Realm through Paul, including casting out demons.
FF. Luke 9:43b-50. The disciples have difficulty understanding the death of	FF'. Acts 19:1-6. Disciples do not fully understand the Realm until they receive the Holy Spirit.

Jesus, greatness, and community in the Realm.	
GG. Luke 9:51-62. When people do not adequately grasp the urgency of the mission of Jesus, they do not become part of the movement to the Realm.	GG'. Acts 18:24-28. Apollos is instructed in the Realm and becomes a full member of the movement toward the Realm.
HH. Luke 10:1-37. Jesus tells the seventy missionaries to shake off their feet the dust of the towns of those who do not receive them In parable of the good Samaritan a Samaritan surprisingly serves as an agent of the Realm.	HH'. Acts 18: 5-23. Paul shakes the dust of the Corinthians off his feet and goes to the Gentiles. Some surprising Corinthians respond positively to the Realm.
II. Luke 10:38-42. Jesus treats Mary as a full fledged disciple by teaching her in the manner of a rabbi, thus pointing to the restoration of women	II'. Acts 18:1-4. Aquila and Priscilla become a teaching couple whose co-operation points to the restoration of male and female relationships.
JJ. Luke 11:1-13. The unknown God of Acts 17 is the God described in Luke 11:1-13.	JJ'. Acts 17:22-34. Paul correlates the unknown God with the God of Israel who is more fully described in Acts 11:1-13.
KK. Luke 11:14-32. Many people think that Satan is the power behind Jesus.	KK'. Acts 17:16-21. In contrast to Jewish people, philosophers seek to understand the power behind Paul and the Realm
LL. Luke 11:33-12:12 Jesus warns the disciples against the Pharisees and then exhorts the disciples to fearless witness.	LL'. Acts 17:1-15. A Jewish mob comes after Paul, Silas and Jason, but the disciples witness fearlessly.
MM. Luke 12:13-34. Jesus teaches the disciples not to be anxious.	MM'. Acts 16:35-40. Paul and Silas are not anxious but witness courageously.
NN. Luke 12:35-59. Jesus tells the disciples to be prepared for social conflict.	NN'. Acts 16:25-34. Social conflict has put Paul and Silas in prison, but God delivers them.
OO. Luke 13:1-9: Those who do not repent will perish.	OO'. Acts 16:16-24. Slave owners should repent.
PP. Luke 13:10-21. The Realm is like a seed growing secretly or yeast leavening a loaf; the healing of the woman possessed by Satan is such a	PP. Acts 16:11-15. Lydia believes and becomes a part of the community of the Realm, a sign that the Realm includes the restoration of women.

sign indicating that the Realm includes the restoration of women.	
QQ. Luke 13:22-30. Despite conflicts, God is gathering a community from east and west, north and south.	QQ'. Acts 15:35-16:1-10. Despite conflicts, God is leading the disciples into international witness.
RR. Luke 13:31-35. Jerusalem laments when it does not welcome the Realm.	RR'. Acts 15:30-35. The disciples are at peace and rejoice serving the Realm.
SS. Luke 14:1-6: On the occasion of healing the person with dropsy, Jesus interprets Torah and healing in relationship with one another	SS'. Acts 15:22-29 The Jerusalem council interprets Torah and the gentile mission in relationship with one another.
TT. Luke 14:7-14. The Realm seeks those who ordinarily would not be invited to a banquet—those who cannot walk, who cannot see, etc.	TT'. Acts 15:6-21. The Realm seeks gentiles, who are in a position vis-à-vis the church similar to those who are poor, who cannot walk, etc., in the parable
UU. Luke 14:15-24. The parable of the great dinner urges the disciples to invite to those who are poor, who cannot see or walk, etc.	UU'. Acts 15:1-5. The church must consider the terms under which to invite gentiles.
VV. Luke 14:25-34. Jesus teaches that the disciples must be prepared to pay the cost.	VV'. Acts 14:1-28 Paul and Barnabas repeatedly pay the cost of discipleship.
WW. Luke 15:1-32. The Realm welcomes the lost, including gentiles (younger heir).	WW'. Acts 13:13-51. The community of the Realm welcomes gentiles.
XX. Luke 16:1-18. The parable of the dishonest manager exposes the depth of corruption in the old age.	XX'. Acts 13:1-12. Barnabas and Saul encounter the false Jewish prophet Bar-Jesus who embodies the corruption of the old.
YY. Luke 16:19-31. In the parable of the rich person and Lazarus, the rich person ignores Lazarus and faces everlasting torment.	YY'. Acts 12:20-25. Herod brutally treats the believers, dies in recompense, and faces everlasting torment.
ZZ. Luke 17:1-10. When Jesus cautions the disciples to be careful not stumble or cause others to do so, the apostles ask Jesus to increase their faith.	ZZ'. Acts 12:12-19. Peter's release from prison increases the faith of the community.
AAA. Luke 17:11-19. While Jesus heals ten lepers, nine Jewish and one	AAA. Acts 12:6-11. While Jewish people were pleased when Herod

Samaritan, the Jewish lepers go on their way while the Samaritan thanks Jesus.	imprisoned Peter, an angel releases Peter.
BBB. Luke 17:20-37. Jesus teaches the disciples that they will suffer in the long transition period between this age and the final manifestation of the Realm.	BBB'. Acts 12:1-5. Herod executes James and imprisons Peter thus validating Jesus's teaching in Luke 17:20-36.
CCC. Luke18:1-8. Through the parable of the widow and the unjust judge, God promises justice.	CCC'. Acts 11:27-30. When a famine breaks out, the community becomes the instrument of justice by sending relief to Jerusalem.
DDD. Luke 18:9-14. The Pharisee trusts in himself whereas the tax collector, trusts in God, repents, and goes home justified.	DDD'. Acts 11:19-26. Traditional Jewish people in Antioch do not welcome the news of the Realm whereas gentiles in large numbers do so.
FFF. Luke 18:15-17. When the disciples try to keep little children away, Jesus welcomes them.	FFF'. Acts 11:1-18. Peter describes how God welcomes gentiles and invites the church to do the same.
GGG. Luke 18:18-30. A rich ruler wants to know how to inherit eternal life, but he goes away sad because he cannot act on Jesus's message.	GGG'. Acts 10:44-48. The Holy Spirit falls on gentiles; these gentiles are more discerning than the Jewish rich ruler.
HHH. Luke 18:31-34. Jesus predicts his death and resurrection.	HHH'. Acts 10:34-43. Peter interprets the death and resurrection of Jesus as the center of the news of the Realm.
III. Luke 18:35-43. Jesus opens the eyes of a person who is blind.	III. Acts 10:1-33. Through a double vision, Jesus opens the eyes of Peter, Cornelius and others.
JJJ. Luke 19:1-10. Jesus welcomes a repentant tax collector into the community of the Realm.	JJJ'. Acts 9:32-43. Peter multiplies the signs of the Realm by healing Aeneas and raising Tabitha (Dorcas)
KKK. Luke 19:11-27. The parable of the pounds urges readers to multiply their witness to the Realm.	KKK'. Acts 9:19b-31. Some responses to the call and initial ministry of Paul are of the five- and ten-pound variety, but some are one-pound responses.
LLL. Luke 19:28-40. Jesus, prophet of the Realm, enters Jerusalem with the news of the Realm.	LLL'. Acts 9:1-19a. The call of Paul is the entry into the mission to invite gentiles into the community of the Realm.

MMM. Luke 19:41-44. Jesus laments the destruction of the temple, a traditional symbol of God's presence.	MMM'. Acts 8:26-40. Philip welcomes a eunuch into the community of the Realm which mediates God's presence;
NNN. Luke 19:45-48. The temple has become a house of robbers.	NNN'. Acts 8:14-25. After attempting to bribe the apostles, Simon repents.
OOO. Luke 20:1-8. People question the authority of Jesus.	OOO'. Acts 8:4-13. Jesus has authority over magic.
PPP. Luke 20:9-18 The parable of the wicked tenants portrays some Jewish leaders as wicked.	PPP'. Acts 6:8-8:3. The stoning of Stephen confirms that some Jewish people are wicked tenants.
RRR. Luke 20:20-26. Jesus exposes Caesar as an idolatrous leader who creates his own abusive domain.	RRR'. Acts 6:1-7. The church elects the deacons as leaders who, in contrast to Caesar serve the Realm of God.
SSS. Luke 20:27-44. Controversy between Jesus and the Sadducees in which Jesus shows his superiority.	SSS'. Acts 5:12-32. Controversy between the apostles and the Sadducees (and some other Jewish leaders) in which the apostles show their superiority.
TTT. Luke 20:45-47. Jesus excoriates the scribes for being self-impressed and devouring widows' houses.	TTT'. Acts 5:33-42. Gamaliel speaks wisely, advising the council not to harass the church.
UUU. Luke 21:1-4. A widow faithfully contributes to the temple treasury, confident that the treasury will provide for her needs.	UUU'. Acts 4:32-5:11. The community holds all things in common, thus providing for the poor. But when Ananias and Sapphira attempt to retain some of their own goods, God kills them.
VVV. Luke 21:5-37. Jesus points to the distress that will accompany the end of the old age, including the destruction of the temple, but the discourse ends with a vision of Jesus' return, thus fulfilling God's promise.	VVV'. Acts 4:13-31. The disciples experience distress as a result of testifying to the coming of the Realm, but the scene ends with the disciples confident that God's promise will be fulfilled.
WWW. Luke 22:1-6. Judas speaks only to betray Jesus.	WWW'. Acts 4:1-12. Peter and John speak boldly before the council.
XXX. Luke 22:7-23. At the last supper, Jesus acknowledges that he will suffer as part of the coming of the Realm.	XXX'. Acts 3:11-26. In his sermon Peter asserts that many in the audience had conspired to cause Jesus's suffering. But God now offers them life, the opportunity to be part of the Realm.

YYY. Luke 22:31-34: Jesus predicts Peter's Denial	YYY'. Acts 3:1-10. Peter is an instrument of healing at the Beautiful Gate
ZZZ. Luke 22:35-38. The disciples had been living from day to day on the hospitality of the people to whom they went, but now must provide for themselves	ZZZ'. Acts 2:43-47. The disciples in the early Jerusalem community become a means of mutual support, thereby embodying the life of the Realm
AAAA. Luke 22:39-46. Jesus urges the disciples to pray they will not come into the time of trial (the great tribulation).	AAAA'. Acts 2:37-42. Many, many people respond to the invitation to repent and join the church in its movement toward the Realm.
BBBB. Luke 22:47-23:25. Some Jewish people conspire with gentiles to put Jesus to death thus illustrating the brokenness of community in the old age.	BBBB'. Acts 2:14-36. Peter asserts that while misguided people crucified Jesus, God now invites all to repent and to become a part of the community moving toward the new age.
CCCC. Luke 23:26-56. The crucifixion of Jesus reveals the old age at its worst and undermines God's purposes to restore human community	CCCC'. Acts 2:5-13. The Spirit begins to reunite the divided human family into an inclusive community of mutual support prefiguring the final community of the Realm.
DDDD. Luke 24:1-12. The resurrection of Jesus confirms the presence of the Realm through the ministry of Jesus	DDDD'. Acts 2:1-4 The Spirit releases the power of the Realm among the followers of Jesus: they now operate with resurrection power.
EEEE. Luke 24:13-35. The risen Jesus appears to disciples on the road to Emmaus	EEEE. Acts 1:15-26. While Judas becomes a definitive sign of the old world by taking his own life, the presence of Jesus reconstitutes the community.
FFFF. Luke 24:36-44. Disciples are empowered together.	FFFF'. Acts 1:12-14. Disciples are empowered together.
GGGG. Luke 24:44-53. The ascension culminates the Gospel of Luke by revealing that Jesus is God's representative in bringing the final manifestation of the Realm. The story of Jesus that has reached this point is completely trustworthy.	GGGG'. Acts 1:1-11. The life and witness of the church in Acts takes place under the ascension which reveals that Jesus is God's agent ruling over all. The church, then, can act with complete confidence in God's purposes.

Appendix 2: Table Correlating Lectionary Readings from Luke with Chiastic Parallels from Acts

The Revised Common Lectionary appoints only a handful of passages from the Book of Acts. The table below makes it possible for a minister preaching from a passage in the Gospel of Luke in the Revised Common Lectionary to locate chiastic parallels from the Book of Acts. The table lists the day of the Christian Year for which a preacher may be developing a sermon, the Lukan Gospel reading from the lectionary, and the parallel from the Book of Acts. The preacher can then incorporate insights from the chiastic parallelism into the sermon on the text from Luke.[1]

Lectionary Year A

Day of the Christian Year	Passage in Luke	Chiastic Parallel in Acts
Nativity of Jesus: Proper 1	Luke 2:1-14 (15-21)	Acts 27:39-44; Acts 27:27-38
Nativity of Jesus: Proper 2	Luke 2(1-7), 8-20	Acts 27:39-44; Acts 27:27-38
Holy Name of Jesus	Luke 2:15-21	Acts 27:27-38
Easter Evening	Luke 24:13-49	Acts 1:15-26; Acts 1:12-14; Acts 1:1-11
Third Sunday of Easter	Luke 24:13-35	Acts 1:15-26
Ascension of Jesus	Luke 24:44-53	Acts 1:1-11
Thanksgiving Day in the United States	Luke 17:11-19	Acts 12:12-29

Lectionary Year B

Day of the Christian Year	Passage from Luke	Chiastic Parallel from Acts

Fourth Sunday of Advent	Luke 1:26-38	Acts 28:17-21
Nativity of Jesus: Proper 1	Luke 2:1-14 (15-20)	Acts 27:39-44; Acts 27:27-38
Nativity of Jesus: Proper 2	Luke 2:(1-7), 8-20	Acts 27:39-44; Acts 27:27-38
First Sunday after Christmas Day	Luke 2:22-40	Acts 27:13-26
Holy Name of Jesus	Luke 2:15-21	Acts 27:27-38
Easter Evening	Luke 24:14-49	Acts 1:15-26; Acts 1:12-14; Acts 1:1-11
Ascension of Jesus	Luke 24:44-53	Acts 1:1-11

Lectionary Year C

Day of Christian Year	Passage in Luke	Chiastic Parallel in Acts
First Sunday of Advent	Luke 21:25-36	Acts 4:13-31
Second Sunday of Advent	Luke 3:1-6	Acts 16:24-32
Third Sunday of Advent	Luke 3:7-18	Acts 16:24-32
Fourth Sunday of Advent	Luke 1:39-45 (46-55)	Acts 28:11-16
Nativity of Jesus 1	Luke 2:1-14 (15-20)	Acts 27:39-44; Acts 27:27-38
Nativity of Jesus 2	Luke 2:(1-7), 8-20	Acts 27:39-44; Acts 27:27-38
First Sunday after Christmas Day	Luke 2:41-52	Acts 27:1-12
Holy Name of Jesus	Luke 2:15-21	Acts 27:27-38
Baptism of Jesus	Luke 3:15-17, 21-22	Acts 26:24-32; Acts 26:1-23
Third Sunday after the Epiphany	Luke 4:14-21	Acts 25:1-12
Fourth Sunday after the Epiphany	Luke 4:21-30	Acts 25:1-12
Fifth Sunday after the Epiphany	Luke 5:1-11	Acts 24:1-9
Sixth Sunday after the Epiphany	Luke 6:17-26	Acts 22:30-23:11; Acts 22:22-29

Appendix 2: Table Correlating Lectionary Readings from Luke with Chiastic Parallels from Acts

Seventh Sunday after the Epiphany	Luke 6:27-38	Acts 22:22-29
Eighth Sunday after the Epiphany	Luke 6:39-49	Acts 21:37-22:21
Ninth Sunday after the Epiphany	Luke 7:1-10	Acts 21:27-36
Transfiguration Sunday	Luke 9:28-36 (37-43a)	Acts 19:21-41
First Sunday in Lent	Luke 4:1-13	Acts 25:13-22
Second Sunday in Lent	Luke 13:31-35 or Luke 9:28-36 (37-43a)	Acts 15:30-35 or Acts 19:21-41
Third Sunday in Lent	Luke 13:1-9	Acts 16:16-24
Fourth Sunday in Lent	Luke 15:1-3, 11b-32	Acts 13:13-51
Liturgy of the Palms	Luke 19:28-40	Acts 9:19a
Liturgy of the Passion	Luke 22:14-56 or Luke 23:1-49	Acts 3:11-26; Acts 3:1-10; Acts 2:43-47; Acts 2:37-42; Acts 2:14-36; Acts 2:5-13
Tuesday of Holy Week	Luke 1:26-38	Acts 28:17-21
Easter Vigil	Luke 24:1-12	Acts 2:1-4
Resurrection of Jesus	Luke 24:1-12	Acts 2:1-4
Easter Evening	Luke 24:13-49	Acts 1:15-26; Acts 1:12-14; Acts 1:1-11
Ascension of Jesus	Luke 24:44-53	Acts 1:1-11
Proper 4	Luke 7:1-10	Acts 21:27-36
Proper 5	Luke 7:11-17	Acts 21:27-36
Proper 6	Luke 7:36-8:3	Acts 21:7-16
Proper 7	Luke 8:26-39	Acts 20:7-17
Proper 8	Luke 9:51-62	Acts 18:24-28
Proper 9	Luke 10:1-11, 16-20	Acts 18:5-23
Proper 10	Luke 10:25-37	Acts 18:5-23
Proper 11	Luke 10:38-42	Acts 18:1-4
Proper 12	Luke 11:1-13	Acts 17:1-13
Proper 13	Luke 12:13-21	Acts 12:13-34
Proper 14	Luke 12:32-40	Acts 16:25-34
Proper 15	Luke 12:49-56	Acts 16:25-34
Proper 16	Luke 13:10-16	Acts 16:11-15

Proper 17	Luke 14:1, 7-14	Acts 15:22-29; Acts 15:6-21
Proper 18	Luke 14:25-33	Acts 14:1-28
Proper 19	Luke 15:1-10	Acts 13:13-51
Proper 20	Luke 16:1-13	Acts 13:1-12
Proper 21	Luke 16:19-31	Acts 12:20-25
Proper 22	Luke 17:5-10	Acts 12:12-19
Proper 23	Luke 17:11-19	Acts 12:6-11
Proper 24	Luke 18:1-8	Acts 11:27-30
Proper 25	Luke 18:9-14	Acts 11:19-26
Proper 26	Luke 19:1-10	Acts 9:32-43
Proper 27	Luke 20:27-38	Acts 5:12-32
Proper 28	Luke 21:5-19	Acts 4:13-31
Reign of Jesus	Luke 23:33-43	Acts 2:5-13

Notes

1. Because the Revised Common Lectionary sometimes divides texts in the Gospel of Luke differently from the way in which they are divided in the chiastic analysis, multiple passages from Acts are sometimes listed in connection with single texts from Luke.

Appendix 3: Sermon Series from the Book of Acts: Representative Texts, Characters, and Themes

In my view, the best way to preach from Acts is usually to engage in *lectio continua*, that is, preaching passage by passage through the book (or through part of the book) from start to finish. However, because of circumstances in the congregation or for the sake of variety, a preacher may do a series of sermons. This appendix proposes three kinds of sermon series—one based on representative texts in Acts, another on characters in the book, and a third on themes in Luke and Acts.

A sermon series of four to eight sermons is usually long enough to cover significant material but short enough that the typical congregation will not weary of the series. Of course, these things vary from congregation to congregation.

Sermon Series on Representative Texts in Acts

A preacher could create a sermon series by focusing on representative texts in Acts.

> 1. Acts 1:6-11: the ascension of Jesus. This passage establishes the fundamental theological grounding of the rest of Acts. The community can count on the coming of the Realm because Jesus is at the right hand of God.
> 2. Acts 2:1-36: the manifestation of the Holy Spirit on the Jewish community. The Holy Spirit is the immediate agent empowering the community's witness to the Realm.
> 3. Acts 2:43-47; 4:32—5:10: the common life of the earliest Jerusalem community. These passages call attention to sharing material resources as a means whereby the church is God's means of bringing the provision of the Realm to the poor in the community and of relieving the rich of the danger of the idolatry of wealth.

> 4. Acts 10:34-48: the Holy Spirit falls on gentiles. This pericope helps the congregation see the reunion of Jewish and gentile peoples as part of the Realm.
> 5. Acts 15:1-29: the Jerusalem council. The church deals theologically and pastorally with the degree to which gentiles should be initiated into Judaism to be full participants in the community of the Realm.
> 6. Acts 18:23—19:20. This passage begins the Third Missionary Journey and gives the preacher the opportunity to help the congregation ponder Paul's missionary travels as well as to consider the incidents in this text.
> 7. Acts 21:17-35: Paul is arrested in the temple. This text reveals the false grounds on which Paul is arrested in the temple and which eventually lead to his journey to Rome. The preacher should consider this text in the context of Acts 21:17-26:32.
> 8. Acts 28:23-32: the ending of Acts. This text gives the preacher the opportunity help the congregation think about what comes next for Paul, and for the contemporary community.

A preacher could select other representative texts to fit other organizing motifs such as texts highlighting women, miracle stories, controversy stories, releases from prison, and testimony before officials.

Sermon Series on Characters in Acts

A preacher might develop a series based around characters who represent important notions in Acts. To develop a sermon on a character, the preacher may need to consider several texts in which the character appears with the goal of helping the congregation recognize how the character functions in Acts.

However, this approach comes with cautions. Preachers often psychologize biblical characters in ways that go beyond anything either in the text itself or that might be presumed on the basis of our knowledge of the first century. Indeed, such sermons are sometimes the epitome of anachronism (discussed in the introduction) in which the preacher reads the contemporary world and its agenda directly into the character. Furthermore, I have heard a number of sermons on biblical characters in which the preacher assumes the role of the character in a first-person narrative. These sermons often become platitudinous and hokey. So, when developing a series on characters, the preacher needs to maintain exegetical, theological, and aesthetic rigor.

> 1. Peter. Peter is the leading figure among the apostles in the Gospel of Luke and represents the Jerusalem tradition in Acts. Important

texts include Luke 5:1-11; 6:12-16; 8:40-55; 9:18-27; 9:28-36; 12:41-48; 18:18-30; 22:7-23; 22:31-34; 22:54-62; 24:1-12; Acts 2:14-41; 3:1-4:22; 5:1-10; 5:17-32 (esp. 29); 8:14-25; 9:32-43; 10:1-11:18; 12:1-18; 15:6-11.

2. Stephen. As the first martyr, Stephen represents the challenge and suffering faced by many in the early community. The important text is Acts 6:8—8:3.

3. Paul. Paul is not only the leading missionary to the gentiles but the central character in Acts 9:1-31; 13:1—14:28; 15:36—18:22; 18:23—20:16; 20:17—28:32.

4. Cornelius. Cornelius represents God-fearers, gentiles who are sympathetic to the God of Israel, and Jewish life but who have not converted. The important text is Acts 10:1—11:15, esp. Acts 10:1-33.

5. Tabitha (Dorcas). Tabitha's story represents faithful women who took a lead in early Christian life and whose ministry testifies to God's desire to restore women in the Realm. The important text is Acts 9:36-42.

6. Gamaliel and the Heirs of Sceva. These two characters represent both the positive and negative strains in Luke's pictures of the Jewish people. The important text for Gamaliel is Acts 5:33-39 while for the heirs of Sceva the text is Acts 19:11-20.

7. Priscilla and Aquila. While Acts mentions this couple in only a few verses, they represent the impulse toward egalitarian relationships between women and men and in leadership in the church in Luke's theology. The important texts are Acts 18:1-4 and Acts 18:20-24.

8. Agrippa. Agrippa represents those who are tied into Roman imperial power. Rome's client ruler of much of Palestine, he is sympathetic to Paul but is unwilling to intervene in Paul's behalf. Acts 25:13—26:32.

A preacher could do a series a single character. For example, since Paul is a leading human actor in Acts, a natural series could summarize the Lukan Paul.

1. Call of Paul (Acts 9:1-31)
2. First missionary journey (Acts 13:1—14:28)
3. Second missionary journey (Acts 15:36—18:22)
4. Third missionary journey (Acts 18:23—21:16)
5. Arrest in Jerusalem (21:17—22:21) and before the council (Acts 22:22—23:35)
6. Before Felix (Acts 24:1-27)
7. Before Festus and Agrippa (Acts 25:1—26:32)
8. The journey to Rome (Acts 27:1—28:10)
9. In Rome (Acts 28:11-32).

A preacher might also compare and contrast Luke's picture of Paul with materials that come from the hand of the historical Paul. For example: the call of Paul and subsequent events (Acts 9:1-30; Galatians 1:11-24) and the Jerusalem council (Acts 15:1-29; Galatians 2:1-21). A preacher could adapt this approach to representative encounters in Acts, representative scenes in the narrative, representative places, or representative groups.

Sermon Series on Themes in Acts

When preaching on a theme, a preacher works not with a single text but with how a motif develops across a series of texts. The theme functions as the organizing center of the sermon in the same way that a single text does in most sermons. The minister typically needs to consider how a number of texts contribute to the theme.[1]

A preacher can focus on themes in Acts alone, but since Luke-Acts is one continuous story in two volumes, the themes run across both books. Consequently, texts relating to themes in both Luke-Acts are listed in the following examples. A preacher could do a series of sermons in which each sermon focuses on a separate theme, or a preacher might develop a series of sermons that focus on one theme.

Here are some themes in Luke-Acts with supporting texts. Many passages relate to more than one theme. These lists are representative and not exhaustive.

1. The Holy Spirit: Luke 1:5-25; 1:26-38; 1:67-80; 2:25-35; 3:15-17; 3:21-22; 4:1-14; 4:16-30; 10:21-22; 11:5-13; 12:8-12; Acts 1:1-5; 1:6-11; 1:15-20; 2: 1-42, esp. 24-31; 5: 1-16; 6:1-16; 7:55-60; 8:15-17; 8:26-40; 9:10-17; 10:1-11:18, esp. 44-46; 13:1-4; 15:6-11; 15:22-29; 16: 6-10; 19: 1-7; 20:17-36; 21:1-16; 28:23-29.

2. Discipleship: Luke 5:1-11; 6:12-16; 6:20-49; 8:19-21; 9:1-17; 9:18-27; 10:1-20; 11:1-13; 12:22-53; 14:25-35; 17:1-10; 22:39-46; 24:44-52; Acts 1:12-26, esp. 21-26; 2:43-47; 4:32-5:1-10; 6:1-6; 9:32-43; 10:1—11:18; 11:19-26; 15:1-29; 19:1-7; 20:7-12; 20:17-35.

3. Mission to the gentiles (the great reunion of the human family). Luke 2:1-20; 2:23-32; 3:1-6; 3:22-38; 4:16-30; 7:1-10; 11:33-36; 14:15-24; 15:1-10; 15:11-32; 24:44-49; Acts 1:6-11; 2:17-21; 3:25-26;9:1-19, esp. 15; 10:1-11:18; 13:46-48; 14:15-17; 15:1-29; 17:22-34 ; 18:5-11; 26:19-29; 28:26-30

4. Women. Luke 1:5-25; 1:26-39; 1:39-56; 1:57-66; 2:1-7; 2:36-38; 4:20-30; 7:11-17; 7:36-50; 8:1-3; 8:40-56; 10:38-42; 13:10-17; 13:20-21; 13:31-34; 15:8-10; 18:1-8; 21:1-4; 20:27-28; 21:21-24; 23:26-55; 24:1-11; 24:22-27; Acts 1:1-4; 2:16-18; 6:1-6; 9:36-43;

Appendix 3: Sermon Series from the Book of Acts: Representative Texts, Characters, and Themes | 227

12:12-17; 16:1; 16:11-15; 16:16-18;17:4-12; 17:34; 18:1-4, 24-28; 21:7-9

5. Religious practices: prayer, baptism, the sacred meal, and the laying on of hands. Luke 1:5-25; 2:36-38; 3:1-20; 3:21-22; 5:12-26; 6:12; 6:27-31; 7:24-30; 9:10-17; 9:28-36; 11:1-13; 12:49-53; 18:1-8; 18:9-14; 22:7-22; 22:39-46; Acts 1:1-4; 5-11; 2:38-41; 2:42-47; 3:1-10; 4:27-31; 6:1-6; 8:9-24; 8:26-40; 9:10-19; 10:1-33;12:1-5; 12:12-17; 13:1-3; 13:16b-25; 14:19-23; 16:11-18; 16:25-34; 18:5-11; 18:24-28; 19:1-7; 21:1-6; 20: 22:17-21; 20:36-38; 22:12-26; 26:24-29; 27:27-32; 27:33-38; 28:7-10. Note: a preacher could easily develop a series on just one of these practices, prayer, baptism, the sacred meal, or the laying on of hands.

6. Use and misuse of material resources as God's means to provide for the community; Luke 1:46-55; 3:10-14; 4:16-30; 5:1-10; 5:27-28; 6:20-26; 7:18-23; 7:40-43; 8:1-3; 9:1-6; 9:57-61; 9:10-7; 11:1-13; 12:13-21; 12:22-34; 14:1-6; 14:7-11; 14:12-24; 14:25-33; 16:1-13; 16:19-31; 18:18-30; 10:1-10; 19:11-27; 21:1-4; Acts 1:15-20; 2:42-47; 4:32-5:11; 6:1-7; 8:14-24; 11:12-30, esp. 27-30; 16:16-24; 20:17-35, esp. 33-35; 24. 24-26

7. Relationship of Judaism and the Community of the Realm. Luke 1:5-25; 1:57-66; 1:67-79; 2:8-20; 2:22-40; 2:41-52: 3:1-20, esp. 7-9; 4:16-30; 5:17-26; 5:27-32; 6:6-11; 7:1-10; 7:29-30; 7:31-35; 7:36-50; 11:29-32; 11:37-12:1; 12:11-12; 13:1-9; 10:10-17; 13:23-30; 13:32-35; 14:1-6; 14:7-24; 15:1-32; 16:14-15; 16:16-18; 16:19-31; 17:11-19; 17:20-21; 18:9-14; 19:11-27; 19:41-44; 19:45-48; 20:1-8; 20:9-19; 20:27-40; 20:41-44; 20:45-47; 21:5-24; 22:1-2; 22:47-54; 22:63-65; 23:1-5; 23:6-12; 23:13-25; 23:26-31; 23:32-38; 23:47-48; 23:50-51; 24:24; 24:47-49; Acts 2:14-42; 3:12-26; 4: 1-4 ;4: 5-22; 4:23-31; 5:12-16; 5:17-42; 6: 8-15; 7:1-60; 9:29-30; 10:1-44; 11:1-18; 12:1-19;8-21; 17:1-9; 17:10-15; 18:1-17; 18:18-19:41; 21:27-40; 22:1-21; 22:30-23:10; 23:12-35; 25:1-7; 25:13-27; 26:1-23; 28:17-28

8. The Roman Empire and the Community of the Realm. Luke 1:32-33; 1:37-55, esp. 52; 1:67-79; 2:1-7; 3:1-20, esp. 10-14; 6:12-15; 6:27-38; 7:1-10; 12:49-53; 13:1-9; 19:28-40; 20:20-26; 21:5-36; 22:24-30; 22:35-38; 23:1-5; 23:6-12; 23:13-25;; 23:27-31: 3:44-49; Acts 5:33-42; 12:1-5, 20-24; 16:19-40; 21:27-40; 22:22-23:35; 24:1-27; 25:1-26:32; 27:1-43; 28:30-32.

These themes are only samples of themes that make their way through the Gospel and Acts. These approaches are only three examples of series that a preacher could develop. There are as many ways to develop sermon series as there are preachers.

Notes

1. For a general approach to preaching on themes, see Ronald J. Allen, *Wholly Scripture: Preaching Biblical Themes* (Saint Louis: Chalice, 2004). On Luke-Acts, see Allen, *Preaching Luke-Acts.* Preaching Classic Texts (Saint Louis: Chalice, 2000).

Appendix 4: Suggestions for Further Reading

This brief bibliography lists some standard works on the Book of Acts—as well as some resources for preaching on the Gospel of Luke and the Book of Acts—that I think preachers would find helpful. In commentary series and in independent commentaries, separate scholars typically interpret the Gospel of Luke and the Book of Acts, thus giving separate interpretations of the Gospel and the Acts. This bibliography includes some works by scholars who have written on both Luke and Acts and thereby bring a single interpretive perspective to both works. This list contains representative works from across the theological spectrum.

Allen, Ronald J. *Preaching Luke-Acts.* Preaching Classic Texts. Saint Louis: Chalice Press, 2000. Explores developing sermons from themes that span both the Gospel of Luke and the Book of Acts. The theme functions as the "text" of the sermon. Themes considered in detail: Realm of God, Holy Spirit, great reunion of the human community, restoration of women, and use of material resources.

Barrett, C. K. *A Critical and Exegetical Commentary on the Acts of the Apostles.* International Critical Commentary. Historical-critical commentary based on the Greek text. Great attention to details.

Bock, Darrell F. *A Theology of Luke-Acts: God's Promised Program Realized for All Nations.* Biblical Theology of the New Testament. Grand Rapids: Zondervan, 2012. Survey of major theological themes in Luke-Acts: God, fulfillment, Messiah, Spirit, salvation, Israel, gentiles, ethics, Luke's opponents, women, Torah, ecclesiology, eschatology, the Scriptures in Luke-Acts.

———. *Acts.* Baker Exegetical Commentary on the New Testament. Grand Rapids: Baker, 2007. Accessible commentary highlighting historical, sociological, and theological concerns.

Borgman, Paul. *The Way according to Luke: Hearing the Whole Story of Luke-Acts.* Grand Rapids: Eerdmans, 2006. A professor of English (with an eye for biblical literature) reads Luke-Acts as a single narrative with attention to literary and rhetorical patterns.

Boring, M. Eugene, and Fred B. Craddock, *The People's New Testament Commentary*. Louisville: Westminster John Knox, 2004, 174–282, 363–465. The best one-volume commentary on the Gospels and Letters reaches a high point with Luke and Acts. Eminently quotable for preaching.

Cadbury, Henry Joel. *The Making of Luke-Acts*. New York: Macmillan, 1927. A classic work on the interplay of Luke and Acts. Foundational to much contemporary scholarship.

Craddock, Fred B. *Luke*. Interpretation: A Bible Commentary for Preaching and Teaching. Louisville: Westminster John Knox, 1990. The dean of Eurocentric male preachers interprets Luke with great exegetical, hermeneutical and homiletical sensitivity. If a preacher can only afford one commentary on Luke, this is the one.

Dunn, James D. G. *The Acts of the Apostles*. Narrative Commentaries. Valley Forge: Trinity International, 1997. Good basic commentary with focus on the narrative as narrative.

Fitzmyer, Joseph. *The Acts of the Apostles*. Anchor Yale Bible Commentary. New Haven: Yale University Press, 1998. A fine historical-critical commentary giving attention to issues of historicity and to Luke's literary art.

———. *The Gospel according to Luke I–IX*. Anchor Bible. Garden City: Doubleday, 1982. Like the commentary on Acts (just above), a fine historical-critical commentary giving attention to issues of historicity and to Luke's literary art.

———. *The Gospel according to Luke X–XXIV*. Anchor Bible. Garden City: Doubleday, 1985.

Fleer, David, and Dave Bland, eds. *Preaching from Luke/Acts*. Abilene: Abilene Christian University Press, 2000. A collection of articles sermons by several scholars and preachers (headlined by Thomas G. Long) on texts and themes from Luke-Acts.

Gaventa, Beverly Roberts. *Acts*. Abingdon New Testament Commentaries. Nashville: Abingdon, 2003. One of best commentaries on Acts. Views Acts as a narrative of God's activity. A great eye for detail while keeping the sweep of Luke-Acts in view. Good on the connections within Acts (and reaching back to Luke).

Haenchen, Ernst. *The Acts of the Apostles: A Commentary*. Philadelphia: Westminster, 1970. Although dated, I continue to be struck by many of Haenchen's insights into particular passages.

Jacobsen, David Schnasa and Günter Wasserberg. *Preaching Luke-Acts.* Nashville: Abingdon, 2001. Views Luke-Acts as a grief document: grief in the church that Jewish contemporaries have not, in large numbers, recognized the work of God through Jesus. Using narrative exegesis, the authors explore seven key passages.

Johnson, Luke Timothy. *The Acts of the Apostles.* Sacra Pagina. Collegeville: Liturgical, 1992. With his *The Gospel of Luke,* the best combination of commentaries on Luke-Acts. Particularly sensitive to literary interplay within the Gospel and the Acts, and gives special attention to Hellenistic literary and rhetorical backgrounds.

———. *The Gospel of Luke.* Sacra Pagina. Collegeville: Michael Glazier, 1992.

Kee, Howard Clark. *Good News to the Ends of the Earth: The Theology of Acts.* Valley Forge: Trinity International, 1991. Basic overview of major theological themes in Acts. Should be used in connection with *To Every Nation Born Under Heaven* (below).

———. *To Every Nation Born under Heaven: The Acts of the Apostles.* The New Testament in Context. Edinburgh: T&T Clark, 1997. Cultural background within which original readers heard Acts with extended notes (very helpful for preaching) on people, places, theological ideas, Roman modes of justice, geographical locales, expression of community.

Keener, Craig S. *Acts: An Exegetical Commentary.* Introduction and Acts 1:1–2:47. Grand Rapids: Baker Academic, 2012. The single most detailed commentary ever published on Acts. Particularly interested in historicity and in literary elements.

Krodel, Gerhard. *Acts.* Augsburg Commentary on the New Testament. Minneapolis: Augsburg Publishing, 1986. Good basic commentary on Acts concentrating on Luke's role as creative theologian and author in shaping material.

Malina, Bruce, and John J. Pilich. *Social Science Commentary on Acts.* Minneapolis: Fortress Press, 2008. Reads Acts from the perspective of cultural values that permeated antiquity such as community, patron-client relationships, kinship, shame, honor, healing, and the work of the Spirit. Attention to recurring scenes and reading scenarios.

Marshall, I. Howard. *Acts.* The Tyndale New Testament Commentaries. Grand Rapids: Eerdmans, 1980. While interested in Luke as theologian and literary artist, this volume is particularly concerned with historicity.

———. *The Gospel of Luke.* New International Greek Testament Commentary. Grand Rapids: Eerdmans, 1978. Detailed commentary on the Greek text with interest both in historicity and in Luke's literary features.

———, and David Peterson, eds. *Witness to the Gospel: The Theology of Acts.* Grand Rapids: Eerdmans, 1998. Twenty-four contributors explore themes in Acts: salvation, the call of God, and the renewing work of God.

Nickle, Keith F. *Preaching the Gospel of Luke: Proclaiming God's Royal Rule.* Louisville: Westminster John Knox, 2000. A commentary with a focus on the preacher from the perspective of the Realm of God as the center of Luke's theology.

Spencer, F. Scott. *The Gospel of Luke and the Acts of the Apostles.* Interpreting Biblical Texts. Nashville: Abingdon, 2008. Basic introduction to Luke and Acts with focus to the relationship of these books to history as well as to the literary-theological world created within the narrative of Luke-Acts.

Talbert, Charles. *Reading Acts: A Literary and Theological Commentary on the Acts of the Apostles.* Smith and Helwys, 2001. Careful literary reading of Acts, building on his earlier literary reading of Luke, calling attention to how the narrative communicates Luke's theology.

———. *Reading Luke: A Literary and Theological Commentary on the Third Gospel.* New York: Crossroad, 1992. Careful literary reading of Luke paving the way for his later literary reading of Acts, calling attention to how the narrative communicates Luke's theology.

Tannehill, Robert S. *The Narrative Unity of Luke-Acts: A Literary Interpretation, vol. 1: The Gospel according to Luke.* Foundations and Facets. Minneapolis: Fortress Press, 1986. This volume and the next show how the Gospel of Luke paves the way for the Acts the Apostles, and how the Acts presumes the Gospel of Luke with discussions of themes: previews of salvation, the beginning of the mission, Jesus as preacher and healer, the oppressed and excluded, the crowd or the people, authorities, disciples, revelation.

———. *The Narrative Unity of Luke-Acts: A Literary Interpretation, vol. 2: The Acts of the Apostles.* Foundations and Facets. Minneapolis: Fortress Press, 1990. The purpose of his volume is described above but the format is more like that of a commentary following Acts from start to finish.

———. *The Shape of Luke's Story: Essays on Luke-Acts.* Eugene: Cascade, 2005. Explorations of theology, poetry, rhetoric, attitude toward the Jewish people, how the narrative functions, and hermeneutics.

Walasky, Paul. *Acts: Westminster Bible Companion.* Louisville: Westminster John Knox, 1998. Reader-friendly, basic commentary. Sees Luke's purposes in writing as educational, theological, and apologetic.

Wall, Robert J. "Acts." In Leander Keck et al., eds. *The New Interpreter's Bible.* Nashville: Abingdon, 2002. Vol. 10. A fine commentary. Each section concludes with questions, issues, and reflections moving toward today.

Willimon, William H. *Acts.* Interpretation: A Bible Commentary for Teaching and Preaching. Louisville: Westminster John Knox, 1988. Energetic commentary with passion for the church. Filled with memorable phrases. Exegetically responsible with comments for preaching through a Barthian lens.

Witherington, Ben. *The Acts of the Apostles: A Socio-Rhetorical Commentary.* Grand Rapids: Eerdmans, 1997. Detailed commentary interpreting Acts through a lens combining social science criticism, ancient rhetoric, and other perspectives. Attention to how Luke shaped the retelling of history in Acts for particular rhetorical effect.

www.ingramcontent.com/pod-product-compliance
Lightning Source LLC
Chambersburg PA
CBHW051940290426
44110CB00015B/2050